SCHOOL LIBRARIES MATTER

SCHOOL LIBRARIES MATTER

Views from the Research

MIRAH J. DOW, EDITOR

LIBRARIES UNLIMITED

AN IMPRINT OF ABC-CLIO, LLC
Santa Barbara, California • Denver, Colorado • Oxford, England

Library of Congress Cataloging-in-Publication Data

School libraries matter : views from the research / Mirah J. Dow, editor.
   pages cm
  Includes index.
  ISBN 978-1-61069-161-1 (hardcopy : alk. paper) — ISBN 978-1-61069-162-8 (ebook)
  1. School libraries. I. Dow, Mirah Jane Ingram, editor of compilation.
  Z675.S3S291144   2013
  027.8—dc23   2013009849

ISBN: 978-1-61069-161-1
EISBN: 978-1-61069-162-8

17 16 15 14 13   1 2 3 4 5

This book is also available on the World Wide Web as an eBook.
Visit www.abc-clio.com for details.

Libraries Unlimited
An Imprint of ABC-CLIO, LLC

ABC-CLIO, LLC
130 Cremona Drive, P.O. Box 1911
Santa Barbara, California 93116–1911

This book is printed on acid-free paper ∞

Manufactured in the United States of America

This book is dedicated to school librarians who are on the front lines of education in today's schools and to the causes of democracy that with education, including schools and school libraries, will continue to exist.

CONTENTS

Illustrations   xiii

Foreword   xv
    Blanche Woolls

Preface   xvii

Introduction   xxi

1   Professional Dispositions of School Librarians   1
    Gail Bush and Jami L. Jones
      Introduction: Exploration of Professional Disposition of
        School Librarians   1
      Dispositions in Action   1
      The Concept of Professional Dispositions   3
      The Question of Professional Dispositions of School Librarians 5
      A Broad Context for a Review of the Literature   6
      The Delphi Study Methodology   7
      Research Design: Delphi Method   7
      Research Findings and Plans of Action   8
      Envisioning a Future   14
      Conclusions: Identification of School Librarian Professional
        Dispositions   15
      References   15

2   School Librarians in Vygotsky's Zone of Proximal Development   19
    Mirah J. Dow and Jacqueline McMahon Lakin
      Introduction: Information Behavior Research   19
      Cutting School Librarians Is a Paradox   19
      What Is Information Behavior?   21

Constructivism   21
   Constructivism in Education and Sociology   21
   Constructivism in Library and Information Science Research   22
   Constructivist Theories of Information Behavior   22
   Vygotsky's Zone of Proximal Development   22
Student Achievement   23
   Annual Yearly Progress: Federal Mandate   24
   Every Student Should Graduate High School Ready for
     College and Career   24
   Students' Growth: State-Level Example   25
Methodology   27
   Dervin's Sense-Making   27
   Kuhlthau's Information Search Process   27
   Information Behaviors Necessary for Achieving Common
     Core State Standards   28
Research Findings: Notably Higher AYP Proficiency with
   School Librarian   29
What More Is Needed?   33
Conclusions: A New Picture of the Presence or Absence of
   School Librarians   34
References   35

3   Influencing Instructional Partnerships in Preservice
   Elementary Education Teachers   39
   Mirah J. Dow, Tonya Davis, and Angela Vietti-Okane
   Introduction: Preparing Future Teachers   39
   Literature Review   39
     Partnering in Instruction   39
     Collaboration Theory   40
   Context: Elementary Teacher and School Library Partner Course 41
   Research Questions   42
   Methodology: Pre- and Post-survey and Procedure   43
   Limitations   44
   Findings   46
   Conclusions   46
   References   49

4   Everyday Life Information Seeking Practices of Upper-Income
   High School Students   51
   Lori L. Franklin
   Introduction: A Focus on Students Today in a New School Library 51
   New Technologies and Today's Young People   51
   A Study Spark for Examining Teenage Students   52
   Literature Pinpoints Need for Studying ELIS Practices in School
     Libraries   52
     Savolainen and the Theoretical Framework for This Study 52

Studying Teens in a Highly Technological School Library   53
Methodology   53
 Choice for a Unique Study Site and Population   53
 A Newly Constructed School: Rivals and Rule Testing   54
 Data Collection   54
  School Librarian Interviews   55
  Student Focus Group Sessions   56
  Print and Virtual Documentation   57
 Generalizability, Substantive Validation, and Reliability   57
 Study Limitations   58
Findings   58
 Theme 1: Students Prefer Own Cell Phones to Library Computers   58
 Theme 2: Students at This Site Require a Specific Type of
  Instructional Model   59
 What Are the ELIS Practices Exhibited by Students at the Study Site? 59
 How Do the Students in This Study Use Physical and Virtual
  Technologies in the School Library?   60
Conclusions: ELIS Practices of Upper-Income High School Students   61
References   63

5 The Impact of School Libraries on Academic Achievement   65
   Keith Curry Lance and Linda Hofschire
   Introduction: Circumstances that Define American Public Education 65
    Site-Based Management   65
    Absence of Reliable, Dedicated Federal Funding   66
    School Staffing Trends   66
    Standards-Based State Tests   66
    Advent of Computers and the Internet   67
    Advent of eBooks, eReaders, and Tablet Computers   67
    Partnership for 21st-Century Skills   68
   Typical School Library Research Questions   68
   Review of the Literature   69
    School Libraries and Student Achievement   69
    Moving Beyond Student Achievement Studies   71
   Methodological Challenges   72
   Five-Step Improvement Plan   73
    Creating Partnerships with Administrators and Teachers   73
    Sharing Research about the Impact of School Libraries and Librarians 73
    Defining the Roles of School Library and Librarian   74
    Creating New Measures of School Library Outputs and Outcomes 74
    Documenting the Impact of Teaching 21st-Century Skills on Student
     Learning   75
   Conclusions: New Questions to Be Studied   75
   References   77

6   The Role of the School Library: Building Collaborations to
    Support School Improvement   79
    Elizabeth A. Lee and Don A. Klinger
        Introduction: Education, A Lightning Rod for Reform and
            Accountability   79
        Topic and Problem   80
        Do School Libraries Matter?   81
            Our Approach to the Question   81
            Our Findings on Exemplary School Libraries   83
        Collaboration as a Path to School Improvement   86
        Conclusions: Moving Forward, Being Effective Regardless of
            Current Status   86
        References   88

7   Perspectives of School Administrators Related to School Libraries 91
    Deborah Levitov
        Introduction: Mixed Methods Study of School Administrators   91
        Lack of Administrative Awareness   91
        Context and Background of the Study   92
        Research Questions   93
        Literature Review   93
        Administrators' Knowledge of School Library Programs   94
        Informing School Administrators about School Library Programs 95
        Methodology: Mixed Methods Approach   96
        Participants   96
        Assumptions   97
        Limitations   97
        Improvement Plan (Summary of Findings)   97
            Administrators' Changed Perceptions   97
            A Shift in Language   101
        Changed Perceptions   102
            University-Level Coursework about Libraries/Librarians   102
            Administrators as Advocates for Librarians/Libraries   102
            School Librarian and Administrator Hold Commonality   103
        Implications   103
            Solutions for Informing Administrators   104
            Informing School Library Specialists   104
        Conclusions: Recommendations for Further Study   105
        References   106

8   A Content Analysis of School Librarian Conferences:
    A Search for Empowering Professional Development   109
    Judi Moreillon
        Introduction: Content of Professional Development Conference
            Offerings   109
        A Line of Inquiry to Improve Teaching in Higher Education   109
        Topic and Problem of Conference Professional Development
            Content   110

Research Questions 111
Literature Review 112
Methodology: Content Analysis 113
Preparation of the Analysis 113
Sample 116
Findings 116
Improvement Plan 117
Conclusions: State-Level Conferences Are Important for
Empowering Professional Development 118
References 118

9   School-Based Technology Integration and School Librarian
Leadership 123
Marcia A. Mardis and Nancy Everhart
Introduction: Solutions to Technology-Related School Challenges 123
Technology Integration 123
Research Questions 124
Theoretical Framework: Formative Leadership Theory 125
Literature Review 125
Leadership in Schools 126
School Librarians and Leadership 126
Methodology: Participatory Research 127
Procedure 128
Validity and Reliability 129
Improvement Plan 130
Conclusions: Questions Answered through Cooperative Inquiry 130
References 134

10   Crossing the Language Barrier: The Potential for School
Librarians in Facilitating Cross-Cultural Teaching and
Learning in the School Library 137
Andrew J. M. Smith and Nancy J. Brown
Introduction: English Language Learners 137
The Multicultural School 137
Problems for Foreign-Born Students 138
The Role of the School Librarian in Standards-Based Education 139
The Changing Environment: From School Library to Learning
Commons 141
Learner Characteristics 142
Strategies for Supporting ELLs from the Research 142
Books and Instructional Materials 142
Instructional Strategies 143
Programming to Support ELLs 144
Technology Applications and Projects 145
Practical Matters 146
Conclusions: Culturally Responsive Leaders 146
References 147

11   Views from Research: From Ideology to Action   151
     Mirah J. Dow
         Introduction: What Must We Say about School Libraries?   151
         The Purpose   151
         The Premise   152
         The Practices   152
         School Libraries Matter   153
         Conclusions: Characteristics of a Professional School Librarian   162
         References   163

Index   165

About the Editor and Contributors   171

ILLUSTRATIONS

FIGURES

1.1. School Library Professional Dispositions Self-Assessment   11

2.1. Summary of Kansas Proficiency Rates by Five Middle School
      Subject Areas   29

3.1. Pre- and Post-survey Question Statements   44

4.1. School Library Map   55

6.1. Exemplary School Library Program Continuum
      (Adapted from Lee & Klinger, 2011)   84

8.1. Domain Matrix   114

9.1. Cycle of Cooperative Inquiry   130

TABLES

2.1a. Kansas Reading: All Students Increase over 10 years,
       2000–2010   25

2.1b. Kansas Mathematics: All Students Increase over 10 years,
       2000–2010   26

2.2.   2006–2009 Kansas Overall Distribution Trends across
       Three Grade Spans   30

2.3.   Kansas Grade Span by Trend Crosstabulation   32

3.1.   Number of Valid Responses by Question   45

3.2a. Questions 1–6 Agree/Strongly Agree Responses,
2008–2010   47

3.2b. Questions 7–12 Agree/Strongly Agree Responses,
2008–2010   48

9.1. Summary of Participants' Cooperative Inquiry Experiences   131

FOREWORD

Solid research is the "lifeblood" of evidence-based practice. Solid research has been the ally of school librarians for the past 60 years and continues to be the ally of school librarians today. The research conducted by Mary Helen Mahar and Doris C. Holladay and published by the U.S. Office of Education in 1964, *Statistics of public school libraries 1960–61 basic tables*, showed that fewer than 50 percent of elementary schools had libraries and attracted the interest of private industry. The lobbying efforts of the American Library Association's Washington office joined with concentrated efforts of key school librarians across the country resulted in the passage of the Elementary and Secondary Education Act (ESEA) with funds specified to purchase library materials and to build elementary and expand secondary school libraries. This new book, a collection of solid research from across North America, is critical to informing today's lobbying efforts in current reauthorization of the ESEA and revising No Child Left Behind, and to all stakeholders who advocate for professional librarians' important, necessary place alongside all 21st-century students and educators.

Keith Curry Lance led the way in showing the impact of school libraries on academic achievement with his landmark study of Colorado that was conducted in 1992 and published in 1993. He has verified these findings with two follow-up studies in Colorado and in studies he and his team have reported from many other states. Other researchers have carried out their own studies in a number of other states, and the results continue to demonstrate that school librarians matter. Other essential research has provided insight into the information seeking behavior of students and the importance of the presence of a school librarian in this process. School library research is informing new roles of school librarians as they facilitate instructional design, curriculum development, and partner with classroom teachings to implement the new Common Core States Standards.

For many years, school librarians have accepted the role of learning about introducing new technologies in their buildings and instructing teachers to use them.

From the earliest days of the computer in the library and classroom, school librarians have been the person to ask for help in their use. Students and teachers learned from school librarians about finding titles in the online catalog and then online searching in the school's databases. The newer technologies so quickly adopted by students remain a challenge for many teachers who lack the confidence to use them for instruction. It is the school librarian who is leading teachers.

The role of the school librarian in helping students become information literate has expanded with new literacies such as digital literacy and health literacy. School librarians are expected not only to help students find information and assess the usefulness of what is found in the ocean of resources available to them in an online environment, but also to help them create new information.

This book includes examples of the continuing research showing the impact of the school library and librarian in the achievement of students. It explains the new role of helping teachers in the implementation of the Common Core State Standards and the possibility for student learning including information retrieval skills in the multiple literacies that go well beyond information literacy. It addresses the need for collaboration at the school building level, as well as in university-based teacher education programs where future school administrators and content teachers are working to discover how to address today's educational challenges. This book explains the need for school librarians to accept a leadership role in their schools, a new role for many and a new definition for some teachers and for many school administrators.

This book offers solid research and realistic, evidence-based models for success. Sharing the contents of this book as widely as possible at local, regional, state, and even national conferences can help pave the way for school reform. One-on-one local conversations can begin the process. Programs at local meetings will capture school librarians who do not attend conferences. School librarians can work together to explain these new roles during their state conferences and to revise what they are doing and how they are offering their services in their schools. Advocates and policy makers can use it as a basis for focusing discussions about what can be accomplished with professional school librarians in every school building, and in writing of new policy that includes school librarians and fully funded school libraries.

The research found in this book should be shared with teachers, school administrators, parents, and others in the community, especially legislators. When these research results showing the value of the school librarian in a school are explained to legislators at the state and national levels so that these decision-makers *truly* understand that school librarians make a difference in the achievement of students, change will occur. This book is an excellent, important step in offering the evidence needed.

—Blanche Woolls
Professor and Director Emerita, School of Library and
Information Science, San Jose State University
Professor Emerita, School of Information Sciences,
University of Pittsburgh

PREFACE

The time has come for state-licensed school librarians in America to assume positions of authority and responsibility along with other educators in teaching today's students. This book provides authoritative library and information science research addressing the school librarian's position as an essential school leader, school-wide resource person, and collaborator who partners with classroom teachers in the design and delivery of instruction. It highlights the school librarian's unique expertise grounded in information seeking research, which conceptualizes information behavior as "how people need, seek, manage, give and use information in different contexts" (Bates in Fisher et al., 2009, p. xix). Taken together, the research in this book makes clear that state-licensed school librarians are necessary educators to teach 21st-century students in the context of core content areas to recognize an information need; search for, access, and evaluate information; use information to develop and communicate new ideas for resolution of human problems. State-licensed school librarians are much more than an educational luxury. For America students, state-licensed school librarians represent a necessity if this country is to move forward with the educational goal to graduate all students prepared for college, jobs, and/or careers.

Chapter authors were identified through a search of school library research from 2006–2011. High-quality research in terms of topical and conceptual significance and well-articulated and appropriate methods has been selected. While there are many other high-quality studies deserving attention, the chapters in this book create a collection of studies, all useful in the establishment of a strong foundation to move forward with new national, state, and local initiatives using innovative methods that will continue to demonstrate the vital importance of school libraries in every school building.

I am passionate about the topic of this book on at least three levels, which I view as parallel. First, the contents of this book encapsulates the essence of why I, as well as many of my colleagues, get up in the morning and hustle to get started teaching and interacting with library and information science graduate students, practicing school librarians, local and state school administrators, and others at the University and beyond who are engaged in educational enterprises. These are people who, because of their common interests in education, have a great opportunity to make positive contributions to improving life in today's society. In this way, my contribution is much greater than if I simply worked alone without a professional network.

Through higher education, college students master a body of knowledge and become informed and able to respect individual differences including intellectual and physical abilities and styles, races, religions, languages, and cultures, as well as differences in socioeconomic status. Through the study of library and information science in particular, college students in our programs become professional librarians, and other information professionals, with the authority and responsibility to resolve human problems through access to information, management of information systems, and to lead positive change in the world. The contents of this book assure me, and I hope others who are similarly situated, that we have not lost sight of real learner-centered intentions for college teaching.

Secondly, as a member of the American Association of Librarians (AASL) Legislation Committee from 2007–2011, I discovered the urgent need to advocate while also quickly and effectively communicating the importance of school librarians in today's schools. Frequently, sometimes weekly depending on the legislative calendar in Washington D.C., the AASL Legislation Committee members are called on by individuals in the American Library Associations' Washington office and/or by the AASL president to provide comments, or evidence, in support of inclusion of state-licensed school librarians and school library programs in federal law. During my term on the committee, our committee provided comments on several crucial pieces of federal legislation including the reauthorization of the Elementary and Secondary Education Act; Race to the Top; the Strengthening Kids Interest in Learning and Libraries (SKILLS) Act; the Literacy Education for All, Results for the Nation (LEARN) Act; and Improving Literacy Through School Libraries. As chair of the committee, it was my task to facilitate best conversations within the committee that would result in accurate, clear, and powerful statements. I learned that even with the input of new and veteran school librarians, library school educators, and other school library leaders from across the United States, it was not easy, or even at times possible, to say enough in limited space about the positive impact of school librarians and fully funded school librarians on student learning and achievement. Sometimes, we needed a book that contains organized "voices" of multiple research contributors and their many references to research-based evidence. Hopefully, this book will begin to fill this need with its 17 contributing researchers, 2 from Canada and 15 from the United States, citing numerous references to publications.

Thirdly, as a teacher of doctoral students, the contents of this book are important because the major scope of each chapter includes a critical–theoretical connection to debates and the progression of thought that characterizes broad realms of theoretical influence in the social sciences, making the research potentially relevant to the larger academic society including other educators and public policy makers. These studies examine data and locate school libraries within operational contexts. Review of the elaborate details in each chapter should be helpful to doctoral students grappling with the challenge of locating their own research in significant theoretical and practical contexts. It would also be important that doctoral students use this collection of studies in their critique of what to do, or not do, when it comes to building theory about what it means to learn, and to measure learning and other user-centered aspects of progress in an information society where computer technology has increased mass creation and use of information and where information seeking has become a fundamental behavior of humans.

This book is written for all who advocate in the best interest of school librarians and fully funded school libraries. It may be of interest to

- Legislators and other educational law and policy makers who want to know what educational programs will effectively and efficiently help to accomplish the U.S. public education goals, as well as goals for education in other countries
- Educators and school administrators who want to achieve the Common Core State Standards that include information retrieval skills and multiple literacies including digital, visual, textual, and technological skills
- Educators and school administrators who want to improve reading skills and growth of comprehension in all children
- Educators and school administrators who want school leadership to achieve technology integration via professional guidelines of state, national, and international organizations
- Educators and school administrators who want to improve learning for English language learners and to discover the capacity of the school librarian as a pivotal resource for learners and teachers
- School librarians taking the lead in educating school communities about the changing nature of today's digital students and the librarian's positive impact on student achievement when partnering with classroom teachers
- Researchers wanting to reshape existing theory and build interdisciplinary theory while asking new questions and moving school library research into the 21st century and linking school libraries to future research in the social, behavioral, and economic science disciplines
- Educators and members of the public who advocate for best practices and communicate research-based links between investment in school libraries and student learning outcomes
- University administrators and teachers who are committed to sharing expertise across professional and disciplinary boundaries that will result in new, innovative content reflecting knowledge, skills, and disposition appropriate for 21st-century school administrators, classroom teachers, and librarians
- Conference planners and other stakeholders who share responsibilities for providing highest quality and relevant professional development topical offerings that support school librarians' development as leaders and meet priorities for best practice set out by national associations

ACKNOWLEDGMENTS

I want to thank all the contributors for their ideas and content for this book. The authors of these chapters were quick to agree when asked to write their respective chapters. Each author was supportive of the purpose of the book, respectful and accepting of my guidance in outlining the task, and enthusiastic about sharing their own research to what may potentially be a worldwide audience. I also want to thank my school's administration and my faculty colleagues for their insightful guidance and encouragement. It is a great pleasure to be part of a school of library and information management and university that has for 110 years offered library education, and from the very beginning included education for school librarians. Thank you to my current and former students in the Midwest and Western states who continually inform me of the pressing issues facing individuals and schools today. Thank you to my family members, Patrick, Hilary, and Geoffrey, whose professional and scholarly experiences broaden the scope of my thinking, teaching, and research, and to our son, Patrick, who without speaking, reading, or writing teaches us all to appreciate the freedom we have to access and use information for the greater good of everyone.

REFERENCE

Bates, M. J. (2009). Preface. In K. E. Fisher, S. Erdelez, & L. (E. F.) McKechnie (Eds.), *Theories of information behavior* (pp. xix–xxii). Medford, NJ: Information Today, Inc.

INTRODUCTION

Today across America, school budgets are being cut and licensed personnel are being slashed from schools. In many states, despite their professional teaching credentials, many state-licensed school librarians have been cut. It is urgent that educational law and policy makers recognize and use what can be learned from empirical evidence about the importance and the positive impact of state-licensed school librarians and school library program on student learning and achievement.

This book provides evidence through a collection of 10 recent studies that the state-licensed school librarian is a leader, instructional partner, information specialist, teacher, and program administer (AASL, 2009) that today's children and youth cannot do without. Chapters explain professional librarians' theory-based pedagogy that enables them to rise above the seemingly random confusion of a complicated society and to understand principles on which to base purposeful, productive action. Each study uses quantitative, qualitative, or mixed research methods to answer important questions. Each chapter ends with conclusions that provide statements that can be used to advocate for the employment of state-licensed school librarians. The chapters are a collection of school library research upon which to improve through the design and implementation of future studies that will contribute to an ongoing theory-building process and to new evidence-based practices. A brief introduction to each chapter follows.

Chapter 1 describes what is meant by professional dispositions of school librarians. Through a review of education literature and the description of a study using the Delphi method to question exemplar school librarians, readers discover a vision for professional dispositions, the professional attitudes, values, and beliefs demonstrated through verbal and nonverbal behavior and necessary for professional educators to interact with students, families, colleagues, and community members. The professional dispositions that are discussed in this chapter are from a school library perspective that emphasizes providing all students access to information. The chapter outlines actions that can and should be taken to guarantee that today's children and youth learn from only those educators, including school librarians, who bring to today's information and technology-based learning environments significant passion for students as individuals, fairness, and belief that all students can learn.

Chapter 2 asserts that information seeking has become a fundamental behavior of humans, particularly in developing countries where computer technology has increased mass communication and use of information. Two prominent theories of information behavior, sense-making (Dervin, 1983) and the information search process (Kuhlthau, 2004), are presented as explanations for school librarians' important roles in helping students to learn to adapt to their environment through development of information seeking and use skills. The chapter outlines a quantitative study of state annual yearly progress data that investigates student success when schools are with and without school librarians.

Effective elementary teacher preparation for successful pedagogical practices in co-teaching information literacy skills is the focus of Chapter 3. A study is detailed based on the premise that professional knowledge about successful integration of information literacy instruction, which requires collaboration and partnerships between school librarians and classroom teachers, can begin during university-based, elementary education programs. The chapter provides evidence that requiring a 1-credit hour course taught by a university instructor, an experienced, state-licensed school librarian who teaches from a library science perspective, can effectively inform future teachers about the roles of state-licensed school librarians in teaching reading and research. The chapter advances the theory that for collaboration to move beyond cooperation to instructional partnerships between teachers and school librarians, there must be engagement by colleges of education and schools of library and information science in large-scale change. This proposed opportunity for education reform involves new university infrastructures that will allow and reward faculty for sharing content areas and responsibilities for instruction.

Chapter 4 highlights recent research that investigates the information behavior of young people who use information and communication technologies to seek personal information, particularly in the school library. This study of student learning demonstrates how school librarians are uniquely positioned to investigate information seeking practices of today's digital generation and to shift toward dynamic, educational concepts of informatics in schools. This study answers "What are the everyday life information seeking practices of students working in a highly technological high school?" The chapter addresses information behaviors of students in a segment of society that needs to be better understood in order for education, school libraries in particular, to better serve all school-aged members of today's society.

Chapter 5 begins with a discussion of seven sets of circumstances that define the context of American public education in today's and in tomorrow's school library programs. It provides in-depth explanations of school library research that has examined school librarians' impact on student achievement and a new research focus on how school librarians are perceived by their fellow teachers as well as by school administrators. The authors of this chapter outline a five-step action plan for how school library research can be used to improve local school library programs. With their sights on the rapid and continuous changes in school environments and computer technologies, the authors identify some new, pressing research questions.

Chapter 6 addresses educational reform and accountability by first introducing the Literacy and Numeracy Secretariat, a branch of the Ministry of Education Ontario, formed in Ontario in 2004 to lead provincial, supportive efforts to increase the proportion of students in Canada meeting the provincial standards in literacy and numeracy. The researchers point out that while the United States has used a policy approach to school improvement, jurisdictions in Canada tend to use a less demanding approach, providing a supportive model to lead to school improvement. The researchers describe their recent, mixed methods study using a developmental program evaluation approach to ask "Do the school library and the teacher librarian add value to the efforts to meet the goals of continuous school improvement and accountability?" Compared to summative approaches to evaluation that use an overall worth and value exploration, this developmental model enables deep exploration of complex interactions that occur among teachers, students, and programs within a school. The researchers developed an exemplary school library program continuum, which offers a way to evaluate the current functioning in a school library program without judging it categorically as meeting or not meeting a set of criteria. This study suggests program personnel opportunities to engage in systematic inquiry and data-informed decision-making.

The author of Chapter 7 presents findings of a mixed methods study that examined the experiences of two groups of administrators who participated in an online course designed to educate school administrators about school library programs and the role of the librarian, and to subsequently create administrative advocates for school libraries. This study addresses the need for educational leadership, as well as the community to recognize, support, and fund the efforts of school librarians. Participant administrators in the study indicated that the course was the first time they had encountered content about development and evaluation of school library programs. They also indicated that course content was important and should become part of university-level administrative coursework.

Focused on the need for empowering professional development for school librarians, the study articulated in Chapter 8 is a content analysis that grew out of a university-level teaching dilemma and faculty motivation to undertake a line of inquiry to improve education for school librarian graduate students. Using a stratified random sample, a content analysis of school librarian conferences held in the 2010–2011 academic year was conducted. A domain matrix was developed, tested, and then used to analyze titles and descriptions of 12 conference program offerings. The researcher concludes with a call for bringing state-level conferences into alignment with national guidelines and priorities.

Chapter 9 identifies technology integration as a crucial element of teaching and learning that requires school-based leadership to be consistent, relevant, and connector between various aspects of students' learning experiences. Using a formative leadership theory (Ash & Persall, 2000) framework, this study, which was funded by the Institute of Museum and Library and Services, asked "How can cooperative inquiry methodology be used to evaluate the outcomes of education for school librarianship leadership in technology integration?" Cooperative inquiry (Oates, 2002), a form of participatory research, was used to merge the participation of school librarians, teachers, technology personnel, administrators, and other key school stakeholders in solving a mutually agreed-upon problem: What is an issue facing our school community that can be addressed with technology?

Chapter 10 points to shifting U.S. population demographics and the increasing numbers of English language learners. The research in this chapter answers two leading questions for more than a decade: "Why does our school need a library when we have access to so much information from our classrooms via the Internet?" And, "What does a new learning commons look like?" Through an exhaustive review of literature, the researchers describe the role of the school librarian as an invaluable, pivotal resource for learners and teachers and examples of successful instructional materials, strategies, programming, and technology.

Chapter 11 summaries key findings from all the chapters and answers the question "What can and will advocates and informed stakeholders say to convince others that school libraries matter?" It provides nine research-based statements drawn from the content of this book. The chapter concludes with a description of the characteristics of a professional that is applied to the school librarian profession.

If anything, this book does not prove that school librarians have no faults or are immune to failure. School librarians, like all educators, experience periods of ups and downs. What sets some educators apart from those who fail and later achieve is their ability to closely examine practices, envision a different result, and willingness to change themselves and their practices. This book demonstrates these strengths. School librarians are professional educations who focus on student learning. Views from research in this book—together with many more worthwhile school library research studies such as Lesley Farmer and Alan Safer's (2010) study, Developing California school library media program standards; Ross Todd's (2012) study, School libraries and the development of intellectual agency: Evidence from New Jersey; and Renee Hill's (2012) study, Strengths and opportunities: School librarians serving students with special needs in central New York State—make clear that school librarians will when funded and involved in today's schools go far beyond textbooks to significantly help to increase all student learning and achievement, and help to make education in the United States more globally competitive.

REFERENCES

American Association of School Librarians (AASL). (2009). *Empowering learners: Guidelines for school library media programs.* Chicago: American Library Association.

Ash, R. C., & Persall, J. M. (2000). The principal as chief learning officer: Developing teacher leaders. *NASSP Bulletin, 84*(616), 15–22.

Dervin, B. (1983). Information as a new construct: The relevance of perceived information needs to synthesis and interpretation. In S. A. Ward & L. J. Reed (Eds.), *Knowledge structure and use: Implications for synthesis and interpretation* (pp. 155–183). Philadelphia: Temple University Press.

Farmer, L., & Safer, A. M. (2010). Developing California school library media program standards. *School Library Research, 13.* Retrieved from http://www.ala.org/aasl/sites/ala.org.aasl/files/content/aaslpubsandjournals/slr/vol13/SLR_Developing California_V13.pdf

Hill, R. F. (2012). Strengths and opportunities: School librarians serving students with special needs in central New York State. *School Library Research, 15.* Retrieved from http://www.ala.org/aasl/sites/ala.org.aasl/files/content/aaslpubsandjournals/slr/vol15/SLR_StrengthsandOpportunities_V15.pdf

Kuhlthau, C. C. (2004). *Seeking meaning: A process approach to library and information services* (2nd ed.). Westport, CT: Libraries Unlimited.

Oates, B. J. (2002). Co-operative inquiry: Reflections on practice. *Electronic Journal of Business Research Methods, 1*(1), 27.

Todd, R. J. (2012). School libraries and the development of intellectual agency: Evidence from New Jersey. *School Library Research, 15*. Retrieved from http://www.ala.org/aasl/sites/ala.org.aasl/files/content/aaslpubsandjournals/slr/vol15/SLR_School LibrariesandDevelopment_V15.pdf

1

———◦•◦•◦———

PROFESSIONAL DISPOSITIONS OF SCHOOL LIBRARIANS

Gail Bush and Jami L. Jones

INTRODUCTION: EXPLORATION OF PROFESSIONAL DISPOSITION OF SCHOOL LIBRARIANS

This chapter discusses an exploratory study to identify professional dispositions of school librarians. The researchers describe the context of the research within school librarianship based on national student learning standards, the research question regarding professional dispositions, and the subsequent selection of the Delphi method— a qualitative research methodology that places an emphasis on expert knowledge within a particular field. The researchers developed a plan of action including a self-assessment and implications for school librarianship graduate program curricula.

DISPOSITIONS IN ACTION

Viewed from an historical context within American education, there are those who might argue that school librarians are coming late to the dispositions party. The teacher education field has been ruminating and swaying around teacher dispositions for decades (Katz & Raths, 1986; Katz, 1993; Murrell, Diez, Feiman-Nemser, & Schussler, 2010). However, it could also be argued that school librarians have not lost much ground and should focus on moving forward rather than looking back. While attention to dispositions in teacher education was initiated by national teacher accreditation standards (National Council for the Accreditation of Teacher Education [NCATE], 2007), school librarians, on the other hand, are motivated by the most meaningful purpose within education—school librarians start with student learning dispositions and find purpose emanating from that core of learning. School librarians' approach to dispositions seems to be a more learner-centered approach that acknowledges that the best way to teach learning dispositions is to model them. And thus, this research agenda emerged.

———————

This chapter is based on Bush, G., & Jones, J.L. (2010, May). Exploration to identify professional dispositions of school librarians: A Delphi study. *School Library Research*, *13*. American Library Association. http://www.ala.org/aasl/sites/ala.org.aasl/files/content/aaslpubsandjournals/slr/vol13/SLR_ExplorationtoIdentify.pdf

It was in October 2007 at the Treasure Mountain Institute in Reno, Nevada, which preceded the American Association of School Librarians (AASL) conference, that the researchers in this study first encountered the *Standards for the 21st-century learner* (AASL, 2007). The initial reaction to the dazzling colors and oversized photos in the 8" × 10" glossy brochures that spilled out of the shrink-wrapped plastic paled in comparison to the subsequent reaction to the "dispositions-in-action" strand of standards. We met the perplexed outcry with our own affective learning dispositions of creative exploration as we synergistically seized upon this open invitation that was presenting itself to us. Our triage of this challenge was that in order for school librarians to aspire to best practices for student learning dispositions, our very own professional dispositions would need identification. We discovered this to be especially true once we started to conduct a literature review and learned from the teacher education literature that educator performance evaluations would be inevitably coming down the road and that dispositions were going to have an important role in both administrator and self-assessments. If school librarians did not identify their own dispositions, others would do it. School librarians needed to take a long, deep look in the mirror before reflecting and modeling student dispositions in action. While possibly arriving late to the party, school librarians were going to make one grand entrance that should attract the attention of the education community writ large.

The research goal became clear as we sought to identify professional dispositions of exemplary school librarians as a step toward teaching for understanding of student learning dispositions. While clarity of purpose catapulted us forward, our steps were measured by the necessity of closely studying school librarianship as a profession, considering what identifying dispositions would mean within a professional "identity," and matching the most appropriate methodology to this research agenda. We took these steps with the firm understanding that exploration into the affective domain of school librarianship has never been particularly welcomed and that much of what has been considered problematic within the field has in fact been identified as personality or temperament or simply behavioral concerns. Having served in various types of librarianship roles, what we knew to be true within school librarianship was confirmed by our research. Often relegated to the poor relation within education, the school librarian was also marginalized within the profession of librarianship.

Within the study of professionalism, school librarians are on "the periphery of librarianship," as school librarians were considered to be "often teachers doubling as librarians" (Abbott, 1988, p. 219). In his 1988 publication, *The system of professions: An essay on the division of expert labor*, Abbott posits in his discussion of the information professions that librarianship has a "highly structured core and very hazy periphery" (p. 218). Abbott asserts that because academic and research librarians have professionals as their clients, their status and organizational standing is high within librarianship. School librarians and youth services within small- and medium-sized public libraries would conversely be at the low end of his measure, which he calls "low-status areas" based on the societal ranking of our young charges (p. 219).

While knowing where school librarians stand within the profession of librarianship and the field of education is certainly inspiration enough to self-identify professional dispositions, there are those who might question the source of self-knowledge that these researchers sought. William James would call this sense of identity "character" (Erikson, 1968, p. 19). Erikson explains that to James this sense of identity is both mental and moral and it comes to one as a recognition. Erikson (1968) also studies Freud's grasp of identity within a communal culture as he emphasizes the complexity of identity formation, which "employs a process of simultaneous reflection and observation" (p. 22). As researchers, we were poised to ask school library colleagues to question not current identity but to challenge school librarians further by requesting that they foresee the professional dispositions of exemplary school librarians—not to bemoan and qualify what could be viewed as broken within school librarianship but what professional dispositions of an exemplary school librarian practitioner would look like and what an administrator would see as those dispositions are demonstrated.

Discussions around methodology became crystal clear the more we researched and learned about the Delphi study methodology. As researchers, we were interested in what leading scholars and exemplary school librarian practitioners would forecast. We determined that many school library scholars and exemplary practitioners were in service to the profession through the editorial and advisory boards of school library journals. This community would serve as a pool of participants who are known as "panelists" in the Delphi study methodology. Additionally, we sought independent thinking, an aggressive timeline, and convenience of correspondence on behalf of participants. The Delphi methodology fulfilled all of identified research needs and offered a manageable and reasoned qualitative approach to this study. While maintaining confidentiality of our panelists, permission was requested through informed consent protocols to subsequently publish the names of the participants and anonymous excerpts of their responses. Finally, the Delphi methodology also allowed for the potential for further rounds of queries as needed.

The research topic and problem seemed to have presented themselves right there in the throes of literally "unpacking" new national standards. The dramatic impact of the moment aside, this opportunity felt timely, within professional capacities, and eminently fascinating. The chance to deeply study the affective domain of the school librarian felt like uncharted territory. As there was no path to follow, these researchers set out to leave a trail behind that promised to invite a shift in school librarianship preparation, performance assessments based on dispositions identified by school librarian scholars, and further research.

THE CONCEPT OF PROFESSIONAL DISPOSITIONS

It was the 2007 release of the *Standards for the 21st-century learner* by the AASL that introduced the concept of dispositions to school librarianship. The hierarchical framework of AASL standards fosters:

> High expectations for today's learners because the skills, dispositions, responsibilities, and self-assessment strategies represented by these standards will provide the foundation for learning throughout life ... and ... serve as guideposts for school library media specialists (SLMSs) and other educators in their teaching because these skills and dispositions are most effectively taught as an integral part of content learning. (AASL, 2009, p. 5)

Even though the focus of these standards is on the learner, the support of a strong school library is assumed and mirrors the thinking of national professional groups that recognize that teacher quality is vital to student learning and achievement (Darling-Hammond & Bransford, 2005). The authors of the *Standards for the 21st-century learner in action* conclude that "a strong school library media program (SLMP) that offers a highly-qualified school library media specialist" is "implicit within every standard and indicator" (AASL, 2009, p. 5). One could assume that the skills, responsibilities, and self-assessment strategies identified in the student learning standards would be met with understanding by practicing school librarians. Only the dispositions strand is unfamiliar territory, having been introduced to the field through these standards. Searching and researching school library media research illuminates the end result that the concept of dispositions is new to school librarian vernacular. The research led the researchers to the teacher education field where a substantive goal focused on dispositional growth and awareness in preservice educators was found, which highlights the comparative urgency of the school librarianship field impetus to impact student learning dispositions (Dottin, 2006; Breese & Nawrocki-Chabin, 2007). Breese and Nawrocki-Chabin (2002) conclude that dispositions must indeed be cultivated through intentional activities in order to ensure that teachers enter the field with acceptable dispositions. Reflection and peer conferencing are two ways to identify specific actions and to engage educators or beginning teachers to analyze and consider the dispositions they need, or need to develop. All the research on dispositions in the teacher education field that was studied began and ended with teacher preparation programs and entry-level teachers. Only in school librarianship are professional dispositions seen as a pathway to modeling student learning dispositions.

The *Standards for the 21st-century learner* (AASL, 2007), which comprise four learning standards each consisting of four strands (skills, dispositions, responsibilities, and self-assessment strategies), are the best examples of dispositions for school librarians. The full spectrum of 21st-century learner dispositions as crafted by AASL is as follows:

- Display initiative, engagement, emotional resilience, persistence, curiosity
- Demonstrate confidence, self-direction, creativity, adaptability, flexibility, personal productivity, leadership, teamwork, motivation
- Maintain (and employ) a critical stance, openness to new ideas
- Use both divergent and convergent thinking
- Have (and show) an appreciation for social responsibility

The dispositions identified in the AASL *Standards for the 21st-century learner* are student dispositions but must be acquired by school librarians who then model these for youth. In essence, the AASL standards become the de facto dispositions of school librarians by virtue of the fact that dispositions are best "acquired, taught, and caught through modelling" (Bush & Jones, 2010).

The AASL dispositions-in-action strand introduced expectations not evident in past standards and led to questions centering on the meaning of student learning dispositions and strategies for best practices in developing them (Jones & Bush, 2009). After much anecdotal discussion with and interest from colleagues from across the country (and at an international meeting of many American school librarians working globally), these concerns confirmed the authors' suspicions that an exploration of the concept of dispositions within the school library profession was warranted. In fact, it was the communal interest in the question of professional dispositions as a response to student learning dispositions that was a springboard for this research.

THE QUESTION OF PROFESSIONAL DISPOSITIONS OF SCHOOL LIBRARIANS

The researchers' introduction to dispositions was as sudden as the first frenzied reading of the hot-off-the-presses 2007 AASL student learning standards. That we recognized a problem inherent in the student dispositions-in-action strand harkens Jean Lave's stance that "finding something problematic is not caused by lack of knowledge but on the contrary subsumes a great deal of knowledge" (Talja, 2010, p. 213). As researchers, our areas of concentration were both in the affective domain, in developing a framework for educator collaboration, and in resiliency. It was with this affective domain lens that both researchers simultaneously saw the problem. We were literally standing on the outside of a group of colleague scholars who were sitting and rapidly reviewing the new standards. As we experienced their response to the dispositions strand, we immediately saw the potential in exploring this problem. Lave suggests that problem solvers freely mold problems to fit the prospective resolution (p. 213). We took the problem of student learning dispositions and reconfigured it in an attempt to take measured steps toward a productive outcome. In order to teach learning dispositions, school librarians would need to model them; in order to model them, school librarians would need to understand them; in order to understand student dispositions, school librarians would need to recognize their own dispositions.

"Know thyself," an ancient Greek aphorism used by Socrates, Plato, and others, was the guiding principle, but with a twist. We saw this exploration as a golden opportunity to better ourselves—in a sense to know ourselves in order to better outgrow ourselves, to be our best selves. For too long, colleagues have bemoaned the fact that many school librarian practitioners seem to be lagging behind the critical mass of research and publications around collaboration and partnerships. School librarians forego the social context of the professional role for the safe, secure, and sadly outdated traditional warehousing managerial tasks. Driven by student learning, the center of the core of all that is meaningful and purposeful within the school librarian field, we are now given the "green light" to turn the mirror on ourselves.

It was never the researchers' focus to explore the current ecosystem of school librarianship. We were not motivated by the divide between would, could, and should. We were engaged by the promise of modeling learning standards and by the possibility of influencing the next generation of school librarians to be freed from outdated traditions of the practice that kept them snugly within the confines of the workroom hidden from view behind book carts of unprocessed donations.

With the ultimate goal of effectively teaching student learning dispositions, the research question—borne out of brilliant and generous colleagues who collaborated to write the 2007 student learning standards—was:

What are the professional dispositions of exemplary school librarians?

A BROAD CONTEXT FOR A REVIEW OF THE LITERATURE

Numerous in-depth searches resulted in the researchers' confidence that there was no published literature available to review in the identification of professional dispositions of school librarians. Defining terms necessitated broadening the context for the research to include the origins of dispositions within the education literature and teacher dispositions within the teacher education field. Affirmation would lie in the discovery that this journey would start with progressive educational philosopher John Dewey's 1922 publication, *Human nature and conduct*. Dewey laid the dispositional foundation by contemplating the question, "Why do some well-educated people function at higher levels than others?" Dewey (1922) attributes this functioning to a "readiness to act overtly in a specific fashion whenever opportunity is presented" (p. 41).

Although it seemed to be undetected within the education field, education scholar Arnstine was first to extend the philosophical discussion about dispositions beyond Dewey's introduction to the concept. Arnstine (1967) views learning as the acquisition of "behaviors, knowledge, skills, habits, and attitudes," the latter he defines as dispositions (p. 13). Learning, therefore, is the continuing and lengthy process of acquiring and developing a great number of abilities and attitudes—or dispositions, or the changing of old ones. While Arstine (1967) may have laid the dispositional foundation in education, it was efforts of Katz and Raths (1986) that propelled the discussion about effectiveness and teacher quality to the forefront of teacher education by proposing that the "goals of teacher education programs should include a class of outcomes we call professional dispositions" that focus "exclusively upon behaviors of teachers related to effective teaching in the classroom" (p. 302).

Katz (1993) defines dispositions as a "tendency to exhibit frequently, consciously, and voluntarily a pattern of behavior that is directed toward a broad goal" (p. 2). Katz and Raths (1986) describe these as a "pattern of acts that were chosen by the teacher in particular contexts and at particular times" (p. 7). Although

> We are not using the term dispositions to indicate a cause of behavior; the construct is descriptive rather than explanatory. For example, a teacher does not praise children because he has a disposition to be supportive. Rather, a teacher observed to make use of praise in a number of contexts and on frequent occasions, might be described as having a supportive disposition. (Katz and Raths, 1986, pp. 301, 302)

A thorough review of the literature of this complex concept of educator dispositions revealed one overwhelming conclusion. The realization that within the school librarian field, school librarians must identify valued dispositions—that there is "no one size fits all" when it comes to dispositions—may lead to uneasiness among some professionals uncomfortable with uncertainty and ambiguity. These notions were abundantly evident in the responses and comments made by Delphi study panelists even though the NCATE definition of dispositions was provided. It is within this context of dispositions and the AASL standards that the researchers sought to investigate the expert thinking about professional dispositions of school librarians, which had not previously been studied.

THE DELPHI STUDY METHODOLOGY

Thinking back to the unveiling of the AASL standards (2007), profoundly insightful researchers might have foreseen the attraction of anecdotal documentation of that moment and taken a straw poll to identify the number of school library scholars present who had ever encountered the concept of dispositions. While conjecture will not hold up in the court of scholarly research, nevertheless, we suggest that the response would be close to zero. An exhaustive search of school library research (and library and information science research) confirmed that as researchers, we were beginning a journey through uncharted territory. Starting from scratch required that terms be defined. Was the search for truth or belief? Would participants be secure enough in their own value systems to forecast "dispositions" with all the ambiguity that the query and the concept proffer? We became completely enamored with participation in this study when those who readily agreed to participate in our study blithely treaded through the sticky-messy-ill-defined waters of professional dispositions. Scholars and skilled practitioners alike did not skip a beat with concerns over an absolute truth (Rorty & Engel, 2007) but understood that we were seeking their own truth as they forecast an unknown. As Margaret Atwood wrote in *True stories*:

> Don't ask for the true story;
> why do you need it?
>
> It's not what I set out with
> or what I carry. (1981, p. 9)

The qualitative research methodology selected for this study was the Delphi method that places an emphasis on expert knowledge within a particular field (Booth, Colomb, & Williams, 2003; Schwandt, 2003). An economical hallmark of Delphi studies that is distinctive is that it reduces the need for panelists to travel to a location to participate in focus groups. Additional rationales against employing focus groups for Delphi studies are consistent with individual contributions to the research.

The specific strengths of the Delphi method as the research technique chosen for this study are highlighted by two renowned research teams in this arena: by Linstone and Turoff (1975) as having a "problem that does not lend itself to precise analytical techniques but can benefit from subjective judgments on a collective basis" (p. 275) and by Van de Ven and Delbecq (1974) who recognize that without the use of focus groups, the "isolation of the participants facilitated a freedom from conformity pressures" (p. 619). While the Delphi method lent itself to the initiation of the conversation started by this study, the researchers anticipate that future studies may certainly take different research paths to deepen this discourse.

RESEARCH DESIGN: DELPHI METHOD

Delphi panelists are required to contribute their opinions in response to specific queries within a short period of time. While subject selection is considered a critical step in the Delphi process, there is little in the way of standards for the selection process. Since "expert" is defined within a discipline, selection is determined by researchers as appropriate within the context of the query and the perceived ability of the participants to respond with vision. Researchers use their discretion to identify appropriate participants for a particular study; this judgment may vary within a field based on the type of information researchers intend to elicit. Commonly chosen panelists across disciplines include positional leaders, authors of publication in the literature, and those who might have direct contact with the issue under investigation (Hsu & Sandford, 2007).

Invited Delphi panelists included members of the editorial boards of *Knowledge Quest, Library Media Connection, School Library Monthly, School Library Media Research*, and *Teacher Librarian*, five journals in the school library field, with select academic scholars and association leaders, a total of 63 invited participants. The researchers considered this selection suitable to this study as it encompassed key leaders in the field who regularly use their scholarly and professional judgment in editorial decisions to share their expert views on a wide range of school librarianship topics. They determine annual themes for the journals and develop column and feature topics that are timely and critical to the advancement of the school library field. The editorials boards as a whole represent both school library scholars and accomplished practitioners from across the country.

We were optimistic that perhaps one-half of the 63 invited Delphi panelists would be willing to participate due to the timely nature of the study and that most likely participant fatigue would continue through the subsequent rounds. This strategy was a backward design with the intent of having approximately 15 panelists participate throughout the entire study, the average number of Delphi panelists as identified by Ludwig in 1997. The participants (referred to as panelists) were informed in the Informed Consent form that the Delphi approach engages experts in responding to a single query and subsequent contributions based on initial responses, that participation was intentionally individual, and that panelists would be asked for independent thought. Since all communication would be through e-mail, participants would not need to consider cost or travel considerations. Delphi panelists were informed that the first query (Round 1) would consist of one question with a request to identify five dispositions with each one including brief substantiation (100 words maximum each). Traditionally, in Delphi studies, the number of rounds or "iterations" depends both on the consensus of the responses and the degree to which the researchers are seeking consensus from the study (Hsu & Sandford, 2007).

RESEARCH FINDINGS AND PLANS OF ACTION

The impetus for the *Exploration to identifying professional dispositions of school librarians: A Delphi study* was the 2007 publication of the AASL *Standards for the 21st-century learner* complete with dispositions in action for the student learner. There was an implied imperative that practicing educators were to provide the requisite modeling of student learning dispositions, which is borne out in the teacher education professional literature (Katz & Raths, 1986; Katz 1993; Mevarech, 1995; Smith, Skarbek, & Hurst 2005; Sockett, 2006). However, when the researchers began to investigate dispositions of school librarians, research uncovered studies regarding professional dispositions of classroom teachers in teacher education literature based on standards only as described in the "Introduction" section of this chapter. It became clear that initial studies needed to be conducted in school librarianship; there had been no research detected, no published studies found, no indication that professional dispositions were identified, discussed in school librarian preparatory programs, topics of professional development, or included in professional evaluations by administrators.

Despite the coupling of the relatively unfamiliar and decidedly complex concept of dispositions and the open-ended qualitative research design of the Delphi study, results were found to (1) indicate a vision for professional dispositions of school librarians recognized predominantly for their quality teaching but from a distinctly school library perspective, (2) provoke a range of emotional responses from dedicated leaders of the field, and (3) highlight the critical importance of grappling with the identified schism between reality and the vision of professional dispositions of school librarians as documented by this study. Evaluation and assessment are inevitable in the accountability-laden educational system. If school librarians do not identify their own vision of the dispositions of school librarians, there is a real risk that professional dispositions will be identified for school librarians. This motivational message was not lost on the thoughtful panelists of this Delphi study and likely influenced decisions to participate notwithstanding the provocative nature of the inquiry.

1. *Results indicate a vision for professional dispositions of school librarians recognized predominantly for their quality teaching but from a distinct school library perspective:*

Panelists identified dispositions that focus on change agency in the practice of teaching and learning. While the identification of teaching was both predominant and problematic, it spoke to the overwhelming response that in one way or another, it is all about teaching, if only school librarians could get ideas sorted out and identify the distinction that school librarians have from our classroom teacher counterparts. School librarians engage with learners in a holistic, communal, and societal context where care and equity are symptoms of the school librarian's respect for each student. School librarians build intellectual character over time through modeling, guiding, and influencing learning through understanding. School librarians share the journey with young charges throughout learning experiences in the school and in authentic learning that reaches local and global communities. School librarians employ instructional strategies, techniques, skills, and applied best practices to bring focus to an inquiry stance that envelops both deep thinking and proven skill sets that create learners rather than the learned.

2. *Results were found to provoke a range of emotional responses from dedicated leaders of the field:*

The subject of this study is one that appears to be unexplored in school librarianship. Best practices that are accepted though rarely evidence-based, student learning is our worthy goal, and new iterations of visionary outcomes demonstrate remarkable contributions by school librarian scholars and leaders. The publication of the 2007 AASL standards shone a light on student learning dispositions and caused the field to turn the mirror on itself. There was a fair amount of cognitive dissonance with the complexity of the concept of dispositions as indicated by Round 2 results. There was an understanding that responses were individual and should come from the panelist's professional tacit knowledge rather than research. Indeed, frustration with this process of query (as in the process of identifying dispositions), even for school librarianship scholars, is identified by Kuhlthau, Maniotes, and Caspari (2007), but "it is during exploration that the most significant learning takes place in the inquiry process" (p. 17).

3. *Results highlight the critical importance of grappling with the identified schism between reality and the vision of professional dispositions of school librarians as documented by this study:*

Participation by the panelists required visionary thinking, not what experience has shown to be our professional dispositions but rather what the panelists forecast to be professional dispositions of *exemplary* school librarians. In Round 3, panelists were reminded that they should "identify what should be—not what is; seek to identify the ideal, do not report on our reality." Naturally, there are no wrong answers and no right answers, there are only responses gathered from recognized experts in the field who are dedicated, visionary, and accustomed to providing profoundly valuable and selfless service to the profession. Additionally, the Delphi methodology requires that panelists be independent in their responses and individually respond to inquiries. These factors illuminated diverse thinking across the field, both geographically and creatively. Regardless of the particular sentiment of any given panelist, there is a distinctly heightened consciousness of the need for the field to identify professional dispositions of school librarians as a compass for professional education programs and professional development.

In the words of National Board for Professional Teaching Standards (NBPTS), accomplished teachers are "models of educated persons, exemplifying the virtues they inspire in students" (NBPTS, 2002). However, the initial step underpinning this theoretical framework is self-assessment. Dispositions that define exemplary professional practice do need to be explicitly identified and recognized within the field. That being said, it is confounding to consider someone other than oneself determining that one is lacking as a professional and subsequently willfully taking the requisite steps to develop into a more effective practitioner without first having an opportunity to self-assess. This also alerts us to the ongoing discussion regarding the "having" thoughts and "doing" behavior dilemma within the field of psychology (Cantor, 1990). Teacher educators Koeppen and Davison-Jenkins (2007) posit that teacher educators can support teacher candidates in developing new dispositions. Perhaps a well-respected mentor is in a position to have a positive impact on both the improvement of inadequate dispositional behaviors and development of new dispositions. It is more likely that upon *self-reflection*, we might identify the dispositions that are recognized as exemplary and that might be lacking as potential areas indicated to improve one's practice (Schön, 1987). Self-assessments might be used as formative assessments throughout professional education and then again as evaluation tools once school librarians are engaged in professional practice.

The proposed self-assessment tool (Figure 1.1) is a framework model that might be used in school library education and also as an evaluation tool for administrators. It is a working draft of a theoretical framework for acquiring dispositions by school librarians. Perhaps it seems that creating an assessment tool is premature in this discussion of dispositions within the school library field. The value of this

DISPOSITION	AWARE	DEVELOPING	MEETS EXPECTATIONS
I DEMONSTRATE CARING, COLLEGIALITY, AND COLLABORATION IN INTERACTIONS AND COMMUNICATION.			

Exemplars:	Comments and Proposed Action:
• I demonstrate care for students through respect for them as unique individuals with full lives and promising futures beyond their experiences in the school environment. • I demonstrate care for students by "creating a warm environment" as documented in the AASL *Standards for 21st-century learners.* I value learning as an exciting, engaging, and inspired lifelong pursuit and demonstrate that value through my practice in the school library media program. • I demonstrate care for students through attention to their interests, motivation, and abilities. • I demonstrate care for students through use of appropriate communication methods and modeling appropriate communication behaviors. I value students as social and expressive learners and understand technology as both an instructional and a communication tool. • I prepare for collaboration with colleagues by studying the general curriculum, identifying optimal interdisciplinary units for collaboration, and by actively listening to my colleagues. • I collaborate with colleagues to best serve all students to reach their potential. • I collaborate with colleagues in the assessment of student learning in the school library to best integrate the library program into the general curriculum. • I seek out collaboration both within and outside of the school learning community to best serve all students. Effective educator collaboration requires that the library is not restricted to the physical facility of the library.	

(Continued)

DISPOSITION	AWARE	DEVELOPING	MEETS EXPECTATIONS
I DEMONSTRATE CARING, COLLEGIALITY, AND COLLABORATION IN INTERACTIONS AND COMMUNICATION.			
• I research and apply best practices to best serve all students. I share best practices with colleagues through professional development. • I demonstrate intellectual curiosity and interest in the scholarship and professional dispositions of others as well as my own. • I share knowledge to enhance the practice of my colleagues. • I demonstrate an attitude of respect toward administrators and colleagues. • I attend to feedback from administrators and colleagues.			
I DEMONSTRATE PROFESSIONALISM THROUGH A COMMITMENT TO INTELLECTUAL FREEDOM, LEADERSHIP, AND PROFESSIONAL ETHICS.	AWARE	DEVELOPING	MEETS EXPECTATIONS
Exemplars: • I demonstrate professionalism through a transparent commitment to intellectual freedom. • I demonstrate leadership through a purposeful and deliberate approach to advocacy. • I demonstrate professionalism by administering an exemplary learner-centered school library program both physically and virtually that meets the needs of all students and faculty through staffing, facilities, budgeting, and collection development. • I demonstrate professionalism through the development of a collection that both supports the general curriculum and fosters independent learners and readers. • I demonstrate professionalism through relevant and engaging programming that inspires learners to pursue individual interests. I share myself as a model of a lifelong reader and learner.	Comments and Proposed Action:		

(*Continued*)

I DEMONSTRATE PROFESSIONALISM THROUGH A COMMITMENT TO INTELLECTUAL FREEDOM, LEADERSHIP, AND PROFESSIONAL ETHICS.	AWARE	DEVELOPING	MEETS EXPECTATIONS
• I demonstrate professionalism through seeking supplemental funding through grants and awards that highlight strengths of the school library program and supports needs as assessed. • I demonstrate professionalism by reporting to administrators and the school learning community regarding the impact of the school library program on student learning. I invite parents to engage with the library in a variety of ways. • I act in accordance with professional standards of practice in the education field including demeanor, behavior, attire, and appropriate response to administrative responsibilities. • I demonstrate leadership by placing a value on the networking relationships of other school library and professional educators locally, regionally, nationally, and internationally. • I actively pursue professional development to ensure that I am best serving my school learning community. I seek to learn emerging technologies and determine their value within the school library media program. • I continually reflect on my practice to identify dispositions, relationships, practices, ideas, and knowledge that would benefit from strengthening.			
I MODEL "DISPOSITIONS IN ACTION" FOR 21ST-CENTURY STANDARDS FOR LEARNERS.	AWARE	DEVELOPING	MEETS EXPECTATIONS
Exemplars: • I display initiative, engagement, emotional resilience, persistence, and curiosity. • I demonstrate confidence, self-direction, creativity, adaptability, flexibility, personal productivity, leadership, teamwork, and motivation. • I maintain and employ a critical stance and openness to new ideas and alternative perspectives.	Comments and Proposed Action:		

(*Continued*)

I MODEL "DISPOSITIONS IN ACTION" FOR 21ST-CENTURY STANDARDS FOR LEARNERS.	AWARE	DEVELOPING	MEETS EXPECTATIONS
• I use both divergent and convergent thinking. • I demonstrate appreciation and commitment for social responsibility. I am fair and nondiscriminatory toward others. I treat all persons with respect and regard for their individual worth and dignity.			

Figure 1.1   School Library Professional Dispositions Self-Assessment

backward design is to identify the strengths and weaknesses of this tool and to use it in further studies of the professional dispositions of exemplary school librarians. How professional dispositions relate to 21st-century learners is embedded in the self-assessment. By measuring dispositions, school librarians can benefit students as they seek to model the dispositions for all learners. This self-assessment is an adaptation for the school library field based upon an internal document in the Reading and Language Department at National Louis University developed for preservice reading specialists (McMahon & Quiroa, 2009).

The discussion of dispositions and the proposed self-assessment contained in this chapter is a bold first step to understand dispositions of school librarians who are preparing students for the 21st century. Naturally, this discussion begs the question about instruction for dispositions in school library education. As this research agenda continues, dispositions are identified and documented, and self-assessment evolves, it is the authors' plan to develop and recommend "signature pedagogies" (Falk, 2006) that will benefit school library educators as they integrate dispositional practices into instruction. It is at that juncture that the school librarian field will have the requisite tools to produce the next generation of practitioners who will serve all 21st-century learners and who, in their caring wisdom, will continue to deepen contributions to the school librarian field and develop into exemplary school librarians.

ENVISIONING A FUTURE

Have a conversation about dispositions, and one inevitable "limitation of the study" will emerge. Panelists were provided with a definition of dispositions from NCATE (2007), but that definition is simply not satisfactorily descriptive. This cognitive dissonance is grounded in the historically challenging attempt to encapsulate the concept of dispositions into a neat and tidy concept. As one panelist commented, "the definition of a disposition is not sufficiently clarified." While the concept of dispositions is complex, the researchers believed that the school library scholars who chose to participate would give this topic their best effort. It is hoped that this study will serve as a starting point for further research, no more and no less.

A logical future step is the development of valid and reliable assessments. Proposed assessments might include assessments used in preservice graduate preparation programs for intake at the time of admissions, benchmark at a midpoint during a program, and evaluative as a summative assessment. These assessments may be both self- and adviser-assessed. Additionally, the same points of ongoing assessment might be developed for building-level practicing school librarians.

CONCLUSIONS: IDENTIFICATION OF SCHOOL LIBRARIAN PROFESSIONAL DISPOSITIONS

To review, this research project sought to investigate the identification of professional dispositions of exemplary school librarians by soliciting input from editorial board members of the leading professional journals in the school librarian field in the United States. The researchers selected the Delphi study methodology, as it was determined that it would best fit this research project investigation. Delphi study panelists independently identified professional dispositions and described their terminology, commented on 11 prominent dispositions that received the most consensuses of responses, and finally ranked and/or combined categories of dispositions. The results of this study provide a foundation for designing and implementing signature pedagogies for use in school library education, appropriate assessment measures for both school library education and practicing school librarians, and a research-based foundation for the discussion of professional dispositions of school librarians.

The exploration each panelist launched multiplied the impact of this study of professional dispositions and broadened the results to initiate a conversation that has only just begun. Panelists shared their experience with their graduate students and local and regional networks. As these researchers continue to mine the data to design appropriate pedagogies in school librarian preparation programs and assessments (intake for graduate programs, preservice, and position evaluation), we invite our colleagues to think freely about what is truly important about the role that school librarians play in education. We believe that this research removes professional constraints from the past and invites us to envision a future for all learners that cannot be imagined without an exemplary school librarian in a vital role.

REFERENCES

AASL. (2007). *Standards for the 21st-century learner.* Retrieved from www.ala.org/ala/mgrps/divs/aasl/aaslproftools/learningstandards/AASL_LearningStandards_2007.pdf

AASL. (2009). *Standards for the 21st-century learner in action.* Chicago, IL: American Library Association.

Abbott, A. (1988). *The system of professions: An essay on the division of expert labor.* Chicago: University of Chicago Press.

Arnstine, D. (1967). *Philosophy of education: Learning and schooling.* New York: Harper & Row.

Atwood, M. (1981). *True stories: Poems.* New York: Simon and Schuster.

Booth, W. C., Colomb, G. G., & Williams, J. M. (2003). *The craft of research* (2nd ed.). Chicago: University of Chicago Press.

Breese, L., & Nawrocki-Chabin, R. (2002, October). *Nurturing dispositions through reflective practice.* Paper presented at the meeting of The Association of Independent Liberal Arts Colleges for Teacher Education, San Diego.

Breese, L., & Nawrocki-Chabin, R. (2007). The social cognitive perspective in dispositional development. In M. E. Diez & J. Raths (Eds.), *Dispositions in teacher education* (pp. 31–52). Charlotte, NC: Information Age Publishing.

Bush, G., & Jones, J. B. (2010). Exploration to identify professional dispositions of school librarians: A Delphi study. *School Library Media Research, 13*. Retrieved from http://www.ala.org/aasl/slr/vol13

Cantor, N. (1990, June). From thought to behavior: "Having" and "Doing" in the study of personality and cognition. *American Psychologist, 45*(6), 735–750.

Darling-Hammond, L., & Bransford, D. (Eds.). (2005). *Preparing teachers for a changing world: What teachers should learn and be able to do.* San Francisco: Jossey-Bass.

Dewey, J. (1922). *Human nature and conduct.* New York: Modern Library.

Dottin, E. S. (2006). A Deweyan approach to the development of moral dispositions in professional teacher education communities: Using a conceptual framework. In H. Sockett (Ed.), *Teacher dispositions: Building a teacher education framework of moral standards* (pp. 27–48). Washington, D.C.: AACTE Publications.

Erikson, E. (1968). *Identity: Youth and crisis.* New York: Norton.

Falk, B. (2006, January). A conversation with Lee Shulman—Signature pedagogies for teacher education: Defining our practices and rethinking our preparation. *The New Educator, 2*(1), 73–82.

Hsu, C., & Sandford, B. A. (2007). The Delphi technique: Making sense of consensus. *Practical Assessment, Research & Evaluation, 12*(10), 1–9. Retrieved from http://pareonline.net/pdf/v12n10.pdf

Jones, J., & Bush, G. (2009, September 2–4). *The dispositions of exemplary school librarians: How professional dispositions relate to student learning in the 21st century.* Proceedings of the 38th Annual Conference of International Association of School Librarianship—Preparing pupils and students for the future: School libraries in the picture, Albano Terme, Italy.

Katz, L. G. (1993). *Dispositions as educational goals* (ERIC EDO-PS-93-10). ED363454. Urbana, IL: ERIC Clearinghouse on Elementary and Early Childhood Education. Retrieved from http://ceep.crc.uiuc.edu/eecearchive/digests/1993/katzdi93.html

Katz, L. G., & Raths, J. D. (1986, July). *Dispositional goals for teacher education: Problems of identification and assessment.* Paper presented at the 33rd World Assembly of the International Council on Education for Teaching, Kingston, Jamaica.

Koeppen, K. E., & Davison-Jenkins, J. (2007). *Teacher dispositions: Envisioning their role in education.* Lanham, MD: Rowman & Littlefield.

Kuhlthau, C. C., Maniotes, L., & Caspari, A. K. (2007). *Guided inquiry: Learning in the 21st century.* Westport, CT: Libraries Unlimited.

Linstone, H. A., & Turoff, M. (1975). *The Delphi method: Techniques and applications.* Reading, MA: Addison-Wesley.

Ludwig, B. (1997). Predicting the future: Have you considered using the Delphi methodology? *Journal of Extension, 35*(5), 1–4. Retrieved from http://joe.org/joe/1997october/tt2.html

McMahon, S. E., & Quiroa, R. (2009). *Scholarly and professional dispositions self-assessment: Reading and language students.* Wheeling, IL: National-Louis University.

Mevarech, Z. R. (1995). Teacher's paths on the way to and from the professional development forum. In T. R. Guskey & M. Huberman (Eds.), *Professional development in education: New paradigms and practices* (pp. 151–170). New York: Teachers College Press.

Murrell, P. C., Diez, M. E., Feiman-Nemser, S., & Schussler, D. L. (Eds.). (2010). *Teaching as a moral practice: Defining, developing, and assessing professional dispositions in teacher education.* Cambridge, MA: Harvard Education Press.

NBPTS. (2002). *What teachers should know and be able to do.* Retrieved from www.nbpts.org/UserFiles/File/what_teachers.pdf

NCATE. (2007). *Professional standards for the accreditation of teacher preparation institutions.* Retrieved from http://www.ncate.org/public/standards.asp

Rorty, R., & Engel, P. (2007). *What's the use of truth?* New York: Columbia University Press.

Schön, D. A. (1987). *Educating the reflective practitioner: Toward a new design for teaching and learning in the professions.* San Francisco: Jossey-Bass.

Schwandt, T. A. (2003). Three epistemological stances for qualitative inquiry: Interpretivism, hermeneutics, and social constructivism. In N. K. Denzin & Y. S. Lincoln (Eds.), *The landscape of qualitative research: Theories and issues.* (2nd ed., pp. 292–331). Thousand Oaks, CA: Sage Publications.

Smith, R. L., Skarbek, D., & Hurst, J. (Eds.). (2005). *The passion of teaching: Dispositions in the schools.* Lanham, MD: Scarecrow Education.

Sockett, H. (2006). *Teacher dispositions: Building a teacher education framework of moral standards.* Washington, D.C.: American Association of Colleges for Teacher Education Publications.

Talja, S. (2010). Jean Lave's practice theory. In G. J. Leckie, L. M. Given, & J. E. Buschman (Eds.), *Critical theory for library and information science: Exploring the social from across the disciplines* (pp. 205–220). Santa Barbara, CA: Libraries Unlimited.

Van de Ven, A. L., & Delbecq, A. H. (1974). The effectiveness of nominal, Delphi, and interacting group decision making processes. *Academy of Management Journal, 17*(4), 605–621.

2

SCHOOL LIBRARIANS IN VYGOTSKY'S ZONE OF PROXIMAL DEVELOPMENT

Mirah J. Dow and Jacqueline McMahon Lakin

INTRODUCTION: INFORMATION BEHAVIOR RESEARCH

Information seeking has become a fundamental behavior of humans, particularly in developing countries where computer technology has increased mass creation and use of information. According to Bates (2009b), "how people need, seek, manage, give and use information in different contexts" (p. xix) is the way to conceptualize information behavior. Information behavior research, based in a constructivist metatheory in which individuals are seen as actively constructing an understanding of their world, is a growing body of knowledge in library and information science (LIS) research. This body of empirical research can improve understandings of educational law and policy makers, educators, and the general public about why state-licensed school librarians are essential in every school building.

In this chapter, Vygotsky's zone of proximal development (ZPD) theory, which influences psychology, education, and now information science research, is used to locate the school librarian's place, alongside other professional educators, for asserting specialized expertise in the process of enabling students to develop new cognitive skills. Two prominent theories of information behavior, sense-making and the information search process (ISP), are applied as explanations for school librarians' important roles in helping students to learn to adapt to their environment through development of information seeking and use skills. Using a quantitative research design to investigate student success when schools are with and without school librarians, this question was answered: "Are there notably higher student annual yearly progress (AYP) proficiency rates in reading, mathematics, science, history/government, and writing curriculum areas when schools employ state-licensed school librarians?" Notably higher student proficiency rates in four years of AYP data were found in five content areas.

CUTTING SCHOOL LIBRARIANS IS A PARADOX

While many public school districts across the United States cut school librarians to save costs, many question what effects this decision will have on student learning.

Will erratic trends of reducing school librarians' hours, or eliminating them all together, hurt students and their abilities to do the kind of research and writing expected in college and other postsecondary experiences? The problem is that cutting school librarians is becoming a paradox because the Common Core State Standards Initiative (2010) accepted by all except two or three of the states articulate high expectations for student learning consistent with the world's academic standards for content areas, as well as for information retrieval skills and multiple literacies, including digital, visual, textual, and technological skills. Often, teachers are not prepared in these areas. It is state-licensed school librarians who frequently train and collaborate with teachers in joint efforts to teach students to recognize an information need; search for, access, and evaluate information; and use information to develop and communicate new ideas for resolution of human problems. School librarians' expertise is very important in a democratic society. With information and the skills to evaluate and use it, citizens can seek effective help, correct abuses, enjoy basic human functioning, and benefit from resources around them. With information, professional and scholarly bodies of knowledge can grow and expand through creation of new scientific knowledge and professional practices.

In today's tight economy, the lack of federal or state mandate for state-licensed school librarians and a lack of understanding of available research explaining the essential impact that school librarians have on student learning and achievement are reasons why LIS researchers must be involved in "unpacking" or "getting behind" school curriculum in an effort to determine what is, or is not, a so-called luxury that students can do without. Unique to this longitudinal, LIS study is an information behavior theory framework derived from systematic studies of human behavior associated with information seeking and use. Not only does our study recognize earlier school library impact studies, but it is also grounded in solid research about what is necessary to enable human intellectual development.

Used in education and psychology and during the past two decades by LIS scholars, Vygotsky's (1978) research offers a theoretical basis for understanding the information behavior of students when confronted with an unfamiliar task or situation and the place in today's schools for school librarians and other educators in facilitating intellectual development necessary for 21st-century learning. Vygotsky's ZPD theory, together with new information behavior theory presented in this chapter, underscores the significance of school librarians in designing and implementing learner-centered information systems such as the school library.

Knowledge of these theories challenged us to investigate the presence or absence of school librarians in schools. While the authors have in the past used qualitative inquiry to learn how school librarians are involved in students' intellectual development, this chapter highlights a quantitative analysis of student achievement scores as represented in AYP data and staffing levels of Kansas state-licensed school librarians as reported in state personnel records. In line with President Barack Obama's imperative to investigate what works and what must work better (U.S. Department of Education, 2010), our question was, "Are there notably higher student AYP proficiency rates in reading, mathematics, science, history/government, and writing curriculum areas when schools employ state-licensed school librarians?" The answer on the basis of AYP data is "yes."

To fully appreciate depth and complexity of well-established and newly proposed conceptual frameworks that researchers may use to study different aspects of information behavior, a discussion of constructivism (a philosophy used to explain how individuals make meaning of their world through a series of individual constructs) in education, sociology, and LIS research is essential. First, presented is a brief definition of information behavior and some observations about its relevance to the discipline of psychology (the scientific study of the human mind and mental processes through analysis of behavior).

WHAT IS INFORMATION BEHAVIOR?

Pettigrew, Fidel, and Bruce (2001) defined information behavior as "how people need, seek, give and use information in different contexts" (p. 44). Information behavior—compared to other areas of psychology such as behavioral psychology (environment shapes human behavior), cognitive psychology (individuals think and develop knowledge), psychoanalytic psychology (psychic energy shapes human behavior), and social psychology (thoughts, feeling, and behavior is influenced by others)—is relatively a "new comer" to the topic of how living persons adapt to their environment. Information seeking has become fundamental behavior of humans, particularly in developing countries where computer technology has increased mass creation and use of information. Human information behavior theory should be, we believe, as basic to the professional and scholarly knowledge base of all educators as are theories of development, learning, personality, motivation, etc. This is particularly necessary given the proliferation of information in today's society and as the educational, political, and technological environment grows more complex. Further, human information theory should be important to all educators concerned with facilitating intellectual growth in today's students as the U.S. population becomes more diverse in terms of culture, race, and ethnicity. Information behavior theory is the content of educational psychology.

CONSTRUCTIVISM

Constructivist theory, referred to as constructivism, is a theory used to explain the way people create meaning of the world through a series of individual constructs. Constructivism is one of the 13 key theoretical concepts, known as metatheories (or philosophically grounded assumptions about a phenomena and how to study it), used by LIS researchers who study information behavior (Bates, 2009a). The focus here is on constructivism rather than other key concepts used to study information behavior because of constructivism's relative dominance that continues to drive educational trends and initiatives. Constructivism is based on the work of major theorists and researchers from education and sociology and informs major theories of information behavior.

Constructivism in Education and Sociology

Educational constructivism—built on the work of early philosophers, psychologists, and educational activists such as John Dewey (1933, 1944), George Kelly (1963), Lev Vygotsky (1978), and others—is a theory that suggests that people create meaning of the world through a series of individual constructs. According to Ritzer (2000), sociological constructivist theory, which questions the primacy of structure or agency in human behavior, resulted from Schutz (English translation 1967, original 1932), Berger and Luckmann (1990 reprint), and Garfinkel (1967). These applications of constructivist philosophy take an "idiographic"

(Oxford University Press, 2012a) approach to theory building, which is the study or discovery of particular scientific facts and processes. This is in contrast to a "nomothetic" (Oxford University Press, 2012b) approach to theory building, which is concerned with the study of the general laws underlying something.

Constructivism in Library and Information Science Research

How and why people seek and use information is central to the nature and scope of LIS research and the questions asked and answered by LIS researchers (Bates, 1999, 2007; Summers, Oppenheim, Meadow, McKnight, & Kinnell, 1999; Taylor, 1966). According to Konrad (2007), LIS is concerned with "humans becoming informed (constructing meaning) via intermediation between inquirers and instrumented records" (p. 660). Librarians of all kinds, including school librarians, attempt to develop theory and construct models to explain making information accessible and useable; how to distinguish between information needs and wants; how to interpret and explain individuals' behavior when they search for information; and how information systems can be designed and used to satisfy human information needs.

Constructivist Theories of Information Behavior

There are two prominent bodies of LIS research that are philosophically anchored in constructivism and currently used to explain how and why people seek and search for information. As early as 1977, Dervin described information seeking as sense-making activity (Dervin, 2009). Dervin (1983, 1999) used a constructivist philosophy to formulate a theory of sense-making, a generalizable approach to thinking about and studying information seeking and information use, specifically human sense-making and sense-unmaking in its different forms. According to Dervin (2009), "Sense-making mandates that problems solving be conceptualized as gap building—not in the purposive, problem solving sense (although that is one subset of all gap-bridgings) but in the sense of gap-bridging as a mandate of the human condition" (p. 27).

Kuhlthau (2004) used constructivism philosophical and educational theories of Dewey, Bruner, Kelly, Vygotsky, and Piaget as the framework for investigation of information seeking behavior from the perspectives on high-school students conducting research in a school library and development of the ISP as a conceptual framework that depicts information seeking as a process of construction in which people build their own view of the world by assimilating and accommodating new information. In six stages, Kuhlthau's ISP describes common patterns in users' experience in the process of information seeking for a complex task that has a discrete beginning and ending, and requires construction and learning to be accomplished. According to Kuhlthau (2009), Vygotsky's concept of a zone of intervention was used to introduce the concept of diagnosing a user's need for assistance and support (p. 233). Kuhlthau's model has been validated in samples of high-school, academic, and public library users.

Vygotsky's Zone of Proximal Development

Kuhlthau's (2004) research leading to the ISP was influenced in part by Vygotsky, a Soviet developmental psychologist and contemporary of Jean Piaget, the one who continues to influence educational constructivism. Vygotsky asserted that action creates thought, development results from dialectical processes, and development occurs in historical and cultural context (Thomas, 1992). According to Winter and Goldfield (1991), Vygotsky's interactionist approach resembles Bruner's (1978) scaffolding, Bandura's (1977) social learning theory, and Kaye's (1982) child-as-apprentice theory. Vygotsky (1978) defined the ZPD as "the distance between the actual development level as determined by independent problem solving and the level of potential development as determined through problem solving under adult guidance or in collaboration with more capable peers" (p. 86). Vygotsky asserted that new cognitive skills are first practiced by children in social interaction with a more experienced adult until the skill is mastered and internalized and the child is able to exercise the skill independently.

Vygotsky's (1978) ZPD theory influenced Kuhlthau's (2004) theory that teaching should be thought of as organizing the learning environment, as well as much that is being done today that emphasizes the collaborative and interpersonal context for the work of students, classroom teachers, and school librarians in partnering to teach reading, core content, and information and technology literacy skills (Achterman, 2008; Church, 2008; Haycock, 2010; Immroth & Lukenbill, 2007; Kachel et al., 2011; Lance, Rodney, & Schwarz, 2010; McGregor, 2003; Moreillon, 2007, 2012; Pickard, 1993; Thomas, Crow, & Franklin, 2011; Todd 2011). Beginning with student's natural curiosity and addressing student's interests and background experiences, ability levels, motivation, and learning styles, students are encouraged to relate ideas to previous knowledge and experience, look for patterns and underlying principles, check evidence and relate it to conclusions, and cautiously and critically examine logic and argument. With the guidance of school librarians, students learn to retrieve information, experiment, publish, and share their new informed viewpoints using the Internet, computers, and other electronic communication devices. Guided inquiry (Kuhlthau, Maniotes, & Caspari, 2007) strategies are integrated into the content of the curriculum; the content of the curriculum is connected to the student's world; and earlier instructional practices of teaching skills in isolation give way to incorporating information location, evaluation, and use concepts throughout the research process.

STUDENT ACHIEVEMENT

While student achievement was once determined by local teachers and expectations for student learning varied within school buildings and from building to building across the county, student achievement is now standardized through federally mandated educational measures and evaluations. Holding teachers and principals responsible for all their students' learning is a governmental strategy for closing the achievement gap between high- and low-performing students, especially the achievement gaps between minority and nonminority students and disadvantaged and more advantaged students, and for demanding what some in the general public perceive to be return on tax-funded investments in U.S. education. Some taxpayers, through their elected officials, now insist that the federal government, particularly the U.S. Congress and the U.S. Department of Education, should establish high standards and uniform road maps for educational accountability. Still others may say that taxpayers have no idea about student achievement and have no "voice"; and therefore, all of that power should be returned to the local level. Already, governmentally determined road maps that have in recent years established required educational measures and evaluations for student achievement may be changing in efforts to relief some states from what educators claim are difficult federal mandates, particularly in schools with large, at-risk populations.

Annual Yearly Progress: Federal Mandate

During the past five decades, U.S. education has focused on eliminating poverty through equal access to education and established high standards and accountability. AYP is a measurement defined by the No Child Left Behind (NCLB) Act of 2001 (P. L. 107–110) that allows the U.S. Department of Education to determine how every public school and school district in the county is academically performing according to results on state summative assessments. The standard method of determining AYP has been a "status model" in which school performance is mainly evaluated in terms of the proportion of students meeting or exceeding proficiency levels on state reading and mathematics assessments.

Since 2010 in a document titled *Priorities in a blueprint for reform* (U.S. Department of Education, 2010), proficiency has been reframed by raising standards for all students with the goal that every student should graduate from high school ready for college and career, regardless of their income, race, ethnic, language, background, or disability status.

Every Student Should Graduate High School Ready for College and Career

Most recently, due to some prevalence of low-performing schools where students are unable to meet adequate proficiency levels, some states have sought alternatives to what they believe to be federal mandates that stand in the way of making best use of teachers' abilities to teach and schools' limited financial resources. According to a press release on February 29, 2012, "Twenty-six states and the District of Columbia have formally submitted requests to the U.S. Department of Education for waivers from key provisions of NCLB along with plans to implement bold education reforms in exchange for relief from burdensome federal mandates" (U.S. Department of Education, 2012).

All 26 states, including Kansas, according to the February 2012 press release,

> Proposed plans to raise standards, improve accountability, and support reforms to improve principal and teacher effectiveness. If their plans are approved, these 26 states and D.C. will set performance targets based on whether students graduate from high school ready for college and career rather than having to meet NCLB's 2014 deadline based on arbitrary target for proficiency; design locally tailored interventions to help student achieve instead of one-size-fits-all remedies prescribed at the federal level; be free to emphasize student growth and progress using multiple measures rather than just one test score; and, have more flexibility in how they spend federal funds to benefit students. (U.S. Department of Education, 2012)

Formal requests from states to the U.S. Department of Education for waivers from key provisions of NCLB are likely to occur in "waves" as schools determine their ability to meet AYP levels.

Students' Growth: State-level Example

Germane to this research is an overview of student academic growth in Kansas. Results from the 2010 Kansas statewide assessments (KSDE, 2010) show a 10-year, statewide growth trend area (Table 2.1a and 2.1b) in reading (59.2–86.3) and mathematics (50.3–83.1). Students performing in the top three performance levels on the reading assessment increased to 86.3 percent in 2010, up from 85.7 percent in 2009. On the mathematics assessment, students in the top three performance levels totaled 83.1 percent in 2010, up from 82.8 percent in 2009. Participation rates topped 99 percent in each subject area. The 2010 Kansas statewide assessment report also indicates some growth in 2009–2010 student achievement in reading by subgroups including free and reduced lunch (76.6–78.0), students with disabilities (SPED; 73.4–73.7), English language learners (ELL; 64.6–66.6), African American students (69.1–70.6), and Hispanic students (73.1–75.0). For 2009–2010 student achievement in reading by subgroup, there was some growth in free and reduced lunch (73.6–74.5), ELL (68.4–70.3), African American (63.1–64.3), and Hispanic (71.0–73.4); and a slight decrease in math subgroup SPED (68.0–67.9).

This academic growth occurred in one state, Kansas, which has long promoted LIS education and employment of state-licensed school librarians. Many Kansas educators, including school librarians, have for the past two decades used a research-based, collaboration model for instruction and multiple criterion-referenced assessments to indicate whether or not the test taker performed well or poorly, to compare the test taker's current and previous performance, and to continually revise and improve instruction. This is in sharp contrast to instructional practices

Table 2.1a   Kansas Reading: All Students Increase over 10 years, 2000–2010

KANSAS READING	ALL STUDENTS 10-YEAR RANGE	ALL STUDENTS READING INCREASE OVER 10 YEARS
2000	59.2–86.3	27.1
2001	60.2–86.3	26.1
2002	61.2–86.3	25.1
2003	66.8–86.3	19.5
2004	70.2–86.3	16.1
2005	73.1–86.3	13.2
2006	78.0–86.3	8.3
2007	82.5–86.3	3.8
2008	84.1–86.3	2.2
2009	85.7–86.3	0.6
2010	86.3	

Table 2.1b   Kansas Mathematics: All Students Increase over 10 years,
2000–2010

KANSAS MATHEMATICS	ALL STUDENTS 10-YEAR RANGE	ALL STUDENTS MATHEMATICS INCREASE OVER 1O YEARS
2000	50.3–83.1	32.8
2001	54.5–83.1	28.6
2002	56.2–83.1	26.9
2003	59.8–83.1	23.3
2004	65.3–83.1	17.8
2005	68.1–83.1	15.0
2006	72.5–83.1	10.6
2007	80.1–83.1	3.0
2008	81.0–83.1	1.8
2009	83.8–83.1	0.7
2010	83.1	

that focus primarily on norm-referenced tests that estimate the position of the tested individual in a particular population with respect to a trait being measured. Norm-referenced tests identify whether the test taker performed better or worse than other test takers, but not whether the test taker knows more or less material than is necessary for a given.

Kansas school librarians have also promoted a school librarian–developed, critical problem-solving model. As early as 1995, both veteran and new school librarians in Kansas began to use *The Handy 5* (Blume, Fox, & Lakin, 2007; Grover, Fox, & Lakin, 2001), an integrated information skills instructional model that establishes a common language and a five-step method for critical problem-solving. This widely accepted model, which continues to be used in many school buildings, correlates with the five steps in mathematic problem-solving: the assignment, plan of action, doing the job, product evaluation, and process evaluation. *The Handy 5* steps are applied to curriculum areas includes reading, writing, mathematics, social studies, science, the arts, and information literacy skills. Analysis of data from a sample of participant schools where teachers used *The Handy 5* yielded multiple findings, including "use of the model had an impact on low achieving students" and "use of the model helped students learn higher order thinking skills, i.e., analysis, synthesis, and evaluation" (Grover et al., 2001, p. 88). This suggests that while mathematics teachers and school librarians might not be teaching in the same room, instructionally they "mirror" each other in their efforts to teach logic, reasoning, problem-solving, and critical thinking.

Kansas criterion-referenced assessments used to inform the instructional process with students include teacher-made classroom assessments, curriculum and test coordinator–made district-level assessments, and standards-based assessments created by the Center for Educational Testing and Evaluation at University of Kansas. This tradition of using multiple criterion-referenced assessments, in addition to state summative assessments, may help to explain a 10-year, Kansas statewide growth trend in reading and mathematics, and is important in Kansas educators' continued efforts to turn around low-performing schools.

METHODOLOGY

This quantitative study is philosophically grounded in the constructivist view of learning. For this, the researchers locate students and their educators, including school librarians, in what Vygotsky (1978) termed the zone of proximal development and theorized that students engaged in information seeking and searching with the help of their school librarians and classroom teachers are essentially engaged in information behavior. Our theoretical framework is based on understandings about information behavior influenced primarily by two prominent, formative information behavior theorists: Dervin (sense-making) and Kuhlthau (ISP), both applicable to understanding significant communication patterns and interactions between and among school librarians, other educators, and their students.

Dervin's Sense-Making

One information behavior theory grounded in constructivism is the human sense-making theory—a methodological, or a generalizable, approach to thinking about human sense- and unsense-making that conceptualizes communication as gap bridging (Dervin, 1983; Dervin, Foreman-Wernet, & Lauterback, 2003). Sense-making methodology is an approach to communication research and practice and the design of communication-based systems and activities. Dervin's research, which began in 1972 and continues today, is "based on three central assumptions regarding communication practice: (a) That it is possible to design and implement communication systems and practices that are responsive to human needs; (b) That it is possible for humans to enlarge their communication repertoires to pursue this vision and to discipline their communications to achieve these possibilities; (c) That achieving these outcomes requires the development of communication-based methodological approaches" (*Dervin's sense-making methodology*). The researchers use Dervin's ideas about design and implementation of communication systems as a way to think about the design and implementation of school libraries operating in an optimal ZPD. Dervin's ideas about moving beyond communication practices influenced by behavioral psychology's stimulus–response model to a model that is "situational and will be predicted by situational conditions" (Dervin, 2003, p. 256) holds promise for improving educators' communication practices with students in a variety of learning situations across time and space and opens new possibilities for bridging gaps and giving meaning to experience in an information rich world. Dervin's most extensive application of sense-making has been with library professions as a "dialogic interface" (Dervin, 2003, p. 335) between librarian and patron in reference interviews.

Kuhlthau's Information Search Process

Secondly and equally important, our assumptions about school librarians operating in an optimal ZPD is further supported by information behavior theory that explains human information searching in terms of an ISP model (Kuhlthau, 2004).

According to Kuhlthau's ISP theory, when individuals are engaged in a directed information search, such as an resource-based project commonly required in today's schools and colleges, information seeking can be viewed as a process of construction that allows a student to experience learning firsthand, which involves some common patterns of human experience. Kuhlthau's theory explains the process of information seeking from a holistic perspective as a complex task that has a clear beginning and end, and requires a series of individual constructs, or use of different mental filters placed over ones realities, to be accomplished. Kuhlthau (2004) points out that while in the ISP, humans experience a range of feeling, including "uncertainty; optimism; confusion, frustration, doubt; clarity; sense of direction/confidence; relief; satisfaction or dissatisfaction" (p. 82), that can without the support and facilitation of a knowledgeable other lead to a cognitive state that can, if left unattended, "shut down" mental processes and potentially the interplay of thoughts, feeling, and actions necessary for the search and learning to be accomplished. Kuhlthau (2009) refers to this as the "uncertainty principle," (p. 232) a cognitive state that commonly causes affective symptoms of anxiety and lack of confidence that may exist in early stages of the search process and is associated with vague or unclear thoughts about a topic or question. The effect of students' experience while in the ISP on the outcome or product of their research, we believe, is an important educator accountability issue.

Information Behaviors Necessary for Achieving Common Core State Standards

Sense-making and ISP information behavior theories provide theory-based support for our claim that state-licensed school librarians are essential to student learning and achievement and, therefore, should be valued and employed as necessary experts to instruct and enable students in sense-making and the ISP. These are information behaviors necessary for common core standards-based expectations for information retrieval skills, as well as digital, visual, textual, and technological skills (Common Core State Standards Initiative, 2010). To examine this claim, Dow, Lakin, and Court (2012) began their study in 2010 with the most current four years of state AYP data. Our hypothesis was that higher and more stable levels of school librarian allocation will yield greater levels of proficiency and greater positive change in proficiency when controlling for differences in prior performance, school characteristics, and student demographics. With SPSS, a computer program for data analysis, analysis of covariance (ANCOVA), a test to determine whether certain factors have an effect on the outcome variable after removing the variance for which quantitative predictors, or covariant, account was used. In this case, ANCOVA was used to examine library media specialist (LMS), the label used for school librarian in the Kansas-licensed personnel data, staffing levels, and student achievement as recorded in Kansas AYP data at the school level. Two general models for analysis were developed. In one model, the dependent variable was proficiency rate; independent variable was full-time equivalent (FTE) allocation; and covariates were prior achievement, socioeconomic status (SES), school size, percent ELL, percent modified test takers, and percent alternate test takers. In the other model, the dependent variable was proficiency rate that changes over time, the independent variable was trend (changes in FTE allocation from 2006 through 2009), and the same covariates. Five subject areas (reading, mathematics, science, social studies, and writing) were examined over a four-year period (2006–2009). Overall, the study examined more than 2.5 million individual assessment results from all 1,389 Kansas schools. Schools, not students, served as the unit of analysis in the study.

RESEARCH FINDINGS: NOTABLY HIGHER AYP PROFICIENCY WITH SCHOOL LIBRARIAN

The results of the study's overall findings show that with at least a part-time school librarian (and, preferably, a full-time school librarian), there are notably higher AYP proficiency rates in schools in all five subject areas (reading, mathematics, science, government/history, and writing) than in schools having no school librarian at all (Figure 2.1).

Below is a summary of additional key findings:

1. Differences in proficiency rates at elementary, middle, and high school levels in reading, mathematics, science, history/government (not elementary), and writing, as well as the effect size magnitudes, indicate that Kansas schools with a school librarian tend to outperform schools with no school librarians (Table 2.2). This finding is consistent across grade spans and subject areas.
2. Of note, 158 schools whose 2008–2009 composite proficiency rate was below the 2009 AYP target of 79.7 percent proficient, 36 schools (23%) would likely have made AYP if they had a full-time school librarian. Conversely, of the 575 schools whose composite proficiency rate was 79.7 percent or better, 26 schools (4.5%) would likely have missed AYP if they had not had a full-time school librarian.
3. FTE allocations (Table 2.3) at particular buildings often varied greatly across the four years. In more than a third of all Kansas schools, the variation involved rather erratic fluctuations; for example, at more than

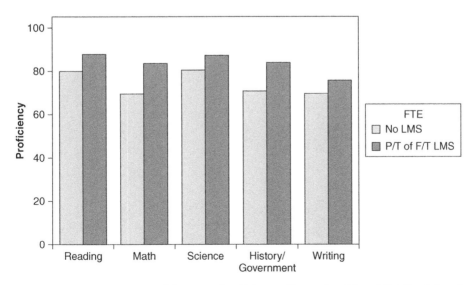

Figure 2.1   Summary of Kansas Proficiency Rates by Five Middle School Subject Areas

Table 2.2 2006–2009 Kansas Overall Distribution Trends across Three Grade Spans

SCHOOL LEVEL	NUMBER OF SCHOOLS	OVERALL PROFICIENCY RATE	LMS VERSUS NO-LMS PROFICIENCY DIFFERENCE (OBSERVED)	EFFECT SIZE (OBSERVED)	LMS VERSUS NO-LMS PROFICIENCY DIFFERENCE (99% CI)	EFFECT SIZE (99% CI)
Reading						
Elementary	796	85.9	2.6	0.23	4.7	0.42
Middle	435	85.7	3.0	0.23	3.9	0.30
Higher Secondary	285	82.8	5.4	0.26	10.9	0.62
Mathematics						
Elementary	796	86.3	4.2	0.38	5.5	0.50
Middle	435	80.1	3.9	0.24	4.1	0.37
Higher Secondary	285	75.2	4.1	0.17	8.8	0.39
Science						
Elementary	692	92.3	2.1	0.18	3.8	0.34

Middle	397	86.0	2.8	0.16	5.3	0.31
Higher Secondary	244	85.1	0.5	0.04	5.4	0.41
History/ Government						
Elementary	n/a	n/a	n/a	n/a	n/a	n/a
Middle	416	81.6	2.8	0.16	5.3	0.36
Higher Secondary	271	80.9	1.6	0.11	5.9	0.41
Writing						
Elementary	638	72.4	2.0	0.10	5.1	0.27
Middle	421	74.6	2.5	0.13	6.6	0.36
Higher Secondary	274	76.4	2.2	0.15	6.4	0.42

Notes: LMS, library media specialist and CI, confidence interval. Kansas does not administer a history/government assessment at the elementary level.

Table 2.3 Kansas Grade Span by Trend Crosstabulation

FTE ALLOCATION TREND (2006–2009)

		NO LMS	STEADY DECREASE	ERRATIC	STEADY INCREASE	STABLE PART-TIME	STABLE FULL-TIME	TOTAL
Grade Span	Elementary Count	127	65	67	82	130	262	733
	Row (%)	17.3	8.9	9.1	11.2	17.7	35.7	100.0
	Middle Count	83	35	32	45	78	126	399
	Row (%)	20.8	8.8	8.0	11.3	19.5	31.6	100.0
	Higher Count	36	21	22	16	3	109	257
	Secondary Row (%)	14.0	8.2	8.6	6.2	20.6	42.4	100.0
Total	Count	246	121	121	143	261	497	1,389
	Row (%)	17.7	8.7	8.7	10.3	18.8	35.8	100.0

Note: LMS, library media specialist; FTE, full-time equivalent.

100 schools, the fluctuation involved no LMS in at least one year, a full-time LMS in at least one other year, and different levels of part-time LMS during the other two years.

4. Schools with a full-time LMS tend to outperform no-LMS schools regardless of their poverty levels. The relationship is generally consistent across all grade spans and all subject areas. In a case study (2006–2009) of high poverty schools, which included unobtrusive observations and interview with school librarians, other educators and staff, and school administrators, our data revealed that the school facilities were modern, aesthetically designed buildings that offered special programs such as English for speakers of other languages (ESOL), special education, and Title I at elementary level. School librarians were highly involved in partnering not only with classroom teachers but also with program specialists in teaching reading, mathematics, and other content areas; implementing before- and after-school programs; making available computer technology equipment and instruction; and supervising support staff. These observations, together with the data in this study, suggest that where there are highly qualified educators and available resources and instruction, students living in poverty can despite many challenges become academically proficient.

5. Small elementary schools, those with fewer than 100 students with valid test scores, outperformed their larger counterparts by 7 to 10 proficiency points. Conversely, in large schools with more than 180 students with valid test scores, there was virtually no difference in proficiency regardless of school librarian staffing, presumably, because the student–school librarian ratio was too high for the school librarian to effectively function. Because the pattern was consistent across all three grade spans and all five subject areas, this finding provides evidence to support an argument that larger schools would benefit greatly from allocating more than one full-time school librarian to the library media center.

WHAT MORE IS NEEDED?

LIS research has as its goal learning how humans become informed or construct meanings through intermediation between inquirers and recorded records. While researchers' assumptions about human information seeking are informed by research-based theory, this study does nothing to build on existing information behavior theory. In order to do so, qualitative methods are needed to learn what more is needed to improve the sense-making process that exists between school librarians and other educators, and between students and their educators. Students today, particularly the ever increasing number of those at risk, are an example of a population for whom issues of power, control, autonomy, and representation have implications for everyday communication interactions, including communication in schools. Also, while the ISP model has been tested in multiple library types and with various sample groups, it seems important to learn more about the ISP experience of students using computer technology and about the zone of intervention as it relates to the work of school librarians in the current digital information age.

CONCLUSIONS: A NEW PICTURE OF THE PRESENCE OR ABSENCE OF SCHOOL LIBRARIANS

This chapter points out that school librarianship is much more than simply knowing how to check books in and out. It makes clear that the school librarians' professional knowledge base is philosophically located, with humanities and social science roots, in educational research (e.g., student learning, teacher training, teaching methods, classroom dynamics, etc.) and LIS research (how and why people seek and use information). This chapter emphasizes that licensed teachers and licensed school librarians share philosophical understandings of pedagogy and both are needed to help students to learn, achieve, and develop the kinds of research and writing expected in college and other postsecondary experiences.

This study examines a claim that state-licensed school librarians are important for student learning and achievement, and takes into account psychological, educational, and information theories that locate students, classroom teachers, and school librarians in a shared environment. The claim is based in information behavior theory and related assumptions about how humans understand information seeking and searching. The claim hypothetically locates students and their educators, including school librarians, in Vygotsky's ZPD and theorizes that the ZPD is optimal when students, with the help of their school librarians and classroom teachers, are engaged in information behavior, particularly sense-making and the ISP.

This study tested the hypothesis that higher and more stable levels of school librarian allocation will yield greater levels of proficiency and greater positive change in proficiency when controlling for differences in prior performance, school characteristics, and student demographics. The research question asked, "Are there notably higher student proficiency rates in reading, mathematics, science, history/government, and writing curriculum areas when schools employ state-licensed school librarians?" Yes, notably higher student proficiency rates were found in five content areas and support for our hypothesis through a quantitative analysis of four years (2006–09) of Kansas AYP data and state-licensed personnel records.

Through the lens of AYP data, this study creates a new "picture" of the presence or absence of school librarians in schools. The researchers believe that this picture, or evidence, has meaning for educational policy makers and others who have a stake in the upcoming reauthorization of the U.S. Elementary and Secondary Act (P. L. 89–10, 79 Stat. 27, 20 U.S.C. Ch.70). This evidence has meaning for those who want to invest in school programs wherein state-licensed personnel are engaged in evidence-based practices that will most positively contribute to the goal that all students will graduate high school and be ready for college and career/job.

The ANCOVA method used in this study to investigate AYP data can be replicated in other states and also with other state-licensed professional education groups. The researchers are in-process of continuing this study, wherein issues of causality will be addressed through propensity-score matching and contributory indices combination to identify the impact of school librarian staffing on student achievement. By using the lens of AYP data, another dimension is added to the body of research known as "school library impact studies" that includes "studies from twenty two states and one Canadian providence" and that "confirms the educational gains that school library programs provide in student learning" (Kachel et al., 2011, p. 4). AYP data should be, as it is in this study, used to inform state departments of education, state boards of education, state and federal education legislation committee members, and others who have responsibilities to be fully informed about school proficiency and to enforce AYP policies.

A challenge for educational leaders is to make certain teachers and librarians are clear about how to collaboratively teach resource-based assignments that enable students to experience guided use of information from elementary through high school and on to college. On the basis of observations in this study, it is possible that all assignments do not encourage or support a process approach to research. When school librarians are not involved in research-based instructional practices, students are not likely to understand their own search process. Further, many students do not learn to ask librarians for expert assistance, or become able to overcome their own uncertainty, particularly in critical initial stages of the search. Lack of school librarian involvement calls for interventions that will hold educators and school principals responsible for student learning and achievement.

REFERENCES

Achterman, D. L. (2008). *Haves, halves, and have-nots: School libraries and student achievement in California.* Denton, TX: UNT Digital Library. Retrieved from http://digital.library.unt.edu/ark:/67531/metadc9800/m1/

Bandura, A. (1977). *Social learning theory.* Englewood Cliffs, NJ: Prentice Hall.

Bates, M. J. (1999). The invisible substrate of information science. *Journal of the American Society for Information Science, 50*(12), 1043–1050.

Bates, M. J. (2007). What is browsing—Really? A model drawing from behavioural science research. *Information Research, 12*(4). Retrieved from http://informationr.net/ir/12-4/paper330.html

Bates, M. J. (2009a). An introduction to metatheories, theories, and models. In K. E. Fisher, S. Erdelez, & L. (E.F.) McKechnie (Eds.), *Theories of information behavior* (pp. 1–24). Medford, NJ: Information Today, Inc.

Bates, M. J. (2009b). Preface. In K. E. Fisher, S. Erdelez, & L. (E.F.) McKechnie (Eds.), *Theories of information behavior* (pp. xix–xxii). Medford, NJ: Information Today, Inc.

Berger, P. L., & Luckmann, T. (1990). *The social construction of reality: A treatise in the sociology of knowledge.* New York: Anchor Books.

Blume, S., Fox, C., & Lakin, J. M. (2007). *The handy 5: Planning and assessing integrated information skills instruction* (2nd ed.). Lanham, MD: Scarecrow Press.

Bruner, J. (1978). The role of dialogue in language acquisition. In A. Sinclair, R. J. Jarvelle, & W. J. M. Levelt (Eds.), *The child's concept of language.* New York: Springer-Verlag.

Center for Educational Testing and Evaluation. *About us.* Lawrence, KS: University of Kansas. Retrieved from http://www.cete.us/about/

Church, A. (2008). The instructional role of the library media specialist as perceived by elementary school principals. *School Library Media Research, 11.* Retrieved from http://www.ala.org/aasl/aaslpubsandjournals/slmrb/slmrcontents/volume11/church

Dervin, B. (1983). Information as a new construct: The relevance of perceived information needs to synthesis and interpretation. In S. A. Ward & L. J. Reed (Eds.), *Knowledge structure and use: implications for synthesis and interpretation* (pp. 155–183). Philadelphia: Temple University Press.

Dervin, B. (1999). On studying information seeking methodologically: The implications of connecting metatheory to method. *Information Processing and Management, 35*(6), 727–750.

Dervin, B. (2009). What methodology does to theory: Sense-making methodology as exemplar. In K. E. Fisher, S. Erdelez, & L. (E.F.) McKechnie (Eds.), *Theories of information behavior* (pp. 25–29). Medford, NJ: Information Today, Inc.

Dervin, B., Foreman-Wernet, L., & Lauterbach, E. (Eds.). (2003). *Sense-making methodology reader: Selected writings of Brenda Dervin.* Cresskill, NJ: Hampton Press.

Dervin's sense-making methodology (SMM): Brief introduction. Retrieved from http://com munication.sbs.ohio-state.edu/sense-making/introSMM.html

Dewey, J. (1933). *How we think*. Lexington, MA: Hearth.

Dewey, J. (1944). *Democracy and education*. New York: Macmillan.

Dow, M. J., Lakin, J. M., & Court, S. (2012). *School librarian staffing levels and student achievement as represented in 2006–09 Kansas annual yearly progress data*. Emporia, KS: ESIRC. Retrieved from http://hdl.handle.net/123456789/1224

Garfinkel, H. (1967). *Studies in ethnomethodology*. Englewood Cliffs, NJ: Prentice-Hall.

Grover, R., Fox, C., & Lakin, J. M. (2001). *The handy 5: Planning and assessing integrated information skills instruction*. Lanham, MD: Scarecrow Press.

Haycock, K. (2010). Leadership from the middle: Building influence for change. In S. Coatney (Ed.), *The many faces of school library leadership* (pp. 1–12). Santa Barbara, CA: Libraries Unlimited.

Immroth, B., & Lukenbill, W. B. (2007). Teacher-school library media specialist collaboration through social marketing strategies: An information behavior study. *School Library Media Research, 10*. Retrieved from http://www.ala.org/aasl/aaslpubsand journals/slmrb/slmrcontents/volume10/immroth_teacherslmscollaboration

Kachel, D. E., et al. (2011). *School library research summarized: A graduate class project*. Mansfield, PA: School of Library & Information Technologies Department, Mansfield University.

Kaye, K. (1982). Organism, apprentice, and person. In E. Z. Tronick (Ed.), *Social interchange in infancy*. Baltimore: University Park Press.

Kelly, G. A. (1963). *A theory of personality: The psychology of personal constructs*. New York: W. W. Norton.

Konrad, A. (2007). *On inquiry: Human concept formation and construction of meaning through library and information science intermediation* (Doctoral dissertation). University of California, Berkeley, CA. Retrieved from http://escholarship.org/uc/item/1s76b6hp#page-1

KSDE. (2010, October 12). *State assessment results show 10 year growth trend*. Retrieved from http://www.ksde.org/Default.aspx?tabid=36&ctl=Details&mid=1030&Ite mID=505

Kuhlthau, C. C. (2004). *Seeking meaning: A process approach to library and information services* (2nd ed.). Westport, CT: Libraries Unlimited.

Kuhlthau, C. C. (2009). Kuhlthau's information search process. In K. E. Fisher, S. Erdelez, & L. (E. F.) McKechnie (Eds.), *Theories of information behavior* (pp. 230–234). Medford, NJ: Information Today, Inc.

Kuhlthau, C. C., Maniotes, L. K., & Caspari, A. K. (2007). Guided *inquiry: Learning in the 21st Century*. Westport, CT: Libraries Unlimited.

Lance, K. C., Rodney, M. C., & Schwarz, B. (2010). The impact of school libraries on academic achievement: A research study based on responses from administrators in Idaho. *School Library Monthly, 26*(9), 14–17.

Moreillon, J. (2007). *Collaborative strategies for teaching reading comprehension: Maximizing your impact*. Chicago: ALA Editions.

Moreillon, J. (2012). *Coteaching reading comprehension strategies in secondary school libraries: Maximizing your impact*. Chicago: ALA Editions.

McGregor, J. (2003). Collaboration and leadership. In B. K. Stripling & S. Hughes-Hassell (Eds.), *Curriculum connections through the library* (pp. 119–219). Westport, CT: Libraries Unlimited.

National Governors Association Center for Best Practices, Council of Chief State School Officers. (2010). Common Core State Standards. Washington, D.C.: National Governors Association Center for Best Practices, Council of Chief State School Officers. Retrieved from http://www.corestandards.org/the-standards

No Child Left Behind Act of 2001 (P. L. 107–110). 115 Statute: 1495–2094. Retrieved from http://www2.ed.gov/policy/elsec/leg/esea02/107-110.pdf

Oxford University Press (2012a). *Oxford dictionaries.* Retrieved from http://oxforddic tionaries.com/definition/idiographic

Oxford University Press (2012b). *Oxford dictionaries.* Retrieved from http://oxforddic tionaries.com/definition/nomothetic?region=uk

Pettigrew, K. E., Fidel, R., & Bruce, H. (2001). Conceptual frameworks in information behavior. *Annual Review of Information Science and Technology, 35,* 43–78.

Pickard, P. W. (1993). The instructional consultant role of the school library media specialist. *School Library Media Quarterly, 21*(2), 115–121.

Ritzer, G. (2000). *Modern sociological theory* (5th ed.). Boston: McGraw-Hill.

Schutz, A. (1967). *The phenomenology of the social world.* Evanston, IL: Northwestern University Press.

Summers, R., Oppenheim, C., Meadows, J., McKnight, C., & Kinnell, M. (1999). Information science in 2010: A Loughborough University view. *Journal of the American Society for Information Science, 50,* 1153–1162.

Taylor, R. S. (1966). Professional aspects of information science and technology. In C. A. Cuadra (Ed.), *Annual review of information science and technology* (Vol. 1, pp. 1–40). New York: Wiley.

Thomas, N. P., Crow, S. R., & Franklin, L. L. (2011). *Information literacy and information skills instruction: Applying research to practice in the 21st century library* (3rd ed.). Santa Barbara, CA: ABC-CLIO, LLC.

Thomas, R. M. (1992). Vygotsky and the Soviet tradition. In R. M. Thomas (Ed.), *Comparing theories of child development* (3rd ed., pp. 319–356). Belmont, CA: Wadsworth.

Todd, R. (2011). "Look for me in the whirlwind": Actions, outcomes and evidence. In D. V. Loertscher & B. Wools (Eds.), *Knowledge building in the learning commons: Moving from research to practice to close the achievement gap* (pp. 34–50). Conference Proceedings of the Mountain Research Retreat #17, Osseo, MN. Spring, TX: LMC Source.

U.S. Department of Education. (2010). *ESEA Blueprint for Reform.* Washington, D.C.: Office of Planning, Evaluation and Policy Development. Retrieved from http://www2 .ed.gov/policy/elsec/leg/blueprint/blueprint.pdf

U.S. Department of Education. (2012, February 29). *26 more states and D.C. seek flexibility from NCLB to drive education reforms in second round of requests.* Retrieved from http://www.ed.gov/news/press-releases/26-more-states-and-dc-seek-flexibility-nclb-drive-education-reforms-second-round

Vygotsky, L. (1978). *Mind in society: The development of higher psychological processes.* Edited and translated by M. Cole, V. John-Steiner, S. Scribner, & E. Souberman. Cambridge, MA: Harvard University Press. (Original work published 1934).

Winter, J. A., & Goldfield, E. C. (1991). Caregiver-child interaction in the development of self: The contributions of Vygotsky, Brunner, and Kay to Mead's theory. *Symbolic Interaction, 14*(4), 433–447.

3

INFLUENCING INSTRUCTIONAL
PARTNERSHIPS IN PRESERVICE
ELEMENTARY EDUCATION TEACHERS

Mirah J. Dow, Tonya Davis, and Angela Vietti-Okane

INTRODUCTION: PREPARING FUTURE TEACHERS

Elementary education programs prepare future educators to teach the next generation of learners. At the locations for this study, a mid-western regional university, talented college students gain knowledge in educational theory and methods and participate in a two-semester professional development school. Through this combination, students develop competencies that enable them to become effective teachers. This study was designed to determine the impact of one elementary education program required course, The Elementary Teacher and the Library Media Specialist: Partners in Teaching Literature Appreciation and Information Literacy, on enrolled elementary education students. The purpose of the course was to shape the preservice teachers' understandings of their joint role with school librarians in teaching students in today's elementary schools (K-6). Participants enrolled over four semesters experienced success in developing perceptions of the school librarian as an instructional partner.

LITERATURE REVIEW

Partnering in Instruction

Teaching language arts and literacy (reading, writing, speaking, listening, and language) are important skills for all K-12 students. As students advance through the grades and master skills, they are able to demonstrate with fluency and regularity the capacity of a literate person. This growth is extremely significant given the amount and formats of information available today. This growth requires "all hands on deck" when it comes to creating a learning environment that responses to students' individual learning abilities, needs, and interests and enables each student to develop a strong base of knowledge across a wide range of subject matter. School librarians through state and national standards (AASL, 2007, 2009b; CCSC, 2010) and instructional best practice guidelines (AASL, 2007, 2009a;

Moreillon, 2007, 2012) are continually directed to assume leadership roles in their schools in teaching students to read, view, and/or listen to information presented in many contexts and to conduct research.

Successful integration of information literacy instruction requires collaboration and partnerships between school librarians and classroom teachers (Achterman, 2008; Church, 2008; Haycock, 2010; Immroth & Lukenbill, 2007; Kachel et al., 2011; Lance, Rodney, & Schwarz, 2010; McGregor, 2003; Moreillon, 2007, 2012; Pickard, 1993; Todd, 2011). Partnerships in this case are a kind of relationship that results from educators working together to accomplish common goals. In a classroom teacher–school librarian partnership, the classroom teacher brings expert knowledge of specific content areas and assumes responsibility for determining what, when, and how to teach specific aspects of the content. Content areas include English and language arts, science, mathematics, history/government, social studies, art, music, physical education, and other subject areas. The school librarian brings expert knowledge of resources and assumes responsibility for facilitating information literacy instruction in the context of the content area. Through information literacy instruction, students learn to recognize information needs; search for, access, and evaluate information; use information to develop; and communicate new ideas for resolution of human problems. According to Woolls (2004), when school librarians and teachers integrate content and information literacy, students learn how to make use of a wide range of resources and broaden their knowledge and understandings of what is taught in the classroom.

Through partnerships, classroom teachers and school librarians share responsibilities for standards-based design and implementation of instruction. Integration of information literacy instruction into the curriculum of the school requires strategies that can be taught and learned in teacher preparation programs. Teacher preparation programs require university-level organizational structures to support sharing of expertise across academic programs within the educational institution.

Collaboration Theory

Collaboration is a popular concept in education but often viewed as being without a consolidated general theory. To fill the need for an operational definition or theoretical foundation for collaboration in library science and an improved way to understand the relationship between classroom teacher–school librarian collaboration and student achievement, Montiel-Overall (2005) studied collaboration as it applies to school librarians and classroom teachers. From a constructivist view of education and a wide range of domains including social, cultural, and educational psychology and the corporate sector, she defined collaboration as "a trusting working relation between two or more equal participants involved in shared thinking, shared planning, and shared creation of integrated instruction. Through a shared vision and shared objectives, student learning opportunities are created that integrate subject content and information literacy by co-planning, co-implementing, and co-evaluating students' progress throughout the instructional process in order to improve student learning in all areas of the curriculum" (Montiel-Overall, 2005, Section A, para. 7). She proposed a model of fully developed collaboration for bringing together educators to share expertise. Her proposed model includes coordination, cooperation/partnership, integrated instruction, and integrated curriculum. She cautions that for this theoretical framework and model to be successful, there are needs for organizational change both at the school and university levels. At the school level, she highlights the need for supportive school principals who enable classroom teachers and school librarians to work together. At the university level, she recommends that colleges of education and schools of library and information science engage in large-scale change, because "these institutions must begin to provide preservice experiences in collaboration" (Montiel-Overall, 2005, Conclusions and Recommendations, para. 3).

CONTEXT: ELEMENTARY TEACHER AND SCHOOL LIBRARY PARTNER COURSE

To instruct preservice teachers about the roles and responsibilities of state-licensed school librarians and infuse participants' learning with collaboration teaching strategies, a course was created for preservice elementary education teachers. In Kansas, state-licensed school librarians have earned an initial elementary or secondary teaching license in a content area, have two years classroom teaching experience, earn a master's degree that emphasizes school librarian content and methods courses, and pass the ETS-PRAXIS exam for school librarians. The decision to create the above-referenced course resulted from collaboration between university-based elementary education and school library faculty, deans, and department heads. Through a series of discussions about the course purpose and structure that took place during a regularly scheduled elementary education curriculum review, the course was finally formally outlined and then submitted for approval through the university, course approval process. The new course became a one-credit hour requirement for all ESU students majoring in elementary education (K-6). This new course was predicated on a decade-long experience by a veteran, state-licensed school librarian's teaching of ESU's elementary education degree program's required course "Children's Literature," and a strong desire by the library school faculty to create a course that would begin to overcome barriers to classroom–library collaboration among teams of educators working together to jointly design, delivery, and assess curriculum.

The approved course was a 1-credit hour course that according to state education policy requires enrolled students to be offered 15 clock hours of instruction. The course was offered in a hybrid course delivery model beginning with one face-to-face class session (five hours) and the remainder of the course delivered using Blackboard, an online platform for technology-assisted instruction. All individuals enrolled in the course were degree-seeking students in the ESU elementary education degree program. The courses, several offered each semester, were scheduled during fall and spring semesters and were taught by two state-licensed school librarians: one with approximately 11 years prior experience as a classroom teacher and approximately 5 years as a school librarian, and the other with approximately 4 years of prior classroom teaching experience and approximately 11 years as a school librarian.

The purpose of the course was an introduction to strategies for enriching children's appreciation of literature, identifying resources for literature-based instruction across the curriculum, and collaboration between the classroom teacher and school librarian in planning and teaching resource-based research. The textbook for the course was *Collaborative strategies for teaching reading comprehension: Maximizing your impact* (Moreillon, 2007). According to Moreillon (2007), this book was written to support the collaborative work of elementary school librarians and for preservice teachers preparing for their career, which would hopefully "embrace the mission of the school library as the hub of the school" (p. ix). The book presents seven research-based strategies for co-teaching reading comprehension in both fictional and informational children's literature: activating background knowledge, using sensory images, questioning, making predictions and inferences, determining main ideas, using fix-up options, and synthesizing. The course learning outcomes outlined in the course syllabus stated that the elementary education student through participation in the course will:

- Know roles and responsibilities of the school library and how they are crucial to the teaching and learning process
- Know the mission of the school library as a hub of learning and a place of opportunity
- Be familiar with Kansas School Library Media and Technology Standards for PreK-12 students
- Be familiar with American Association for School Librarians' (2007) *Standards for the 21st-century learner*
- Develop dynamic collaboration strategies that can be used among equal partners who strive to reach excellence and increase achievement for all learners
- Develop co-teaching reading comprehension strategies to ensure student achievement
- Describe and model strategies for collaboration between classroom teachers and school librarians in planning, guiding, and evaluating student research projects and resource-based learning.
- Identify and use strategies to foster independent reading, independent information seeking, and literature enjoyment
- Identify and use print and electronic fictional and informational resources that support learning in the elementary classroom
- Identify and use professional resources that support the creative use of children's literature in teaching and learning

Course learning activities included in-class participation in lecture and demonstration, partnering activities, and large and small group discussions; assigned readings and written reactions to readings; a school library observation and report; development of a collaborative assignment; and scheduled, structured self-reflections.

RESEARCH QUESTIONS

To determine whether the new course achieved its purpose, the question "Are elementary education majors' perceptions of school librarians as partners in teaching changed through a 1-credit hours course taught by library school faculty?" was asked. The newest of this course and the concept of teaching strategies for effective classroom teacher and school librarian partnerships as a requirement in elementary education program provides opportunities to broaden our understandings of innovative, higher education instruction.

METHODOLOGY: PRE- AND POST-SURVEY AND PROCEDURE

A case study methodology (Creswell, 2007) was used in this study wherein the researchers explored a bounded system over time. While course instructors observed and noted students' progress throughout the course learning process and gathered end-of-course feedback from participants that was utilized in analysis of student learning, the data collection, analysis, and findings articulated in this chapter are only from the longitudinal pre- and post-survey; wherein, we collected the same information from all the participants in the given case study. According to Blaxter, Hughes, and Tight (2006), questionnaires, or surveys, are a widely used social research technique for formulating precise written questions to be answered by those whose opinions or experience specifically are of interest (p. 179).

During fall 2008 (88 students enrolled), spring 2009 (113 students enrolled), fall 2009 (90 students enrolled), and spring 2010 (118 students enrolled), a pre- and post-survey was administered in all courses titled "The Elementary Teacher and the Library Media Specialist: Partners in Teaching Literature Appreciation and Information Literacy Skills" to determine the effectiveness of the course in fostering the perception of school librarian as teachers' instructional partners. The findings were intended for use in revision of the course, as well as to inform the stakeholders about the value of the course.

Not only was the college course context for this study strongly influenced by Judi Moreillon's knowledge of co-teaching strategies, but the method was also based on her research "Two heads are better than one: Influencing preservice classroom teachers' understandings and practice of classroom-library collaboration" (2008), wherein Moreillon studied 14 undergraduate teacher preparation students in a program offered by a state university in Arizona at a campus located in a local community. Twelve questions from Moreillon's survey were identified and recommended by Moreillon for use in this study (Figure 3.1). Using a Likert scale model for construction of responses, each question offered respondents five response choices: strongly agree, agree, disagree, strongly disagree, and don't know.

Each semester, the course began with a five-hour face-to-face class session. The pre-survey was administered during the opening session of the first class. Each student was given an informed consent document. Each student voluntarily and anonymously completed the survey and handed it in. The post-survey was administered at the end of the course in the Blackboard course forum as part of a final assignment, which included a required reflection and completion and submission of the post-survey (10 points). The completed post-surveys were electronically submitted by the student. By design, the instructor printed the completed survey without keeping track of students' names. All survey paper copies were mailed to the university faculty member in charge of the research project. The data were analyzed using SPSS, a computer software program. Student's pre- and post-surveys were not paired. Completed surveys were not separated by instructor name. If a survey completer failed to mark two or more response statements, none of that survey completer's responses were included in the data. Table 3.1 shows the pre- and post-survey number of valid question responses by question number for each semester.

QUESTION NUMBER	STATEMENT
Question 1	School librarians should be responsible for teaching reading.
Question 2	School librarians should be responsible for teaching research skills.
Question 3	School librarians should be responsible for teaching every area of the school curriculum.
Question 4	School librarians should help classroom teachers find materials.
Question 5	School librarians should help classroom teachers design and plan lessons and units of instruction.
Question 6	School librarians should help classroom teachers co-teach lessons and units of instruction.
Question 7	School librarians should assess students' learning on projects in which they have taught some or many components.
Question 8	School librarians should provide in-service for classroom teachers to help improve teaching practices.
Question 9	School librarians should help classroom teachers learn new technologies.
Question 10	School library media programs should be a critical part of the literacy program of the school.
Question 11	School principals should set the expectation for classroom–library collaboration.
Question 12	When school librarians and classroom teachers collaborate for instruction, student achievement should increase.

Figure 3.1   Pre- and Post-survey Question Statements

LIMITATIONS

The single data collection method reported in this chapter causes the study design to fall short of Creswell's (2007) recommendation for "in-depth data collection involving multiple sources of information (e.g., observations, interviews, audiovisual materials, and documents and reports)" (p. 73). As is mentioned in the methodology section of this chapter, multiple methods were used but not all data are reported in this chapter. The data from instructor observations and end-of-course student feedback to instructors were used by university faculty from semester-to-semester to improve the course. Given the fragile nature of many college classrooms in terms of what may potentially disrupt teaching–learning interactions between instructor and students, the researchers decided to only confront the undergraduate participants in this study, many of whom were only one, two, or three years beyond high school, with this pre-survey data collection process. It was a concern that securing consent for multiple data collections and collecting data in more than one

Table 3.1 Number of Valid Responses by Question

	VALID RESPONSES			
QUESTION	2008 FALL	2009 SPRING	2009 FALL	2010 SPRING
Q1-Pretest	86	105	89	79
Q1-Posttest	70	97	88	82
Q2-Pretest	85	105	89	79
Q2-Posttest	69	96	88	82
Q3-Pretest	85	105	89	79
Q3-Posttest	69	96	87	82
Q4-Pretest	85	104	89	79
Q4-Posttest	70	97	88	82
Q5-Pretest	85	105	89	79
Q5-Posttest	69	96	88	82
Q6-Pretest	86	105	89	79
Q6-Posttest	69	96	88	82
Q7-Pretest	86	105	89	79
Q7-Posttest	70	97	88	82
Q8-Pretest	86	105	89	79
Q8-Posttest	70	97	88	82
Q9-Pretest	86	105	89	79
Q9-Posttest	70	97	88	82
Q10-Pretest	86	105	89	79
Q10-Posttest	70	97	88	82
Q11-Pretest	86	105	89	79
Q11-Posttest	70	97	88	82
Q12-Pretest	86	105	89	79
Q12-Posttest	70	97	88	82

way, for example to add structured interviews, could potentially interfere with the primary purpose of the course, which was infusing the preservice educators with knowledge about the mission of school libraries and instructional partnerships with state-licensed school librarians. The design of this study also falls short of experimental methods used for assessing causal relationship by determining the impact of an intervention, in this case teaching of specific content. A quasi-experimental design (Wildemuth, 2009), often used in information and library science including "instruction, evaluation, information seeking, and professional development" (p. 94), could be used in further study using a time series design with data collected at two data collection points in total: pre- and post-treatment. The challenge for using a quasi-experimental design may be in maintaining appropriate controls given the unpredictable nature of instruction that is likely to take place through a continual process throughout several weeks or a semester as was the case in this study. In addition, future studies can move beyond the use of descriptive to inferential statistics that assess the statistical significance of the data and results.

FINDINGS

Elementary education majors' perceptions of school librarians as partners in teaching positively changed through participation in a one-credit hour course in the university's elementary education degree program taught by library school faculty. In fall 2008, agree and strongly agree combined responses increased for questions 1 (16–31), 3 (5–15), 5 (24–51), 6 (39–63), and 7 (47–64). Agree and strongly agree combined responses slightly decreased for responses to questions 2 (66–65), 4 (79–69), 8 (52–51), 9 (66–62), 10 (75–68), 11 (63–57), and 12 (85–69). Overall for the semester fall 2008, the number of participants who agreed or strongly agreed with each statement was above 50 percent (44) of participants except for questions 1 (33/88) and 3 (15/88). In spring 2009, agree and strongly agree combined responses increased for questions 1 (19–50), 2 (85–87), 3 (7–43), 5 (26–86), 6 (40–83), 7 (69–88), 8 (58–83), and 9 (94–95). Agree and strongly agree combined slightly decreased for questions 4 (101–97), 10 (100–97), 11 (82–80), and 12 (103–97). Overall for the semester spring 2009, the number of participants who agreed or strongly agreed with each statement was above 50 percent (56) of participants except for questions 1 (50/88) and 3 (43/88). In fall 2009, agree and strongly agree combined responses increased for questions 1 (18–46), 2 (76–79), 3 (8–30), 5 (25–73), 6 (35–85), 7 (58–84), 8 (51–76), and 9 (94–95). Agree and strongly agree combined responses slightly decreased for questions 4 (101–97), 10 (100–97), 11 (82–80), and 12(103–97). Overall for semester fall 2009, the number of participants who agreed or strongly agreed with each statement was above 50 percent (57) of participants except for questions 1 (46/113) and 3 (30/113). In spring 2010, agree and strongly agree combined responses increased for all 12 questions. Overall for semester spring 2010, the number of participants who agreed or strongly agreed with each statement was above 50 percent (45) of participants. Over the four semesters presented in this study, the concept of school librarians as responsible for teaching research skills (question 2) varied the least in fall 2008 (66–65), spring 2009 (85–87), and fall 2009 (76–79). The concept of that school librarians should help classroom teachers design and plan lessons and units of instruction (question 5) increased more than any other question number during all semesters in spring 2009 (26–86).

CONCLUSIONS

On the basis of this study, a university-based elementary education (K-6) course that teaches co-teaching strategies for classroom teachers and school librarians can improve participants' perceptions about the school library media program and school librarians' involvement in teaching reading and research skills. Through careful selection of instructors, required reading, and learning activities, preservice teachers (undergraduate students) in this study were introduced to collaborative strategies for teaching reading and how to partner with school librarians to maximize impact. The how-to lessons presented in Moreillon (2007) textbook provided models to be learned and practiced with the guidance of university instructors for the course who are both experienced classroom teachers and school librarians. The lessons are likely to have positively influenced perceptions about the school librarians' role in co-teaching lessons and units of instruction, as well as perceptions of school librarians as in-service provider for classroom teachers and

Table 3.2a   Questions 1–6 Agree/Strongly Agree Responses, 2008–2010

QUESTION	RESPONSES	PRESURVEY (POSTSURVEY)			
		2008 FALL	2009 SPRING	2009 FALL	2010 SPRING
Q1. School librarians should be responsible for teaching reading.	Agree	14–27 (16.3–38.6)	17–40 (16.2–41.2)	17–35 (19.1–39.8)	16–40 (20.3–48.8)
	Strongly agree	2–4 (2.3–5.7)	2–10 (1.9–10.3)	1–11 (1.1–12.5)	1–11 (1.3–13.4)
Q2. School librarians should be responsible for teaching research skills.	Agree	50–39 (58.1–55.7)	66–53 (62.0–54.6)	59–47 (66.3–53.4)	47–45 (59.4–54.9)
	Strongly agree	16–26 (18.6–37.1)	19–34 (18.1–35.1)	17–32 (19.1–36.4)	15–30 (19.0–36.6)
Q3. School librarians should be responsible for teaching every area of the curriculum.	Agree	4–12 (4.7–17.1)	7–34 (6.7–35.1)	8–25 (9.0–28.4)	4–33 (5.1–40.2)
	Strongly agree	1–3 (1.2–4.3)	0–9 (0.0–9.3)	0–5 (0.0–5.7)	2–6 (2.5–7.3)
Q4. School librarians should help classroom teacher find materials.	Agree	52–21 (60.5–30.0)	58–36 (55.2–37.1)	53–35 (59.6–39.8)	43–20 (54.4–24.4)
	Strongly agree	27–48 (31.4–68.6)	43–61 (41.0–62.9)	34–51 (38.2–58.0)	33–62 (41.8–75.6)
Q5. School librarians should help classroom teachers design and plan lessons and units of instruction.	Agree	22–30 (25.6–42.9)	25–51 (23.8–52.6)	21–46 (23.6–52.3)	24–41 (30.4–50.0)
	Strongly agree	2–21 (2.3–30.0)	1–35 (1.0–36.1)	4–27 (4.5–30.7)	1–32 (1.1–39.0)
Q6. School librarians should help classroom teachers co-teach lessons and units of instruction.	Agree	36–24 (41.9–34.3)	36–52 (34.3–53.6)	30–35 (33.7–39.8)	28–33 (35.4–40.2)
	Strongly agree	3–39 (3.5–55.7)	4–41 (3.8–42.3)	5–50 (5.6–56.8)	2–47 (2.5–57.3)

Table 3.2b   Questions 7–12 Agree/Strongly Agree Responses, 2008–2010

QUESTION	RESPONSES	PRESURVEY (POSTSURVEY)			
		2008 FALL	2009 SPRING	2009 FALL	2010 SPRING
Q7. School librarians should assess students' learning on projects in which they have taught some or many components.	Agree	44–36 (51.2–51.4)	61–51 (58.1–52.6)	53–43 (59.6–48.9)	46–39 (58.2–47.6)
	Strongly agree	3–28 (3.5–40.0)	8–37 (7.6–38.1)	5–41 (5.6–46.6)	6–38 (7.6–46.4)
Q8. School librarians should provide in-service for classroom teachers to help improve teaching practices.	Agree	43–30 (50.0–42.9)	54–47 (51.4–48.5)	45–46 (50.6–52.3)	37–32 (46.8–39.0)
	Strongly agree	8–21 (9.3–30.0)	4–36 (3.8–37.1)	6–30 (6.7–34.1)	10–41 (12.7–50.0)
Q9. School librarians should help classroom teachers learn new technologies.	Agree	50–29 (58.1–41.4)	70–35 (66.7–36.1)	54–38 (60.7–43.2)	50–19 (63.3–23.2)
	Strongly agree	16–33 (18.6–47.0)	24–60 (22.0–61.9)	22–50 (24.7–56.8)	17–61 (21.5–74.4)
Q10. School library media programs should be a critical part of the literacy program of the school.	Agree	43–26 (50.0–37.1)	66–33 (62.9–34.0)	54–35 (60.7–39.8)	44–30 (55.7–36.6)
	Strongly agree	32–42 (37.2–60.0)	34–64 (32.4–66.0)	26–51 (29.2–58.0)	31–51 (39.2–62.2)
Q11. School principals should set the expectation for classroom–library collaboration.	Agree	49–28 (57.0–40.0)	61–42 (58.1–43.3)	57–36 (64.0–40.9)	47–35 (59.5–42.7)
	Strongly agree	14–29 (16.3–41.4)	21–38 (20.0–39.2)	16–34 (18.0–38.5)	17–33 (21.5–40.2)
Q12. When school librarians and classroom teachers collaborate for instruction, student achievement should increase.	Agree	48–8 (55.8–11.4)	49–18 (46.7–18.6)	48–18 (53.9–20.5)	37–41 (46.8–51.9)
	Strongly agree	37–61 (43.0–87.1)	54–79 (51.4–81.4)	38–68 (42.7–77.3)	41–67 (51.9–81.7)

perceptions of school librarians in assessing students' learning on projects in which school librarians have taught some of many components.

The greatest increases between pre- and post-survey responses took place in the second, third, and forth semesters. Instructors' new knowledge gleaned during the first semester of the study about their undergraduate student audience, as well as about how to best present the content in a hybrid learning environment, was used to revise and improve instruction. Instructors' also exerted a great deal of energy to make the course interesting and worthwhile for enrolled students who in many cases did not feel that the course was necessary, should be required, or should be held on Saturday morning.

Some students in these classes seemed to recognize upon beginning the class that school librarians help classroom teachers to learn new technology; school library media programs should be critical part of the literacy program; school principals should set expectations for classroom–library collaboration; and when school librarians and classroom teachers collaborate for instruction, student's achievement should increase. It is possible that these are perceptions based as much on participants' fairly recent K-12 experience in their own elementary, middle, and high schools with effective state-licensed school librarians as it is based on the content of the course.

This study, albeit indirectly, explored Montiel-Overall (2005) theory that for collaboration to move beyond cooperation to instructional partnerships, there must be engagement by college of education and schools of library and information science in large-scale change that provides preservice educators experiences in collaboration. While this course resulted from ideal university faculty–administrator collaboration during a regularly scheduled curriculum review, it did not develop "roots" deep enough to overcome the harsh effects of a period of growing economic tension and/or some faculty competition for ownership of the reading curriculum area. There was a debate about who should pay for the instructors for the course that ultimately lead to discontinuing this degree program requirement. Until all members of higher education communities are willing and able to cross-list courses and manage inter department teaching loads of faculty, preservice classroom teachers and school librarians are unlikely to experience real partnerships at the university level.

REFERENCES

AASL. (2007). *Standards for the 21st-century learner*. Chicago: American Association of School Libraries. Retrieved from http://www.ala.org/aasl/sites/ala.org.aasl/files/content/guidelinesandstandards/learningstandards/AASL_LearningStandards.pdf

AASL. (2009a). *Empowering learners: Guidelines for school library media programs*. Chicago: American Library Association.

AASL. (2009b). *Standards for the 21st-century learner in action*. Chicago: American Association of School Libraries.

Achterman, D. L. (2008). *Haves, halves, and have-nots: School libraries and student achievement in California*. Denton, TX: UNT Digital Library. Retrieved from http://digital.library.unt.edu/ark:/67531/metadc9800/m1/

Blaxter, L., Hughes, C., & Tight, M. (2006). *How to research* (3rd ed.). Maidenhead, Berkshire: Open University Press.

Church, A. (2008). The instructional role of the library media specialist as perceived by elementary school principals. *School Library Media Research, 11*. Retrieved from http://www.ala.org/aasl/aaslpubsandjournals/slmrb/slmrcontents/volume11/church

Creswell, J. W. (2007). *Qualitative inquiry & research design: Choosing among five approaches.* Thousand Oaks, CA: SAGE Publications.

Emporia State University (ESU). Retrieved from http://emporia.edu

Haycock, K. (2010). Leadership from the middle: Building influence for change. In S. Coatney (Ed.), *The many faces of school library leadership* (pp. 1–12). Santa Barbara, CA: Libraries Unlimited.

Immroth, B., & Lukenbill, W. B. (2007). Teacher-school library media specialist collaboration through social marketing strategies: An information behavior study. *School Library Media Research, 10.* Retrieved from http://www.ala.org/aasl/aaslpubsandjournals/slmrb/slmrcontents/volume10/immroth_teacherslmscollaboration

Kachel, D. E., et al. (2011). *School library research summarized: A graduate class project.* Mansfield, PA: School of Library & Information Technologies Department, Mansfield University.

Lance, K. C., Rodney, M. C., & Schwarz, B. (2010). The impact of school libraries on academic achievement: A research study based on responses from administrators in Idaho. *School Library Monthly, 26*(9), 14–17.

McGregor, J. (2003). Collaboration and leadership. In B. K. Stripling & S. Hughes-Hassell (Eds.), *Curriculum connections through the library* (pp. 119–219). Westport, CT: Libraries Unlimited.

Montiel-Overall, P. (2005). Toward a theory of collaboration for teachers and librarians. *School Library Media Research, 8*(1). Retrieved from http://www.ala.org/aasl/aaslpubsandjournals/slmrb/slmrcontents/volume82005/theory

Moreillon, J. (2007). *Collaborative strategies for teaching reading comprehension: Maximizing your impact.* Chicago: ALA Editions.

Moreillon, J. (2008). Two heads are better than one: The factors influencing the understanding and practice of classroom-library collaboration. *School Library Media Research, 11.* Retrieved from http://www.ala.org/aasl/aaslpubsandjournals/slmrb/slmrcontents/volume11/moreillon

Moreillon, J. (2012). *Coteaching reading comprehension strategies in secondary school libraries: Maximizing your impact.* Chicago: ALA Editions.

National Governors Association Center for Best Practices, Council of Chief State School Officers. (2010). *Common Core State Standards.* Washington, D.C.: National Governors Association Center for Best Practices, Council of Chief State School Officers. Retrieved from http://www.corestandards.org/the-standards

Pickard, P. W. (1993). The instructional consultant role of the school library media specialist. *School Library Media Quarterly, 21*(2), 115–121.

Todd, R. (2011). "Look for me in the whirlwind": Actions, outcomes and evidence. In D. V. Loertscher & B. Wools (Eds.), *Knowledge building in the learning commons: Moving from research to practice to close the achievement gap* (pp. 34–50). Conference Proceedings of the Treasure Mountain Research Retreat #17, Osseo, MN. Spring, TX: LMC Source.

Wildemuth, B. M. (2009). *Applications of social research methods to questions in library and information science.* Westport, CT: Libraries Unlimited.

Woolls, B. (2004). *The school librarian manager* (3rd ed.). Westport, CT: Libraries Unlimited.

4

EVERYDAY LIFE INFORMATION
SEEKING PRACTICES OF UPPER-
INCOME HIGH SCHOOL STUDENTS

Lori L. Franklin

INTRODUCTION: A FOCUS ON STUDENTS TODAY IN A NEW SCHOOL LIBRARY

As a beginning researcher, this author shares findings from school librarian interviews conducted during a case study designed to uncover the everyday life information seeking (ELIS) practices of students working in a highly technological high school. The theoretical framework for this study is based on Savolainen's ELIS theory, which was informed by Bourdieu (1984) and his ideas about *habitus*, the recent research by Agosto and Hughes-Hassell's (2005, 2006a, 2006b) urban teen study, and Havighurst's (1972) adolescent developmental tasks and theories. A literature search pinpoints the need for exploring ELIS practices with students working in school libraries. Findings indicate that students from affluent families are deeply concerned with academic achievement and gaining entry into prestigious colleges and universities, and thus require a type of "instructional model" to assure success. Participants in this study accomplish ELIS practices by using their own devices, particularly smartphones, to bypass school district–required filtering and enjoy accessing a variety of information seeking topics. The school librarian roles, as outlined in the *Empowering learners* (2009) guidelines, are discussed within the context of the study and the students' ELIS practices, and recommendations are provided for working with 21st-century students in school libraries.

NEW TECHNOLOGIES AND TODAY'S YOUNG PEOPLE

The world today hangs at a precipice as new computer technologies are developed, making advancement in all areas of life and global reach possible. School librarians are uniquely positioned to teach young people who eagerly adopt and modify technological innovations to suit their own social and learning needs. Research is needed that investigates the information behavior of young people who use information and communication technologies (ICTs) to seek personal information, particularly in the school library. School librarians are in a unique position to study

information behavior while observing and interacting with students using their fa-
vored technological devices; to lead in the development of new, best instructional
practices; and to advance the idea of dynamic education informatics in education.
To improve educators' practices with students, this study asks, "What are the ELIS
practices of students working in a highly technological high school?"

A STUDY SPARK FOR EXAMINING TEENAGE STUDENTS

While working in school libraries, a question started this quest to find out how students find information of a personal nature: Why do students enter school libraries
and then choose to stay there, beyond the parameters of classroom assignments
or formal class visits? Having read Denise Agosto and Sandra Hughes-Hassell's
(2005, 2006a, 2006b) urban teen study, further investigation of their discoveries, this time with a different population, teens from affluent families who use the
school library, was appropriate. In the Agosto and Hughes-Hassell study, urban adolescents who attended public schools and lived in inner city housing and who also
spent time in public libraries were studied. The researchers developed theoretical
and empirical models of their participants' ELI practices in relation to their public
library use. Their work was built upon the ELIS theory developed by Savolainen
(2005, 2008) who based much of his theoretical foundation on the research and
writing by Bourdieu (1984), who details class structures and information behaviors. Agosto and Hughes-Hassell questioned urban teens in a context other than
paper-based assignments. They sought to find out what types of information their
participants looked for, how they went about finding it, who their trusted information sources were, and what information channels they used.

LITERATURE PINPOINTS NEED FOR STUDYING ELIS
PRACTICES IN SCHOOL LIBRARIES

Earliest school library studies focused on locations of school libraries within school
campuses, funding school libraries, and collection development (Willson, 1967;
Wofford, 1940). The shift toward conducting critical research investigating school
libraries is outlined in the dual 2003 and 2009 *Library Trends* research agenda
themes; here, Neuman's (2003) call for studying student learning is echoed by
Mardis (2009), who suggests that change must occur "to begin to shift staid conceptions of school librarianship within the LIS academy to the idea of dynamic
educational informatics in schools; this shift in perception can have a tremendous
impact on preparation curriculum, professional practice, and research trajectories
in all areas of library and information science" (p. 1).

Savolainen and the Theoretical Framework for This Study

The foundation upon which ELIS behavior studies can exist is one created by
Reijo Savolainen, who developed his theory in 1984, refining his ideas in 2008
to add the concept of "practices" to ELIS activities. He pays credit in his writings to Bourdieu (1984) and his notions about *habitus* and *way and mastery of
life*. An additional influence on Savolainen's writings is Brenda Dervin. He has
written about her sense-making theory in depth (Savolainen, 1993), hailing its
user-centered approach and multidisciplinary influences. As his interest in ELIS

behaviors began to develop, Savolainen (1993) reminds readers that Dervin's work is a true turning point in the movement of LIS research into a user-centered framework, and also suggests that more research is necessary to gain "insights into the development of other user-centered conceptions trying to combine the elements of structure and action" (p. 27).

Savolainen (1995) defines ELIS as a way to legitimate *nonwork information seeking*, a phrase that by itself might be construed as an ambiguous concept (p. 266). "Broadly defined, the concept of ELIS refers to the acquisition of various informational (both cognitive and expressive) elements which people employ to orient themselves in daily life or to solve problems not directly connected with the performance of occupational tasks" (Savolainen, 1995, p. 267). His ELIS theory paves the way for explorations into the practices exhibited by individuals as they go about meeting their ELI needs, and his theory is useful for informing a study of adolescents working in school libraries.

STUDYING TEENS IN A HIGHLY TECHNOLOGICAL SCHOOL LIBRARY

The researcher's interest in the urban teen study, which took place in public library settings, raised the question about similar findings that might occur with students in a different setting. For this case study, the information behavior of upper-income students attending a newly constructed, highly technological Midwestern high school was chosen to study. The school library in this location is small in contrast to many school libraries. It was designed to primarily facilitate virtual computer technologies that allow students access to resources beyond the walls of the structure itself. While this school library was not selected for the study because of its new, architectural presence, it is noteworthy that the physical school campus is remarkable. The school library has soaring windows that provide natural lighting, sleek seating, and work areas that invite students and adults to be comfortable while completing tasks or socializing.

METHODOLOGY

Using the urban teen study (Agosto and Hughes-Hassell, 2006a, 2006b) as a starting place, the research question was asked: "What are the ELIS practices exhibited by upper-income students working in a highly technological school library?" In this chapter, the focus is on the central research question and two of five subquestions: (1) How do students in a highly technological school library environment use physical and virtual technologies and other information resources provided by the school library? (2) How do findings from this study affect implications for school librarians administering best practices for working with students?

Choice for a Unique Study Site and Population

The purposive sampling method by Creswell (2009) was used to select the study site and participants in this study. The study site, a newly constructed, highly technological high school in Kansas, was selected specifically because the school library was designed with today's digital learners in mind and because students at this site are uniquely different in contrast to those discussed in the urban teen study (Figure 4.1). This school library is unique because it takes up a smaller physical "footprint" than many other school libraries in the region. The population being studied is remarkable because 96 percent of the area residents have earned high school diplomas, in contrast with 27 percent of the U.S. population (U.S. Census Bureau, 2011). The median household income for the city in which the study site is located was just over $71,000 annually, compared with $51,425 for the rest of the nation (U.S. Census Bureau, 2011). Students attending the high school typically live in large homes with multicar garages, have parents who are at least high school educated and typically hold postsecondary degrees, and rarely drop out of high school (less than 1% in 2008–2009). Clearly, the demographic makeup of participants is very different than that of the student participants in the urban teen study. As study authors Agosto and Hughes-Hassell (2006a) note, "Many inner-city teens face a harsh reality of poverty, prejudice, and a lack of strong role models, making this process [growing up] even more difficult than for teens living in more advantaged situations" (p. 1394).

For relative purposes, in 2009, the state of Kansas, where this study took place, had 2.8 million residents (U.S. Census Bureau, 2011). Ethnicities were 88.5 percent white, 9.3 percent Hispanic, 6.2 percent African American, and 2.3 percent Asian. The United States, for the same time frame, had a population of more than 301 million residents. Ethnicities in similar categories were listed as 74.5 percent white, 15.1 percent Hispanic or Latino, 13.2 percent African American, and 4.4 percent Asian. While my study population was not ethnically diverse, it provides a contrasting context for studying ELIS practices of adolescents.

A Newly Constructed School: Rivals and Rule Testing

Because the school is new, public information regarding attendance data is still being compiled from the Kansas State Department of Education. Enrollment data, however, begin to "paint a portrait" of the students who attend this school. Total enrollment is listed as being 839 students, with 250 enrolled in 9th grade, 234 in 10th grade, 248 in 11th grade, and 107 in 12th grade; 58 percent of students are male and 49 percent are female.

This study has captured a moment in time that will never again exist at this school. School policies were in a state of flux and still being developed and tested for usefulness and/or success. For example, students at this particular school do not have to physically attend class.

The developing attendance policy had built-in safety nets to assure that all students received an education; yet, this policy is relaxed in comparison to those provided in other schools.

Data Collection

Data collection methods informed by Krathwohl (1998) and Rubin and Rubin (2005) include 2 school librarian interviews, one that lasted 38 minutes and the other lasting 40 minutes, for a combined total of 78 minutes; 4 student focus group sessions that varied in times from 13 to 29 minutes and totaled 78 minutes, observation occurring on 7 different sessions and totaling 52 hours, and review of virtual and print documentation conducted over 1 semester (9 weeks) while school was in session.

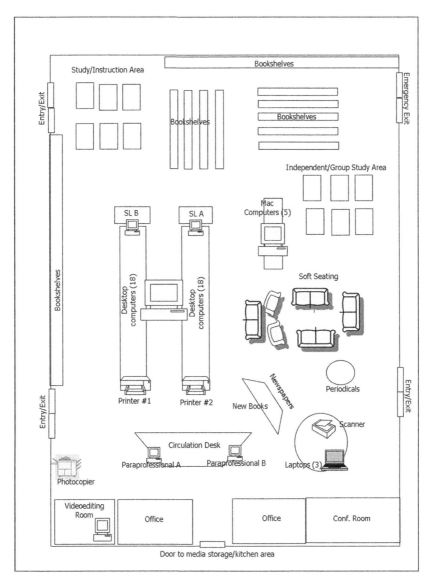

Figure 4.1   School Library Map

School Librarian Interviews

The school librarians, who informed this study and who have varying levels of experience, are assisted by two full-time paraprofessional staff and a full-time technology teacher. During the school librarian interviews, each librarian was asked the same 10 questions:

1. Can you provide me with a description of your typical students?
2. Why do you think students come into your library?
3. What types or kinds of information do you see students looking for?
4. Describe some typical interactions you have with students during day-to-day library operations.

5. How do you use Web 2.0 or virtual technologies in your work with students?
6. What have students taught you about digital age technologies and their place in the school library?
7. How do you see students interacting with one another when they come to your library to find information?
8. Can you close your eyes for me for a moment, and think back to a time when a student came to you for ELI? How did it go?
9. Tell me about an experience you can remember when you interacted with a student or a group of students and later wished the interaction had gone differently.
10. If you were to describe the students at your school to a visiting educational team from another country, how would you describe them? What would be important for the visiting team to know about your adolescent population?

Student Focus Group Sessions

Student participants in this study ranged from age 14 through 19, and were enrolled in grades 9 through 12. The senior class numbered approximately 100 students, as the school enrollment was not populated to capacity yet. Student informants were chosen by the school librarians from assigned advisory class participants. Advisory class is a special time set aside each week for student team–building and general informational sharing, and is designed to help students ease into the new school setting and to interact with peers. Advisory classes were chosen randomly by the school information computing system—the same system that sorts students into different classes according to grade level, required classes, and academic pursuits. Advisory class students might interact with one another only in their advisory classes even as they attend other scheduled classes with different peers. Forming student focus groups during advisory class time was necessary so that regular classroom instruction was not interrupted.

Four student focus group sessions were held in a conference room attached to the school library. A total of 27 students participated: 15 females and 12 males. Ethnicity was nearly 100 percent Caucasian, with the exception of 3 Asian students. A library paraprofessional took notes during the sessions; she sat in a corner and did not participate in the discussion. Students were provided with snacks and water. Six interview questions for both sessions were chosen from the urban teen study, with necessary changes made to reflect the different setting and population, and asked:

1. Why do you come to the library?
2. What types of information do you need? Can you tell me what you are looking for when you come here to find information?
3. Who helps you find information when you need it?
4. What technology do you use when you are in the library?
5. What technology is missing in the library?
6. Can you close your eyes for a moment, and recall a time when you came to the school library to find personal information (not school related)? Thinking back, how did this experience go?

Interview and focus group sessions were audiotaped and transcribed into a total of 113 pages by a local, secure transcription service. Proper institutional review board protocol was obtained and followed, and librarians and students were provided with informed consent forms and descriptions of the study purpose and their role in the process. Observations were also conducted on site, with the researcher acting as an outsider with little if any interaction with students working in the library. Wildemuth's (2009) constant monitoring method was used, and two-column note-taking evolved from pen and paper to computer-based notation.

Print and Virtual Documentation

Print documentation artifacts include the library's daily management paperwork: scheduling, student assignment planners, student newspapers, district newspapers, and circulation statistics. Sixty four digital photographs were taken of the site to help inform an understanding of the setting and some of the 3-D print or media artifacts, such as bulletin board displays. Photographs were taken to use in creating contextual maps and to capture specific details about the study site and various activities occurring in the library.

Virtual documentation included the library website, which makes available much of the virtually accessed library collection and database programs, as well as direct access to many social media Web 2.0 programs used by the librarians with scheduled classes. Five polls with a total of five checklist-response questions and one open-ended response opportunities were created and disseminated online through Edmodo (a secure educational site developed as a social networking tool for teachers to mutually share online information, assignments, photos, and videos with students). Checklist items included technology used in the previous day by students, topics of interest students search for, information sources, general media use, and the school library. The open-ended question asked students to relate what they like about the school library. The five polls were administered on five separate occasions during a nine-week time frame, and were completed by students who were assigned to be in the library for their weekly advisory class. A total of 84 individuals participated in the polls, and responses yielded 10 pages of data transcription. Poll topics included technology use, what students look for when searching for personal information, what people sources students consult when looking for information, what media the students use in their information quests, and how they use the school library website. Each poll was designed to be accessible, brief, and to tap into questions that aligned to a degree with similar questions asked of students in the urban teen study.

Generalizability, Substantive Validation, and Reliability

Transferability rather than generalizability is a goal for this study. In their examination of urban teen ELIS behaviors, Agosto and Hughes-Hassell (2006a) note that one limitation of their study is that the results, because they are based on a small, unique population, are not generalizable. They refer to Lincoln and Gubas's (1985) notion of "transferability" instead, an idea that inferences about homogeneous populations may be made, but that generalizations are not necessarily the expectation for qualitative studies.

Study Limitations

A limitation of this single case study is that it is does not provide a wide view across several technologically modern school sites, numerous librarians, or a racial diversity of students. It was conducted during a finite point in time frame, with restrictions on the amount of hours available for observing and interviewing informants. The students studied represent a homogenous group and do not provide a diverse pool of participants. With only two librarians at the school, data they provided may contain elements of bias from their working closely together. While detailing the study site and participants was an exciting process as a beginning researcher, the work also came with the realization that this study would be challenging to replicate in a similar setting with similar participants.

FINDINGS

The initial coding process for the school librarian interviews yielded 2,374 responses for 203 codes. From this initial code list, codes were collapsed into 21 second cycle codes, which resulted in five core categories: learning, school librarians, students, school, and families, and two dominate themes discussed below.

Theme I: Students Prefer Own Cell Phones to Library Computers

Students at this study site strongly prefer to use their cellular phones and smartphones in lieu of using library-supplied Microsoft Windows and Apple Macintosh desktop computers. As described by both school librarians in interviews, students do this is to search and visit websites and applications that are blocked by the district's filtering policy. Student's phones, then, can easily take them places where their access is denied on school computers. Students' cell phones are in essence "another screen" to locate information in a private manner. Mobile phone use enables students to have the choice to either keep what they discover to themselves or to share their discoveries with peers. Perhaps, one of the reasons this phenomena is so strongly exhibited is that the school library at the study site allows and encourages cell phone use as part of the staff's desire to create a relaxing, low-key atmosphere. When students talk on their phones, which the school librarians said rarely happens, they are asked to step outside into a nearby courtyard. One of the actions most frequently observed was that of sending text messages (texting) and random Internet surfing on smartphones. School Librarian B described students' preferred use of cell phones in the library, especially while they are working on classroom assignments at desktop computers, as "the best of both worlds, because they are getting their work done and they are not breaking any rules but they are getting what they want, like Facebook updates on their phone. You know what I mean? They're happy."

That the school librarians have embraced cell phone and smartphone usage is notable. Students in the various focus group sessions reported that they would not typically be visiting the library outside of a scheduled classroom visit or a need to print out work for an upcoming deadline. Because the library is the one location in the school where students are allowed to openly use their personal devices; it has become a place that students frequently visit.

Theme 2: Students at This Site Require a Specific Type of Instructional Model

Students, because they are trained to be successful academically to assure their entrance into desirable postsecondary educational institutions, require a different type of instructional approach than might be found in other socioeconomic scenarios. School Librarian A spent a significant portion of her interview session describing how students at this study site prefer a type of *instructional model* when asked to complete assigned tasks and projects for a grade. She referred to a professional book she was reading, *The price of privilege: How parental pressure and material advantage are creating a generation of disconnected and unhappy kids* (Levine, 2006), and said one of the strongest ideas she discovered from the book was the notion that some students in affluence strongly desire to achieve the best grades possible and demand specific instructions for accomplishing this. "They are overly dependent on the opinions of parents, teachers, coaches, and peers and frequently rely on others not only to pave the way with difficult tasks but also to grease the wheels of everyday life as well" (Levine, 2006, pp. 5, 6).

At this study site, end products are typically dictated by teachers, who then rely on the school librarians to provide potential pathways for creating the final projects, often using social media Web 2.0 programs to encourage sharing and teamwork during the process. Students want explicit directions so that they can be assured they will successfully complete their assignment. As School Librarian A explained: "They want to not only see an example but they want to know how many slides, they want to know . . . very, very detailed, so they don't mess up. And it's almost worse with our AP [advanced placement] kids than it is with our, you know, other classes."

When students are given more freedom to complete work in alternative ways, School Librarian A says "it's the panic"—they shut down creatively and ask for help before proceeding. Students at this study site have taken school, district, and state assessments nearly every year; School Librarian A said that their familiarity with a "testing culture" and desire to make exemplary scores on assessments also drives their requirement for teaching methods that align with assessment formatting. She describes these behaviors in more detail, calling for more of a teaching influence into "inferencing" (how students analyze and compare potential product outcomes).

> Because we don't always have the necessary step one, two, three with them, there are kids that are like I don't know how to use this. Like [student's name deleted], I don't know how to use this. And there are some girls that are like, I can't get it to upload. I can't get, you know, and they just shut down. They're done. Just that problem solving . . . I wish more and more people would watch the process that kids go through to bring them in and have them do more of that, because . . . they've got to not only figure out the content but then they've got to do all this other problem solving.

What Are the ELIS Practices Exhibited by Students at the Study Site?

Students use their cell phones and smartphones so that their information quest is quick, private, and bypasses district-required filtering. School librarian interviews show that students are most interested in looking for everyday life items that include grades, college information, online shopping for clothing and cars, sports scores, court records (to see if their peers were arrested or received traffic tickets), online news, online photos from dances and team sport events, music and music videos for personal enjoyment, travel information, and YouTube videos. Both school librarians admitted that they did not witness frequent information seeking activities, other than the practice of searching for grade reports online, and added that they believe students use their smartphones for accessing the blocked sites they prefer to visit, such as Facebook and YouTube.

Students look for information of a personal nature while they are physically in the school library study site. Their information practices are not limited by the availability of school computers or a school-provided server and network. Student participants held their own information quest destinies in their hands in the forms of cell phones and, specifically, smartphones. Students' daily practices, then, are heavily influenced by ownership of and access to devices and accompanying (unfiltered) networks. If, as stated by School Librarian B, this ability provides them with the "best of both worlds," then the argument should be made that school librarians should embrace the devices students use in an effort to integrate them into learning scenarios. Librarians have a ready audience at the study site. Their device-friendly library encourages student visits beyond required class visits and sets the playing field for ongoing, deeper learning that moves beyond creating end products.

How Do the Students in This Study Use Physical and Virtual Technologies in the School Library?

Students in this setting use the library primarily for printing papers for assignment completion. Students also use the library as a place to freely use their cell phones and smartphones, and as a place to eat, drink, and simply relax. School Librarian A observed students using the library as a place to "hide out" from pressures of eating lunch with peers or as a way to avoid being in the classroom. They rarely use the library to find print materials, such as books, for either resource or pleasure needs. Librarians reported that although they had heavily invested the library budget into eBook purchases (nonfiction and fiction), the eBooks were not "selling well" yet and students were not taking advantage of this resource.

The most important virtual technology for student use is the school's wireless broadband network. This is fraught with problems because students expressly reported that they do not like the requirement to login through the school network in order to access the Internet. Students complained, at length, about the amount of time it takes to login to the school computers.

Another heavily used technology in this library is desktop computers used for accessing grade reports through the district-provided online program. Students can easily check their grades, assignments, and assessment reports by logging into the program from any school computer. Students at this study site do not only examine their grades, but also scrutinize them and then locate their teachers to question and even argue the veracity of the reported information. School Librarian A's responses indicate that this behavior is a function of students' family affluence. Students are groomed to perform well academically; this is an expectation of their families and students are not shy about questioning grades and ascertaining if current grade reports are up-to-date. That students might question teachers and the school librarians about their grades may seem disrespectful; however, when viewed in light of students upbringing in affluent families, it is possible that students' actions have been encouraged by families as proactive, even necessary behaviors for making certain academic achievement is occurring and being recorded.

CONCLUSIONS: ELIS PRACTICES OF UPPER-INCOME HIGH SCHOOL STUDENTS

The interviews with the school librarians begin to "paint a picture" of the ELIS practices exhibited by upper-income students working in a highly technological school library setting. Students prefer to use cell phones and smartphones instead of library computers; they use these devices to bypass the district-required Internet filtering system in order to access information of a personal nature. Their primary reason for visiting the school library is to print assignments and projects. Because the school librarians embrace usage of cell phones, smartphones, and other devices, students visit the library to both perform both information work and play. Students at this school prefer "instructional models" to help them accurately and successfully complete written assignments and they seek models to satisfy this need.

Student participants in this study have knowledge from their experiences about life in upper-income families who value education. They are motivated to make excellent grades that will help them gain entry into prestigious colleges and universities, and according to the school librarians, it is this desire that makes them demand explicit directions—the instructional model—for completing assignments. While there are some similarities with personal information seeking practices detailed by the urban teens in Agosto and Hughes-Hassell's study (2005, 2006a, 2006b), students at this study site are strongly motivated to check grades online for the purpose of verifying information and seeking teacher interactions when the information does not suit them. At the same time, they take breaks from academic work being performed in the library to seek out music, music videos, and social media and social networking sites, and use their smartphones to bypass the filtering system. That they can access these sites of interest while performing academic work in the library is unique.

The central research question is an all-encompassing one, and further data analysis is necessary to fully answer it. Student focus group sessions lend another context to the school librarian responses, and the researcher's observations, combined with print and virtual documentation, provide details that thoroughly describe what occurred during this study. Full analysis of this data helps to flesh out what was earlier construed about Agosto and Hughes-Hassell's (2006a) theoretical model of the "selves" and how student and librarian responses mesh with Havighurst's (1972) adolescent developmental tasks. Still, the emerging picture indicates that in this one location, at this one point in time, student participants enjoy access to computer technologies that allow them to freely search for items of a personal information nature, information that School Librarian B describes as their "everyday life needs." These behaviors are ELIS practices, and the uncovering of their existence in this setting provides an exciting foundation for future study.

The librarians at this study site are in a distinctive and exciting position. They are poised to be the knowledgeable teachers of information skills even as they learn how to use newer technologies alongside students in ways that help them reach for deeper levels of learning. An understanding of adolescent developmental needs and tasks is necessary so that school librarians can learn and exhibit best practices for approaching students on their own digital playing fields. For this particular study scenario, it is also imperative that the librarians educate themselves about how students from affluent families go about navigating their educational and postedu- cational lives. When developing the proposal, the caution was given not to rely too closely on socioeconomic facts as data was uncovered; however, as data collection and analysis occurred, there was clear evidence that affluence has a strong effect on the population studied. While there is no evidence of a causal relationship between affluence and students ELIS practices in this school, affluence is no doubt a strong contributing factor to their access of computer technologies that allows them to independently fulfill their personal information needs. This finding points to the need for school administrators to reconsider how technology budgets are spent for equipment taking into consideration the importance of students' learning needs. For example, investments in equipment such as iPads that can be handheld and available to all students may be necessary to ultimately realize the desired combina- tion of academic and ELI needs.

Because of the digital disconnect (Smith & Evans, 2010) mentioned earlier in this chapter, students need to be able to use the devices they already own in school settings. The need for access to such devices is not addressed here, because the students in this study already own cell phones, smartphones, tablet computers, and other devices. The librarians at this study site have already taken a crucial first step—they have opened their doors to cell phone and smartphone and other device use, and are gently approaching students to determine ways they can integrate use of such technologies into rich learning experiences. Students are eager to use their cell phones and smartphones while at school, and need guidance in ways they use them for learning in both educational and social arenas. As information specialists, school librarians are there to make those connections meaningful and to fill the gaps that currently exist between ways student devices are used in school libraries and ways they might potentially be used for learning.

As shared in the *Empowering learners* (2009) guidelines, "The SLMS is also cog- nizant of the varied teaching and learning styles of classroom teachers and students. These multiple knowledge bases allow the SLMS [school library media specialist] to lead from the center, guiding learning to meet the needs of all 21st-century learners" (p. 19). Piaget (1954) reported that children and adolescents make sense out of their world through use of a schema, or a mental framework or concept. Be- cause the way students learn is impacted by their understanding of concrete mental frameworks, one can see that a preference for an instructional model is a part of their cognitive growth as they progress through early and late stages of formal op- erational growth. Stated another way, "a certain level of complexity in organization must be achieved by the brain before it can acquire a concept of a given level of abstraction" (Havighurst, 1972, p. 27).

A concern for creating instructional models for students is that they might not explore creative solutions for assignment scenarios. Instead, they want step-by- step directions so they can accomplish requirements quickly and efficiently. An understanding of how student learn to first think in concrete ways before moving into abstract thought affects how school librarians prepare and present instruction. One aspect of this role should include seeking input from students into their own learning process. As reported by School Librarian A, a small percentage (0.63% or

15 responses) of students performed ably and competently on assignments when an instructional model was *not* provided; these were students who were not typically high achieving. What occurs in their learning processes that makes them leave a "comfort zone" in order to explore and employ creativity to satisfy assignment requirements? The school librarians need to investigate these "other" types of students and to determine what made the learning scenario so different.

As a final point, school librarians must think outside of the academic box and understand that students have varying information needs. Librarians should be challenged to consider how students' information needs are met in a private, unfiltered manner through use, for example, of their smartphones. This recommendation informs a holistic library experience for students, one where their ELIS practices can exist alongside academic pursuits. There is a unique coexistence with work and play occurring in this setting, and students are able to enjoy "the best of both worlds"— observation and documentation photos show they nearly always have their cell phones, smartphones, tablet devices, and other "toys" handy in a location right next to the keyboard. They are merging their educational and social worlds nearly seamlessly; school librarians should take note of this and determine ways to infuse that sense of work and play into learning, even as they also acknowledge and aid students with personal information seeking practices in the school library setting.

REFERENCES

AASL (Ed.). (2009). *Empowering learners: Guidelines for school library media programs.* Chicago: American Library Association.

Agosto, D.E., & Hughes-Hassell, S. (2005). People, places, and questions: An investigation into the everyday life information-seeking behaviors of urban young adults. *Library & Information Science Research, 27*, 141–163.

Agosto, D.E., & Hughes-Hassell, S. (2006a). Toward a model of the everyday life information needs of urban teenagers, Part 1: Theoretical model. *Journal of the American Society for Information Science and Technology, 57*(10), 1394–1403.

Agosto, D.E., & Hughes-Hassell, S. (2006b). Toward a model of the everyday life information needs of urban teenagers, Part 2: Empirical model. *Journal of the American Society for Information Science and Technology, 57*(11), 1418–1426.

Bourdieu, P. (1984). *Distinction: A social critique of the judgment of taste* [La Distinction: Critique sociale du jugement]. Cambridge, MA: Harvard University Press.

Creswell, J.W. (2009). *Research design: Qualitative, quantitative, and mixed methods approaches* (3rd ed.). Los Angeles: Sage Publications, Inc.

Havighurst, R.J. (1972). *Developmental tasks and education* (3rd ed.). New York: Longman.

Krathwohl, D.R. (1998). *Methods of educational & social science research: An integrated approach* (2nd ed.). New York: Longman.

Levine, M. (2006). *The price of privilege: How parental pressure and material advantage are creating generation of disconnected and unhappy kids.* New York: HarperCollins.

Lincoln, Y.S., & Guba, E.G. (1985). *Naturalistic inquiry.* Newbury Park, CA: Sage Publications, Inc.

Mardis, M.A. (2009). Introduction: A gentle manifesto on the relevance and obscurity of school libraries in LIS research. *Library Trends, 58*(1), 1–8.

Neuman, D. (2003). Research in school library media for the next decade: Polishing the diamond. *Library Trends, 51*(4), 503–524.

Piaget, J. (1954). *The construction of reality in the child.* New York: Basic Books.

Rubin, H.J., & Rubin, I.S. (2005). *Qualitative interviewing: The art of hearing data* (2nd ed.). Thousand Oaks, CA: Sage Publications.

Savolainen, R. (1993). The sense-making theory: Reviewing the interests of a user-centered approach to information seeking and use. *Information Processing, 29*(1), 13–28.

Savolainen, R. (1995). Everyday life information seeking: Approaching information seeking in the context of "way of life." *Library and Information Science Research, 17,* 259–294.

Savolainen, R. (2005). Everyday life information seeking. In K. E. Fisher, S. Erdelez, & L. McKechnie (Eds.), *Theories of information behavior* (pp. 143–148). Medford, NJ: Information Today, Inc.

Savolainen, R. (2008). *Everyday information practices: A social phenomenological perspective.* Lanham, MD: The Scarecrow Press, Inc.

Smith, L., & Evans, J. (2010). Speak up: Student embrace digital resources for learning. *Knowledge Quest, 39*(2), 20–26.

U.S. Department of Commerce, United States Census Bureau (Ed.). (2011). *American FactFinder.* Retrieved from http://factfinder2.census.gov/faces/nav/jsf/pages/index.xhtml

Wildemuth, B. M. (2009). *Applications of social research methods to questions in information and library science.* Westport, CT: Sage Publications, Inc.

Willson, E. (1967). Research on the elementary school library. *Theory into Practice, 6*(1), 30–35.

Wofford, A. (1940). School library evolution. *Phi Delta Kappan, 22*(6), 285–291.

5

THE IMPACT OF SCHOOL LIBRARIES ON ACADEMIC ACHIEVEMENT

Keith Curry Lance and Linda Hofschire

INTRODUCTION: CIRCUMSTANCES THAT DEFINE AMERICAN PUBLIC EDUCATION

That at least one school library impact study has been reported almost every year since 2000 is of little surprise. A series of issues that have arisen over the past decade or so continue to challenge those who seek to develop, maintain, and strengthen school library programs that enable high-performance teaching and academic excellence.

Seven sets of circumstances that define the context of American public education loom especially large in defining the circumstances of today's and tomorrow's school library programs. They are

- Site-based management
- Absence of reliable, dedicated federal funding
- School staffing trends
- Standards-based state tests
- Advent of computers and the Internet
- Advent of eBooks, eReaders, and tablet computers
- Partnership for 21st-century skills

Site-Based Management

Since the mid-1980s, site-based management has become the norm in U.S. public schools. Prior to that time, the need for school librarians was a commonplace assumption, if not a district policy or state-imposed legal requirement. Since the advent of site-based management, it has been necessary to advocate for the creation or preservation of librarian positions on a school-by-school basis. Given that many of today's school administrators are still old enough to have attended public schools in the 1960s or earlier—before the advent of professional school librarians—it is often difficult to make the case for a position foreign to the decision-maker's own student experience. Further, because some administrators have limited understanding of school libraries and limited experience with school librarians, they tend to make decisions about school librarian positions based on their experience with an individual librarian. For instance, a principal who would consider it absurd to eliminate a math teacher position because of one poorly performing math teacher thinks nothing of eliminating a school librarian position because of a poorly performing librarian. This circumstance alone contributed much—and continues to contribute—to the ongoing need for research that demonstrates the impact of highly qualified school librarians.

Absence of Reliable, Dedicated Federal Funding

Prior to the mid-1980s, the federal Elementary and Secondary Education Act (ESEA) earmarked specific funds for school library collections. When many parts of ESEA were converted to "block grant" programs, those funds disappeared. Much more recently—in 2007–2008 and in 2011–2012—the American Library Association and others championed the SKILLS (Strengthening Kids' Interest in Learning and Libraries) Act, first as part of the ESEA reauthorization, and later as separate legislation. As of this writing, the SKILLS Act has not been enacted. Perhaps, its single most valuable requirement—a full-time state-certified school librarian in every school—is also probably responsible for its failure to be enacted. After almost a generation of site-based management, too many regard such a requirement—no matter how defensible by research and practice—as too strictly prescriptive an action. So, the case remains to be made, school-by-school: Why do we need state-certified school librarians to run school library programs?

School Staffing Trends

Since the Great Recession of 2007–2009, school funding has decreased at all levels—local, state, and federal. Predictably, staffing cuts—especially cuts of positions beyond the classroom—have followed. Site-based management and the absence of a federal mandate for school libraries and librarians make school library positions especially vulnerable. School librarian positions are now the exception rather than the rule at the elementary level, where many school libraries operate at the most minimal level under the direction of library assistants who are not supervised by state-certified school librarians. Many high schools still retain a certified school librarian; though likely only because regional accrediting associations require having one.

Standards-Based State Tests

Since the 2000s, thanks to their being required by George W. Bush's No Child Left Behind Act (which replaced ESEA), standards-based state achievement tests have become ubiquitous. The tests rapidly came to be characterized as "high-stakes" tests, because of the questionably excessive reliance on them in evaluating both students and teachers alike. Despite growing concerns about the validity and reliability of the tests themselves, as well as the counterproductive results of their overuse and abuse, few states show any signs of even considering abandoning them. In less than two decades, such tests have become established as the key indicators of academic achievement. The flurry of school library impact studies in recent years was, and still is, clearly motivated in large part by the fact that each state has its own "brand name" test, on which the impact of school libraries and librarians needed to be demonstrated.

Advent of Computers and the Internet

The first Colorado study of school library impact was reported in 1993; the second, in 2000. During that interval, computers and the Internet became an integral part of public schools; so much so that many began to wonder if school libraries were still needed. If students have access to networked computers and the Internet at school (in computer labs or classrooms) and likely even at home, aren't all the information resources they could need at their fingertips 24/7? Not only is the answer to that rather naïve question a resounding NO, but the introduction of electronic information also suggested a new role for school librarians to play in teaching essential online learning skills to both students and their teachers. Successively, this skill set has been called computer literacy, information literacy, ICT (information, communication, and technology) literacy, digital literacy, and—most recently—21st-century skills. While its name changes and its definition expands, the essential fact in the Information Age is that the world of online information is a very complex place that requires critical thinking and a whole new set of ethics about information use. It has been and remains a challenge for school librarians themselves to keep pace with rapid technological change, to embrace this new role, and to communicate about it effectively with teachers and administrators, among others. As school library impact studies have evolved, more and more attention has been given to this newer and very vital "curriculum" of school librarians.

Advent of eBooks, eReaders, and Tablet Computers

By 2009, the availability of hundreds of thousands of books in electronic format as well as the release of affordable eBook readers, such as Amazon's Kindle and Barnes and Noble's Nook, set the stage for a revolution in book publishing and distribution. In 2010, the introduction of Apple's multifunction iPad—an eBook reader and a way to access newspapers and magazines online—not only increased the demand for eBooks, but also forced a lowering of prices on single-purpose eBook readers like Kindle and Nook. Many, even within the library community, wondered if these developments threatened the existence of libraries, especially public libraries. Once the initial shock subsided, most realized that the advent of streaming media—eBooks; movies downloaded via Netflix, Blockbuster, Hulu, etc.; and music and audiobooks downloaded from iTunes, Napster, etc.—was less of a threat to libraries than to the "library-as-warehouse" paradigm. The economic incentives underlying the existence of libraries remain: most organizations and individuals cannot afford to purchase all the information they need; at least some will continue to need a way to share access to it. The value-added and learning incentives underlying libraries also remain. Libraries offer a wide variety of information in all formats, and facilitate access to it by organizing it and providing librarians who can help people to navigate the ever-expanding universe of information as both consumers and producers of ideas. Although there has not yet been time for a school library impact study to address this particular information revolution, no future study can afford to neglect it.

Partnership for 21st-Century Skills

The partnership for 21st-century skills (P21, 2011) is a national organization that advocates for 21st-century readiness for every student. It provides tools and resources that are helping public schools to fuse the 3Rs and 4Cs (critical thinking and problem solving, communication, collaboration, and creativity and innovation). Building on efforts of leading districts and schools, P21 promotes local, state, and federal policies to extend this approach to every school.

As a member of P21, and as a major part of its contribution to that partnership, the American Association of School Librarians (AASL) has promulgated *Standards for the 21st century learner* (2007). These standards are based on the premises that learners must be able to inquire, think critically, apply and share knowledge, create new knowledge, and pursue personal and aesthetic growth.

This set of ideas—which incorporates and builds upon earlier conceptions of information literacy—constitutes the "theoretical" underpinnings of most school library impact studies. As with the recent phenomena involving eBooks, eReaders, and tablet computers, these ideas, as presently constituted, have not yet been fully addressed by school library impact studies. Extant studies, however, have demonstrated repeatedly the value of some of the specific ideas incorporated in these standards, including

- Reading motivation
- Collaborative inquiry-based learning
- Access to and use of technology
- Information and ICT literacy
- Information ethics

TYPICAL SCHOOL LIBRARY RESEARCH QUESTIONS

School library research has typically focused on the impact of school libraries on student achievement. Examples of research questions that have been explored over the past two decades include:

- What are the measurable contributions to the academic achievement of school librarians and other school library staff?
- What are the measurable contributions to the academic achievement of specific activities of school library staff (e.g., information literacy instruction, collaboration with classroom teachers, technology integration)?
- What are the measurable contributions to the academic achievement of school library resources (e.g., print, digital resources)?
- What are the measurable contributions to the academic achievement of school library capacity, reach, and use (e.g., hours of service, visits, circulation)?

These questions have been answered in a variety of ways in many different places across the United States. For the best extant detailed summary of those answers, visit the Mansfield University's *School library impact studies project* at http://library.mansfield.edu/impact.asp. As noted on the Mansfield project site, it complements two other sources that summarize this research:

- Scholastic Library Publishing's *School libraries work!* (accessible at http://list builder.scholastic.com/content/stores/LibraryStore/pages/images/SLW3 .pdf)
- Library Research Service website's *School library impact studies* page (accessible at: http://www.lrs.org/impact.php)

REVIEW OF THE LITERATURE

Much of our research has also examined the impact of school libraries on student achievement. For example, our first two Colorado school library impact studies, which were conducted in the 1990s, examined the relationships between various aspects of school libraries (e.g., librarian/teacher collaboration, student visits, expenditures) and students' standardized test scores (Lance, 1993, 2000). Over the past decade, we have conducted three additional studies—two in Colorado and one national study—that have further teased out the impact of school libraries on student achievement.

School Libraries and Student Achievement

The first of these studies was conducted during the 2007–2008 school year in Colorado. We examined the impact of school library inputs and outputs (e.g., staffing, collection, visits) on Colorado Student Assessment Program (CSAP) scores (Francis, Lance, & Leitzau, 2010).

We found that inputs including library staffing, expenditures, and video and periodical collections were significantly related to CSAP scores. In terms of staffing, elementary schools with at least one full-time endorsed librarian averaged better CSAP reading scores than those with less than one full-time endorsed librarian. Specifically, more students earned proficient or advanced reading scores and fewer students earned unsatisfactory scores in schools where there was a full-time endorsed librarian. For expenditures and video and periodical collections, we compared schools that were at or above the median on each of these variables with those that were below it. In each instance, elementary schools that were at the median level or above averaged better CSAP reading scores than those that were below it.

In terms of outputs, we found that the number of student visits to the school library significantly impacted CSAP scores. When we compared elementary schools that were at or above the median for weekly number of visits to school libraries with those below it, we found that the schools with more visits averaged better CSAP reading performance than those that reported less visits. More students earned proficient or advanced reading scores and fewer students earned unsatisfactory scores in schools that were at or above the median for weekly visits.

For our second study during the past decade that examined the impact of school libraries on student achievement, we turned to the national level and examined trends in librarian staffing and National Assessment of Educational Progress (NAEP) scores from 2004–2005 to 2008–2009 (Lance & Hofschire, 2011). This study improved upon our previous school library impact studies in three ways. First, we looked at trends in staffing and school achievement over time, instead of doing a snapshot, single-year analysis. Second, because data were publicly available, we were able to compare scores not only for all students, but also for poor students (i.e., those eligible for the National School Lunch Program), black and Hispanic students, and English language learners (ELL). Examining these subgroups is important because each may significantly moderate the results of standardized test score analysis. Third, we controlled for changes in overall staffing over time. This is meaningful because it addresses a common argument skeptics make: that decreases in test scores over time simply reflect school-wide staffing cuts, as opposed to cuts specifically to the school library.

Our study compared NAEP fourth-grade reading scores for states that lost school librarians from 2004–2005 to 2008–2009 with states that gained librarians during this time period. We found that states that gained librarians consistently demonstrated greater reading score increases over time than states that lost librarians. Proportionally, these increases were particularly pronounced for poor students, whose scores increased almost twice as much as all students and four times as much compared with their counterparts in states that lost librarians.

We also found that the percent change in the number of school librarians from 2004–2005 to 2008–2009 was significantly and positively correlated with the percent change in reading scores for all groups (i.e., all students, poor students, Hispanic students, and ELL students) except for black students. That is, for all students except black students, when the percentage of school librarians increased over time, there was a corresponding percentage increase in reading scores.

Then, to examine whether changes in school librarian staffing had an impact on student test scores even when controlling for overall staff changes, we conducted partial correlation analysis. This analysis showed that the relationship between librarian staffing and test performance remained significant when taking into account overall staff changes in schools.

Our third school library impact study during the past decade followed a similar model as our national study—examining the relationship between school library staffing and reading scores over time—but improved on it in two important ways (Lance & Hofschire, 2012). First, we examined Colorado trends in staffing and reading scores at the building level instead of the state level (NAEP scores are only available at the state level). Second, we parsed out endorsed school librarians from their counterparts who did not have an endorsement. This type of staffing data is not available at the national level.

We examined trends in endorsed librarian staffing and CSAP reading scores (advanced or unsatisfactory) from 2005 to 2011. Our analysis of advanced reading scores indicated that schools that either maintained or gained an endorsed librarian over time had more students scoring advanced in reading in 2011, and had improved their performance more since 2005 than schools that either lost their librarians or did not have one in either year. In contrast, schools that lost librarians or never had one had fewer students scoring advanced in reading in 2011, as well as lesser gains in advanced reading scores, compared with schools that maintained or gained a librarian.

Our analysis of unsatisfactory reading scores also supported the argument that school libraries have a positive impact on student achievement. We found that schools that either maintained or gained an endorsed librarian between 2005 and 2011 had fewer students scoring unsatisfactory in reading in 2011, and they reduced the number of unsatisfactory scores over time at a greater rate than schools that lost librarians or never had one. In contrast, schools in this latter group had more students with unsatisfactory scores in 2011, and their percentage of students scoring unsatisfactorily increased over time.

In addition to our analyses of librarian staffing and achievement scores over time, we also examined the impact of various staffing models on 2011 achievement scores. We compared schools with at least one full-time equivalent (FTE) endorsed librarian to schools with less than one FTE endorsed librarian, and found that schools in the former group averaged significantly higher advanced reading scores and significantly lower unsatisfactory scores than schools in the latter group. In contrast, our comparisons of 2011 reading scores for schools with and without nonendorsed librarians and with and without library assistants (working unsupervised) were not statistically significant. That is, CSAP reading scores were not impacted by school library programs that were not managed by endorsed librarians.

Finally, we introduced an important control variable into our study—poverty (percentage of students in a school who were eligible for free and reduced-cost meals)—to determine whether school library programs still impacted test scores, even when taking poverty into account. Using partial correlation analysis, we found that in 2011, both endorsed and nonendorsed librarians were positively correlated with advanced CSAP reading scores and negatively correlated with unsatisfactory scores when controlling for poverty. In contrast, the relationship between library assistants and reading scores was not significant.

Moving Beyond Student Achievement Studies

Over the past decade, we also conducted two studies that broke away from this traditional research model—examining school libraries' impact on student achievement—and instead focused on how school librarians were perceived by their fellow teachers as well as by school administrators.

For the first of these studies (Lance, Rodney, & Russell, 2007), we conducted a survey of principals, classroom teachers, and librarians in Indiana. We asked principals to identify their desired roles for librarians in their schools. The most common roles they selected were "reading motivator" and "teacher," followed by "in-service provider" and "school leader." We also asked principals whether they learned about school libraries/librarians through personal experience, and found that those who reported learning about them this way were less likely to identify "teacher" as a desired role for school librarians. Conversely, those principals who reported learning about school libraries/librarians through in-service professional development were more likely to identify "teacher" as a desired role for school librarians.

We asked teachers to identify the roles they perceived school librarians filling in their schools. They most often indicated the role of "reading motivator," followed by "teacher" and then "instructional resources manager." Elementary school teachers were most likely to identify their librarian as a teacher, followed by middle and high school teachers.

The second of these studies examined the importance of collaboration for instructional design and delivery between teachers and school librarians in Idaho (Lance, Rodney, & Schwarz, 2009). We surveyed principals and other administrators, classroom teachers, and librarians regarding how much they valued this type of collaboration and how often it occurred. Most administrators reported that collaboration was either essential or desirable. However, both teachers and school librarians indicated that collaboration did not occur on a frequent basis.

We also examined the relationship between the value administrators placed on collaboration and how they viewed their school's implementation of ICT standards, finding that the more importance they placed on collaboration, the better they rated their school's ICT standards implementation. Similarly, the more frequently classroom teachers and school librarians reported collaborating with each other, the higher they rated their solo teaching of ICT standards.

We also found impacts on student achievement scores. There was a positive relationship between administrators' beliefs that collaboration was essential and middle school students' reading scores. In addition, more frequent librarian–classroom teacher collaboration at the elementary and middle school levels (i.e., at least monthly) was positively related to higher reading and language arts scores. Similarly, high schools where librarians reported at least monthly teacher-initiated collaboration were more likely to have advanced reading and language arts scores.

Taken together, the results of our Indiana and Idaho studies indicate that it is important for school librarians to be intentional in seeking opportunities—such as professional development and collaboration activities—to demonstrate their capabilities to principals and classroom teachers. By taking advantage of these opportunities, school librarians may raise their visibility within their schools and be more valued in their roles as teachers.

METHODOLOGICAL CHALLENGES

Across the studies discussed above, we experienced a variety of methodological challenges related to our use of available data. These challenges complicated our analyses and had implications for our results. What follows is a brief discussion of these challenges, as well as how our methods have evolved over time in response to these challenges.

Much of school library impact research relies on available data, such as student achievement scores and school staffing data. All four of our Colorado school library impact studies used these data sources, as well as our national study of NAEP scores. Although using available data sources reduces the reporting burden for schools and districts, it posed a variety of issues for us, as we had no control over what was being collected. For example, the level of detail with which achievement score and staffing data are collected varies between the national and state levels. NAEP scores are only available at the state level, meaning that our national study by necessity took a 30,000-foot view when examining the impact of school libraries on student achievement. In contrast, in Colorado, student achievement test scores are available at the building level, which allowed us to get closer to the ground and conduct more detailed analyses. However, scores by various subgroups (e.g., race and ethnicity, ELL) are not available, which limited the number of control variables we could introduce into our analyses.

Staffing data also posed challenges. At the national level, the Common Core of Data provides school staffing information, but it lumps all library staff (whether endorsed, nonendorsed, or aides) into one category. However, it does provide information about overall school staffing, which enabled us to use this as a control variable in our analyses. In Colorado, the opposite types of data are available—we can obtain library staffing data that distinguishes endorsed librarians from those who are not endorsed as well as aides, but overall school staffing numbers are not available. Therefore, we could not control overall staffing changes in our Colorado analyses.

Regarding staffing data, we were also limited by the ways that individual districts choose to report their staffing information to the state. For example, a large school district in Colorado reported staffing data for one year during the past decade at the district level instead of the building level, making that year not eligible for inclusion in our building level analyses.

The issues discussed above—many of which are inherent when relying on available data sources—combined with our interest in including additional measures in our research, served as the impetus to conduct the Idaho and Indiana studies. In these studies, we focused on gathering original data by surveying school administrators, classroom teachers, and school librarians. This approach added another dimension to our available data studies discussed above, as we learned from school staff that endorsed librarians were having a positive impact on their students. Additionally, by correlating our survey results with student achievement scores in the Idaho study, we were able to demonstrate that these positive perceptions of school librarians by school administrators and staff were indeed associated with higher test scores.

FIVE-STEP IMPROVEMENT PLAN

How can the research discussed above be used to improve local school library programs? We recommend a five-step plan of action.

Creating Partnerships with Administrators and Teachers

The critical first step is creating partnerships with administrators and teachers. More than anything else, this is a matter of engagement and ongoing communication. Among the most consistent findings of the school library studies that have examined these partnerships is the importance of the school librarian being perceived as a school leader, a school-wide resource person, and a collaborator with classroom teachers in the design and delivery of instruction. Such roles can only be created and sustained in the context of partnerships between librarian and principal, and librarian and teacher. This context for communication about school library research is essential.

Sharing Research about the Impact of School Libraries and Librarians

Given some degree of rapport in partnerships with administrators and teachers, school librarians can share the findings of the school library impact studies with confidence that their partners will be open to learning about them. The earlier studies provide evidence of the links between test scores and school library staffing levels, specific staff activities, collections, technology, use, and funding. Later studies reinforce these findings by confirming that more successful schools have administrators who value highly and teachers and librarians who implement frequently practices that characterize strong library programs, such as

- Flexible scheduling of library access based on instructional needs
- Collaboration between classroom teachers and librarians on instructional design and delivery
- In-house professional development for faculty provided by librarians
- Librarian participation in key school committees
- Regular meetings between principal and librarian

In addition, the latest studies provide further evidence of the relationships between factors characterizing strong school libraries and better student test performance by confirming that, during and since the Great Recession, increasing librarian staffing tended to lead to stronger improvements in test scores, while losses of librarian positions tended to lead to weaker improvements or declines in test scores.

Defining the Roles of School Library and Librarian

Based on these research findings, the librarian's next step is to establish, redefine, or reinforce the positive roles that the library program and the librarian can play in the school. Achieving this goal will require persuasive delivery, energetic mobilization, and exemplary demonstration of the potential benefits of essential practices.

Creating New Measures of School Library Outputs and Outcomes

As the day-to-day business of the school library program continues to evolve rapidly, the librarian's next step will be to reinforce the messages of the school library impact studies with compelling local data. As with public and academic libraries, measures of school library output and outcomes are not evolving rapidly enough to keep up with the pace of change. We are in an era that requires widespread experimentation with alternative new measures of service output and outcomes. Local school librarians should feel encouraged and empowered to develop and test new measures based on their programs' collections, technology, and services. It is urgent that this kind of experimentation begins, and that local librarians share their experiences in these efforts with each other. AASL, the National Center for Education Statistics, and several state library agencies collect data regularly on school library programs and school librarians. These organizations need input about effective new measures. Such input will be most useful if it is based on some practical experience of collecting data. The days of getting by only on counts of traditional measures (e.g., hours of service, usage transactions, dollars) are passing rapidly. New measures appropriate to the era of streaming media and libraries-without-walls are needed urgently. The good news is that those who invest in this difficult work may see it pay dividends locally long before a new consensus about such measures is reached at the state or national level.

Documenting the Impact of Teaching 21st-Century Skills on Student Learning

The single, most important reason to create new output and outcome measures is to be able to document the impact of teaching 21st-century skills on student learning. Using the so-called "action research" strategies, it will likely be possible to do this at the local level long before it can be done at state and national levels. While the primary and most urgent uses of the fruits of such efforts may be local, it is important to remember how valuable it will be to others to share action research results. Only once there is more comprehensive knowledge of such efforts can any assessment be made that might create a new consensus about how to proceed at state and national levels to document the impact of teaching 21st-century skills.

An even greater challenge than measuring what librarians and library programs contribute to teaching 21st-century skills is expanding the options for large-scale measurement of that particular conception of what students need to learn. For about two decades, many have equated student learning with academic achievement, and that in turn with test scores. Many others offer persuasive arguments against such simplistic reductionism. The problem is, at this juncture, we have no real alternatives. While instruments exist with which to measure some aspects of 21st-century skills, those instruments are not in sufficiently widespread use to yield data for large-scale studies (e.g., state-level studies). One of the more promising efforts has involved crosswalking the 21st-century skills standards with the Common Core standards. Perhaps, in time, this will lead to improvements in state testing, and more detailed results from those tests would permit the use of state-mandated test data to measure the teaching of 21st-century skills. In the meantime, local librarians can employ detailed local test results and/or alternative instruments (e.g., tests, surveys) to measure specific aspects of 21st-century skills.

CONCLUSIONS: NEW QUESTIONS TO BE STUDIED

As we look toward the future of school library research, it is clear that the rapid and continuous changes in the school environment and technology raise a variety of new questions that will need to be studied. Some of the questions that we consider to be the most pressing include

With what do we replace "No Child Left Behind" era standards-based testing that we can use to measure the impact of school libraries and librarians?

Because of the failed promise of standards-based achievement testing to lead to dramatic improvements in student success, many are pressing for such tests to be scrapped or at least revised dramatically. AASL's *Standards for the 21st century* learner (2007) suggests a broader emphasis on student learning and indeed lifelong learning, constructs that are not the focus of large-scale, nationally mandated testing. Determining effective measures that tap into these constructs is critical.

To document the contributions of school librarians and other library staff to student learning, what do we need to know now about how they spend their time, with whom they interact, and how?

Many of the school library impact studies of the past two decades have documented the measurable impact on test scores of state-certified school librarians, especially when they are supported by library aides. Those studies also assessed the impact of a variety of activities of librarians and their staff, chief among them, those associated with school-wide leadership, instructional collaboration with classroom teachers, and technology integration. With the advent of the 21st-century skills framework, new kinds of data about library staff and their activities are required.

How do we measure access to, and use of, online content and streaming media in ways that will generate the data required to measure their contributions to student learning?

In many of the earlier school library impact studies, measures of school library resources that could be relied upon to correlate with test scores included the total number of books in a school library, the number of library books per student, and the average age of books in certain subject areas (e.g., astronomy). During the past two decades, when many studies have been done, the nature of school library collections has been changing dramatically. It has been a truism for at least a generation that students rely excessively on the Internet and the World Wide Web as a first, and often only, resort when seeking information. School librarians have focused more and more on their electronic collections—vetted websites on the free Web and licensed databases—that have all but replaced traditional periodical literature as the leading source of current topical information. In very recent years, a new technological revolution has begun with the advent of eBook formats and eBook readers (as well as tablet computers) that students and teachers are adopting rapidly. An important task of school library researchers is to devise measures that assess the access to and use of these new technologies.

How do we measure the capacity and reach of school library programs in ways that acknowledge a rapidly changing technological environment and the new contributions of school librarians to student learning?

Traditionally, the capacity and reach of a school library was determined by physical parameters, such as hours of service, square footage, numbers of classrooms, and networked computers. While these physical parameters are still meaningful, alone they are no longer adequate to describe the capacity and reach of a school library. Why? Because, ideally at least, the school library is no longer limited to a physical space; a strong school library program permeates the entire school. Indeed, with the introduction of the 24/7 presences of websites, content-rich databases, blogs, wikis, Facebook groups, and virtual reference services, most school library programs can no longer be confined to the school building or the school schedule. Developing innovative approaches to measuring the capacity and reach of school library programs in a virtual era is critical.

At a time when endorsed school librarian positions are being slashed and school library program cuts have become the norm, it is urgent that researchers examine these questions as well as others to provide empirical evidence of the impact of school libraries on student achievement. School library studies from the past two decades have established a strong foundation on which this research can be based. However, it is time to move forward with new initiatives at the national, state, and local levels using innovative methods that demonstrate the vital importance of school libraries in the 21st century.

REFERENCES

AASL. (2007). *Standards for the 21st century learner.* Chicago: American Association of School Librarians. Retrieved from http://www.ala.org/aasl/sites/ala.org.aasl/files/content/guidelinesandstandards/learningstandards/AASL_LearningStandards.pdf

Francis, H. B., Lance, C. K., & Lietzau Z. (2010). *School librarians continue to help students achieve standards: The third Colorado study (2010).* Retrieved from http://www.lrs.org/documents/closer_look/CO3_2010_Closer_Look_Report.pdf

Lance, K. C. (1993). *The impact of school library media centers on academic achievement.* Salt Lake City: Hi Willow Research and Publishing.

Lance, K. C. (2000). *How school librarians help kids achieve standards: The second Colorado study.* Salt Lake City: Hi Willow Research and Publishing.

Lance, K. C., & Hofschire, L. (2011, September 1). Something to shout about: New research shows that more librarians means higher reading scores. *School Library Journal, 57*(9). Retrieved from http://www.schoollibraryjournal.com/slj/printissue/currentissue/891612–427/something_to_shout_about_new.html.csp

Lance, K. C., & Hofschire, L. (2012). *Change in school librarian staffing linked with change in CSAP reading performance, 2005 to 2011.* Denver, CO: Colorado State Library, Library Research Service. Retrieved from http://www.lrs.org/documents/closer_look/CO4_2012_Closer_Look_Report.pdf

Lance, K. C., Rodney, M. J., & Russell, B. (2007). *How students, teachers and principals benefit from strong school libraries: The Indiana study.* Indianapolis: Association for Indiana Media Educators. Retrieved from http://www.ilfonline.org/clientuploads/AIME/2007MSArticle.pdf

Lance, K. C., Rodney, M. J., & Schwarz, B. (2010). *Idaho school library impact study—2009: How Idaho librarians, teachers and administrators collaborate for student success.* Boise, ID: Idaho Commission for Libraries. Retrieved from http://libraries.idaho.gov/doc/idaho-school-library-impact-study-2009

Library Research Service. (2012). *School library impact studies.* Retrieved from http://www.lrs.org/impact.php

Mansfield University. (2011, February 23). *School library impact studies project.* Retrieved from http://library.mansfield.edu/impact.asp

Partnership for 21st century skills. (2011). Retrieved from http://www.p21.org

Scholastic Research & Results. (2008). *School libraries work!* New York: Scholastic Library Publishing. Retrieved from http://listbuilder.scholastic.com/content/stores/LibraryStore/pages/images/SLW3.pdf

Todd, R. (2008, April 1). The evidence-based manifesto for school librarians. *School Library Journal, 54*(4). Retrieved from http://www.schoollibraryjournal.com/article/CA6545434.html

6

THE ROLE OF THE SCHOOL LIBRARY: BUILDING COLLABORATIONS TO SUPPORT SCHOOL IMPROVEMENT

Elizabeth A. Lee and Don A. Klinger

INTRODUCTION: EDUCATION, A LIGHTNING ROD FOR REFORM AND ACCOUNTABILITY

Education remains a lightning rod for reform and accountability policies and initiatives. Examples include Race to the Top and No Child Left Behind in the United States. The desired result of such efforts is one of school improvement, with the intention of providing explicit evidence of increased student outcomes. "Accountability," "data-driven decision-making," and "evidence-based practice" have become commonly used expressions and associated with ongoing and newly implemented reform efforts to improve the educational outcomes of students. Success is commonly measured by school and system improvements on large-scale tests, most notably in literacy or numeracy scores. While the United States has used a policy approach to school improvement, jurisdictions in Canada tend to use a less-demanding approach, providing a more supportive model to lead to school improvement. As an example, the Literacy and Numeracy Secretariat (LNS) was formed in Ontario in 2004 to lead provincial efforts to increase the proportion of students meeting the provincial standards in literacy and numeracy. As one of the branches of the Ministry of Education Ontario, the LNS has been engaged in supporting school and district–based efforts to improve teaching and learning, with the majority of the effort being directed toward literacy.

Certainly, school improvement is not a new focus in either research or practice. There is a large body of research that explores a multitude of policies and practices that have been associated with improved student outcomes. Further, the research has examined aspects of schooling from different levels: for example those system-wide school, principal, and individual teacher practices and characteristics that appear to impact both school climate and student outcomes. As an example, investigations into effective schools in the 1980s (e.g., Good & Brophy, 1989) identified specific patterns of interaction between teachers and students within the classroom that resulted in effective teaching. Other research also explored how individual teacher differences affected education through teacher efficacy (Evans & Tribble, 1986) or teacher agency (Oakes & Lipton, 1999) that emphasized the importance of social and emotional factors in teacher empowerment for educational change. A recent meta-analysis of the educational effectiveness research on school-level factors confirms much of this previous research, demonstrating that effective schools maximized teaching time, extended curriculum beyond the basics, and worked to improve classroom teaching (Kyriakides, Creemers, Antounious, & Demetrious, 2010).

The concept of continuous school improvement became increasingly popular in the 1990s and it continues today (e.g., Fullen, 1993, 2002; Fullen & Hargreaves, 1996; Langer, 2000; Leithwood, Leonard, & Sharratt, 1998). Whether it is under the banner of school improvement or accountability, the principles of continuous school improvement support policies and practices that encourage ongoing efforts to improve teaching and learning. A central tenet to these efforts is the central role of school leaders in creating a school climate that was open and focused on educational purpose and direction. At second tenet, the focus was on creating learning communities in schools, now commonly called professional learning communities (Grossman, Wineberg, & Woolworth, 2001; Louis & Marks, 1998; McLaughlin & Talbert, 2001). The intent of such communities was to enhance collaborative learning and practices in order to improve teaching practice and students' learning outcomes. Combined, the school effectiveness research and the more recent work around continuous school improvement highlight the importance of creating school climates that empower teachers to work together and collaborate with a focus on students' learning and achievement.

TOPIC AND PROBLEM

While educational reform and accountability issues remain prevalent and the focus on school improvement has become paramount, challenges in global economies have resulted in efforts to introduce financial restraints across the public sector. Education is not immune to such pressure, and educational jurisdictions are searching for ways to minimize costs while also demonstrating that the educational needs of children are being met. Classroom teachers and building operations tend to be immune to funding cuts, and reductions to education spending are most commonly achieved through cuts to educational support services. Given the critical importance of the school principal and the classroom teachers to school improvement, financial restraints are sought in other aspects, including class size or support services. The school library has been especially vulnerable to reduced financial support, whether it be through reductions in resources or in staffing (Alberta Learning Resources Council, 2005; American Library Association, 2005; Coish, 2005; Literacy Coalition of New Brunswick, 2005).

Yet, it is highly likely that the reductions in school library resources and staffing are hindering the efforts to increase students' literacy outcomes. Previous research provides a link between school libraries and increased student achievement (e.g., Haycock, 1998; Lance, Rodney, & Hamilton-Pennell, 2000, 2002). The Expert Panel on Early Reading in Ontario (2003) identified several supports that appeared to be important for student literacy success. Along with school leadership, classroom teaching, and the home environment, "a well-equipped and professionally staffed school library" (p. 38) was considered an important school-wide resource for promoting literacy. Our own research in Ontario (e.g., Blackett & Klinger, 2006; Klinger & Blackett, 2006) found a positive link between school library staffing and student achievement on large-scale measures of reading achievement. Further, we found that students in schools that had a professionally staffed school library reported more positive attitudes toward reading. While previous research has identified positive associations between a well-resourced and professionally staffed school library, the nature of these associations have not been carefully studied. Our subsequent work has endeavored to better understand the activities of school libraries, especially those that have been identified as exemplary (Klinger, Lee, Stephenson, DeLuca, & Luu, 2009; Lee & Klinger, 2009).

DO SCHOOL LIBRARIES MATTER?

Our Approach to the Question

Given that the school library and the teacher librarian represent a school program, our work has focused on the role of the school library to support increased student outcomes within the school. Do the school library and the teacher librarian add value to the efforts to meet the goals of continuous school improvement and accountability? While it is difficult to provided direct evidence of such an impact, it is possible to examine how the services and programs offered by the school library and school librarian can support teaching and learning in a school. While our initial work with school libraries identified positive association between well-staffed school libraries and students' literacy achievement and attitudes toward reading (Klinger & Blackett, 2006), we were unable to fully examine these associations. As an example, the survey data used in this original study could not be used to demonstrate causal relationships. At best, such studies provide interesting avenues for subsequent research.

Our more recent work used a developmental program evaluation approach to explore the potential of the school library to support learning in the school. Evaluation approaches have evolved in recognition that program contexts shape the needs of program users and that program contexts change. In contrast to the early summative approaches of evaluation that tended to use a cursory exploration of overall worth and value, the more recent developmental models enable the deeper exploration of complex interactions that likely occur amongst teachers, students, and programs within a school. These models may be used to support learning about how programs work, and provide program personnel with opportunities engage directly in systematic inquiry and data-informed decision-making (Alkin, 2004; Preskill & Catsambas, 2006). Our approach has enabled us to work more closely with schools and teacher librarians to understand how the school library functions within its school context. We can determine the potential of the school library to support teaching and learning, and identify the conditions that either hinder or support the attainment of that potential. We believed that this broader approach to evaluation was better suited to evaluate the complex program goals and purposes that are currently espoused in the expectations for school librarians and school library programs.

As with the first study, we focused our attention on elementary school libraries in Ontario, Canada. Although our first study obtained data from a broad spectrum of school libraries across Ontario, with data obtained from over 800 schools, our more recent evaluation included only 8 schools. This enabled us to examine school libraries from a different and much closer vantage point. Rather than combining data collected from other agencies as done in our first research study, our second project used a mixed methods research approach. The small sample allowed us to deeply explore the complex issues associated with school libraries. Further, we focused solely on school library programs that were identified as being exemplary, as chosen by the Ontario Library Association.

The focus on a small sample of exemplary school libraries led to a decision to use a multistaged case study approach. Hence, we began with two intensive case studies. Interviews, document analysis, observations, and student surveys provided a wealth of data about these two elementary school library programs. Interviews were conducted with the school administration, teachers, and teacher librarians. At each school, we completed a 45-minute interview with the principal, 60-minute interviews with four teachers (Grades 3–6), and two 60-minute interviews with the teacher librarian. Classroom teachers were chosen based on their ability to provide rich information about the current library programs and class use of the library. These interviews focused on the functioning of the school library and the working partnerships that existed between the teacher librarian and classroom teachers.

The document analyses were completed using library documents and materials that illustrated the school activities and working partnerships that involved the school library. These materials included those related to extracurricular activities involving the school library of teacher librarian, library schedules, classroom teacher and teacher-librarian partnerships, and distinct library activities. The interviews and documents provided us with a foundation to focus our observations of the school library and the teacher librarian. These observations occurred over one to two days. We followed the teacher librarian as he or she completed his or her professional responsibilities. Field notes supplemented our observations.

Lastly, we administered student surveys to students in Grades 3–6. Four classes in each school were sampled (between 100 and 120 students per school), and we had a completion rate of approximately 50 percent. In order to minimize the impact on teachers, the surveys were sent home to complete. The 20-minute surveys focused on students' literacy activities, their use of the library, their perceptions about the role of the library and the librarian, and their library experiences. The survey included five sections: (a) student background and attitudes toward school, (b) in-class and out-of-class library activities, (c) items used in the library and the resources students used to choose books, (d) perceptions of the teacher librarian, and (e) students' reading attitudes and perceptions.

After we completed our initial case studies, we expanded the case studies to include six more schools. The initial two cases allowed us to focus our data collection in the subsequent schools. The case studies in the six schools were not only shorter in time and data collection, but were also more focused. While we did not complete observations in these school libraries, we did conduct interviews, document analyses, and student surveys. Based on the initial case studies, the interviews were modified and shortened. Our intentions for the six case studies were not only to further explore our initial findings from the first two case studies, but also to identify important similarities and differences that existed across these exemplary school library programs.

The various types of data we collected provided an ideal situation for a mixed methods approach to research. We had over 40 hours of interview data, field notes from our observations, documents from each school library, and surveys completed by 331 students from 7 of the 8 schools. The mixed methods approach enabled us to obtain the perspectives from different stakeholders in the school, including administrators, teachers, teacher librarians, and students. As we had multiple sources of data, in particular the in-depth interview data and observations of practice, we were able to link information from the interviews with practice. The full-day observations provided a powerful lens for interpretation; we could see how concrete instances of behavior could be understood as representing a recommended professional practice that had been described in documents or in the interviews. These types of data are time consuming to collect and analyzes, and are consequently used less frequently in school library research. However, we found these to be invaluable for our evaluation and allowed us insights that we would have been unlikely to discover otherwise. We were not looking for consistency across stakeholders, but it was our belief that the perceptions of these stakeholders could be combined with our observations to develop a deeper understanding of exemplary school libraries.

Our Findings on Exemplary School Libraries

When we began our evaluation study, it was our intention to provide stories that highlighted the critical features of exemplary school libraries. Instead, we found variability across our interviews and surveys. Importantly, there was consistency in the positive perceptions toward the importance of each school library and the teacher librarian; however, the reasons for these perceptions varied. The multiple types of data that we compiled in our evaluation allowed us consider why these very different programs were considered exemplary. The multiple perspectives allowed us to see beneath surface differences. School library programs varied due to the differing contextual constraints within which they operated. However, all had been nominated as exemplary programs. We came to recognize it was not the specific components of the library programs as one would look for in a standards-based approach but it was the interaction between program and the school context that made them all exemplary. Context was multifaceted and composed of interacting factors, and through their interaction facilitated or hindered the implementation of exemplary practices. We believe we were able to recognize the single importance of context because we had multiple forms and sources of data that enabled us to see the interactions, to view how the instantiation of library practice was the consequence of mediation in a dynamic system.

The school libraries we observed in our research functioned in very different ways. In analyzing these differences, it became clear that a multitude of factors existed in each school that resulted in a set of unique library programs created a unique context for each library program. The continuum that we created was built on our findings of three consistently found features that we identified in each of the exemplary school library programs, and appeared central to the functioning of these libraries (see Figure 6.1). These included the role of the school library and the teacher librarian within school context, teacher librarians who focused on teaching, and teacher librarians who were agents of change through the collaborations they initiated and the programs they developed or offered. The continuum also recognized two important support mechanisms, specifically, the school administration and financial support for the school library and the teacher librarian.

	LEVEL 1	LEVEL 2	LEVEL 3	LEVEL 4
Library's role in school	Operates independently within school culture.	Collaborative partnerships are building.	Library is central to learning. Strong library–teacher collaborations.	Level 3 features plus systematic support.
Teacher librarian's role in school	Seen as a secondary resource.	Library is an important resource.	Equal partner and strong collaborator.	
Teaching and instruction	Library has peripheral support role. Parallel or independent teaching. Librarian capitalizes on administrative and teacher decisions.	Opportunities for teaching (but viewed as add-ons. Cooperative teaching. Actively changing culture.	Central role in instruction. Collaborative teaching. Established a new culture in school.	
Program	Library "skills." Some teaching is unconnected to classroom instruction.	Curriculum and library instruction are coordinated.	Integration of classroom and library instruction. Innovative and opportunistic. Finds solutions to barriers.	
Administration	Library viewed as peripheral.	Library valued but not seen as central to school's purpose. Decision-making about the library may not involve the librarian.	Seen as central to school's purpose. Proactive in support of the library. Shared decision-making. Librarian involved in school leadership.	Shared understanding across staff and system (board) of library role (as defined in Level 3). System-wide valuing and support for library programs (e.g., Board-level consultant).
Finance	Library finance decided by administration. Regular allocation.	Administration provides additional funding on occasion.	Methods to address financial constraints as a regular part of school planning.	Finances on a firm foundation.

Figure 6.1 Exemplary School Library Program Continuum (Adapted from Lee & Klinger, 2011)

These exemplary library programs were embedded within a context that acted as both an enabler and as a constraint on the librarian and program. Context incorporated factors such as administrative support at the school and board level, school culture, teacher expertise, funding, history of the school library, school climate, professional knowledge of the librarian, and tech/volunteer support in the library. These factors interacted amongst each other and may have both direct and indirect effects upon the implementation of an exemplary program. For example, collaboration between the teacher librarian and teachers for jointly planned and carried out teaching is often described as exemplary practice. It is sometimes held up as the ideal. However, teacher expertise interacts with school culture and school history to create an environment that is to a greater or lesser degree open to collaboration. A program with extensive collaboration between the school librarian and teachers may be exemplary but so may be a program in which the teacher librarian carries out the teaching independently. New teachers who lack expertise in teaching may not know the benefits of or be open to collaboration. This is where the second defining feature of exemplary programs came into play. The librarian is a catalyst for change. In such a context, it is the efforts of the librarian to demonstrate the benefits of collaboration to new teachers that makes the program an exemplary one even though the amount of collaboration may be low.

Exemplary school library programs are ones in which the focus of the program is on teaching students. The teacher librarian we observed sought to maximize the amount of time devoted to this within each specific school context. Programs that differed substantially on the amount and form of teaching could be equally exemplary given the different contexts. A simple quantitative judgment based upon the amount of teaching or form of teaching was not sufficient.

The third defining feature of exemplary school library programs was that the teacher librarian continuously worked to change the context in which the school library operated. This was a purposeful effort on the part of the librarian to shift the balance amongst the factors that made up the context to enable more teaching. These teacher librarians worked to build networks with the classroom teachers. These teacher librarians were active agents of change, working to build connections with classroom teachers, school administrators, and the broader community. Thus, the knowledge, expertise, experience, and communication skills of the teacher librarian were vitally important in creating the conditions for this evolution of context to occur. Ultimately, the degree and rate of change was the result of the interaction between the current context and the efforts of the librarian.

Developing the continuum offered a way to evaluate the current functioning of a school library program without judging it categorically as meeting or not meeting a set of criteria. As a continuum, it does recognize that there are no singular set of "best practices." Rather, the continuum highlights the important interactions that occur between the school context and the programs that operate within this context, as in the school libraries in our evaluation.

Overall, the mixed methods approach that we employed in our evaluation allowed us to develop a deeper understanding of the complexity of school library programs. We were able to explore the interactions among multiple factors because of variety of data collection sources and methods. In particular, the observational data gave us a richer and more nuanced understanding than that obtained from the interviews and surveys. This was the key to our discovery of the role of context in school library programs and led to the development of the continuum as a description and the possibility of it being a mechanism for planning improvement. As the context of a school library program changes, through the efforts of the teacher librarian, the possibilities and potentials also change.

COLLABORATION AS A PATH TO SCHOOL IMPROVEMENT

The ongoing research and practice in school improvement research has identified ongoing collaborations and networks amongst teachers to support teaching and learning. Our evaluation witnessed the real potential of such collaborative efforts that the school library and the teacher librarian can create and facilitate. Certainly, the types of collaborations varied, as did the success of these collaborations. Yet, it appeared to be the school context, perhaps analogous to the school climate described in other educational research, that either constrained or fostered such collaborations. Teacher librarians play a critical role in shaping such contexts within their professional practice, while also being responsive to the changing demands faced by schools. As recognized by the professional standards for teacher librarians, school library programs play a key instructional role through collaboration (Branch & Oberg, 2001; Todd, 2008). The underlying premise of the school library program is integration through collaboration (Oberg, 2009). Moreover, Oberg (2009) argues this collaboration should function to support change: "Changing the organizational culture of the school constitutes the key role and goal for the school library professional and requires deep knowledge of the particular culture of the school and the complexities of the change process" (p. 2). This role requires the librarian to mediate amongst competing goals and to consider the larger educational picture. As such, the librarian needs not only to be competent in meeting the current needs of those he or she collaborates with but also to be actively working to shift these goals.

Similarly, the standards and curriculum documents developed by the school library profession emphasize that collaboration is a key aspect of the teacher librarian's role (AASL, 2009; AASL & AECT, 1998; Ontario Ministry of Education 1982; Ontario School Library Association, 2010). School library leaders promote collaboration between the librarian and teachers (Buzzeo, 2002; Haycock, 1998, 2002; Kuhlthau, 1994, 2003; Kuhlthau, Maniotes & Caspari, 2007; Montiel-Overall, 2008). Through these collaborative efforts, the teacher librarian becomes a vital change agent in the school. Perhaps, most importantly, our research and evaluation suggest that these networks and collaborative efforts can truly improve teaching and learning. The teachers we spoke with acknowledged the critical role that the teacher librarian played in supporting their practice and improving the educational opportunities for students. These teachers described how their students' engagement in learning was deeper and more enriching when they worked closely alongside the teacher librarian.

CONCLUSIONS: MOVING FORWARD, BEING EFFECTIVE REGARDLESS OF CURRENT STATUS

Not surprisingly, there is great variability on the manner in which school libraries operate within and between educational jurisdictions. School administrators commonly spoke of the challenges to find the funding to support the school library program and the teacher librarian. School districts in Ontario have a large amount of control with respect to how they allocate the funds they receive from the Ministry of Education, but these funds are limited. In order to provide a balanced budget, difficult decisions regarding educational programs and resources are required. The result is that some districts choose to reduce the funding to school libraries, while others reduce funding to other educational programs and resources. We observed teacher librarians who worked interactively with teachers, while others whose primary role appeared to be the source of teacher preparation relief. Some had full-time positions, while others were at the school for only two to three days per week.

In spite of the ongoing threats to funding for school libraries in Ontario, there are school library programs that meet and exceed our expectations. These exemplary school library programs demonstrate that the school library can be a central hub in the school, leading and supporting literacy initiatives across a school. These library programs provide critical educational opportunities to the students they serve. Perhaps not surprisingly, it appears that such programs exist in the presence of a dedicated and enthusiastic teacher librarian. These teacher librarians are excellent teachers, who use the library to truly support students' learning. They find ways to build educational partnerships with other teachers and the community. They not only offer independent programs within the school, but they also work to improve and support current programs and practices.

Yet even for these exemplary programs, real challenges remain, and this was an important aspect of our evaluation. These challenges are largely created by the context in which the school library operates, and are important factors in determining the current effectiveness of the school library and the teacher librarian. First and foremost, school library programs face a unique challenge in demonstrating their value and worth to both school administrators and teachers. Administrators and teachers' conceptualizations of what a school library program could provide is often uninformed or extremely narrow, and does not align with current conceptions of effective practices for the school library (Church, 2008). This is not completely unexpected considering that neither principals nor teachers have had the opportunity in their professional training to learn about the role of the school library program and the teacher librarian (Asselin & Doiron, 2003; Wilson & Blake, 1993). Thus, teacher librarians frequently must take on an educative or advocacy role with the administrator and teachers in addition to or in order to be able to collaborate and provide important instructional opportunities of support to teachers and students.

However, these challenges also illustrate opportunities and directions that can help school library programs become more effective, regardless of their current status. By situating school library programs within operational contexts, we identified an evolving process that likely occurs along a continuum. School library programs that are placed in a Level 1 or 2 on the continuum are limited, but they may still be seen as exemplary given the limitations imposed on them by their school context. This shift from an absolute standard to a contextually based one moves evaluation from a static judgmental model of practice to a future-directed flexible model of practice. It is critically important to recognize where a program is and using this to create goals and directions for change. The continuum can validate current practices, identifying the current strengths and providing directions to move forward to better support ongoing school improvement efforts. We believe this positive orientation reflects the principles illustrated in the school change and professional learning communities literature. As described in this research, the change process is effective when participants are empowered and validated. Individuals are open to change when it offers positive benefits.

The continuum may serve as a tool for a school library program to situate itself among other schools' programs and to establish goals for improvement through seeking to move along the continuum. Lastly, our findings highlighted the need for teacher librarians to be highly adaptable, changing their manner of approach to suit the styles of the teachers with whom he or she works and the current school context. The most successful programs are characterized by teacher librarian and teacher collaborations, in terms of teaching, learning, and library use.

REFERENCES

AASL. (2009). *Empowering learners: Guidelines for school library media programs.* Chicago: American Library Association.

AASL & AECT. (1998). *Information power: Building partnerships for learning.* Chicago: American Library Association.

Alberta Learning Resources Council. (2005). *Role of the teacher-librarian.* Retrieved from www.learningresources.ab.ca/pdf/role.pdf

Alkin, M. C. (2004). *Evaluation roots: Tracing theorists' views and influences.* Thousand Oaks, CA: Sage Publications.

American Library Association. (2005). *Student achievement.* Retrieved from www.ala.org/aaslTemplate.cfm?Section=studentachieve

Asselin, M., & Doiron, R. (2003). An analysis of the inclusion of school library programs and services in the preparation of preservice teachers in Canadian universities. *Behavioral and Social Sciences Librarian, 22*(1), 19–32.

Blackett, K., & Klinger, D. A. (2006). Canadian study strengthens the link between school library staffing with student achievement and reading enjoyment. *School Library Media Activities Monthly, 23*(3), 56–58.

Branch, J., & Oberg. D. (2001). The teacher librarian in the 21st century: The teacher librarian as instructional leader. *School Libraries in Canada, 21*(2), 9–11.

Buzzeo, T (2002). *Collaborating to meet standards: Teacher/librarian partnership for K-6.* Worthington, OH: Linwood Publishing.

Church, A. (2008). *The instructional role of the library media specialist as perceived by elementary school principals.* School Library Media Research, 11. Retrieved from http://www.eric.ed.gov/PDFS/EJ823034.pdf

Coish, D. (2005, May 4). *Canadian school libraries and teacher-librarians.* Statistics Canada. Retrieved from www.statcan.ca/english/research/81-595-MIE/81-595MIE2005028.pdf

Evans, E. D., & Tribble, M. (1986). Perceived teaching problems, self efficacy and commitment to teaching among preservice teachers. *Journal of Educational Research, 80,* 81–85.

Expert Panel on Early Reading in Ontario. (2003). *Early reading strategy.* Ontario: Ministry of Education. Retrieved from www.edu.gov.on.ca/eng/document/reports/reading/reading.pdf

Fullen, M. (1993). *Change forces: Probing the depths of educational reform.* London: Falmer Press.

Fullen, M. (2002). Educational reform as continuous improvement. In W. D. Hawley & D. L. Rollie (Eds.), *The keys to effective schools: Educational reform as continuous improvement* (pp. 1–9). Thousand Oaks, CA: Corwin.

Fullen, M., & Hargreaves, A. (1996). *What's worth fighting for in your school.* New York: Teachers College Press.

Good, T., & Brophy, J. (1989). School effects. In M. Whitrock (Ed.), *Third handbook on of research on teaching.* New York: Macmillan.

Grossman, P., Wineberg, S., & Woolworth, S. (2001). Toward a theory of teacher community. *Teachers College Record, 103*(6), 942–1012.

Haycock, K. (1998). The impact of scheduling on cooperative program planning & teaching (CPPT) & information skills instruction. *School Libraries in Canada, 18*(1), 20.

Haycock, K. (2002). Collaboration: Critical success factors for student learning. *School Libraries Worldwide, 13*(1), 25–35.

Klinger, D. A., & Blackett, K. (2006, April). *School libraries & student achievement in Ontario.* Toronto: Ontario Library Association. Retrieved from http://www.accessola .com/data/6/rec_docs/137_eqao_pfe_study_2006.pdf

Klinger, D. A., Lee, E., Stephenson, G., DeLuca, C., & Luu, K. (2009). *Exemplary school libraries in Ontario.* Toronto: Ontario Library Association.

Kuhlthau, C. C. (1994). Students and the information search process: Zones of intervention for librarians. *Advances in Librarianship, 18*, 57–72.

Kuhlthau, C. C. (2003). Rethinking libraries for the information age school: Vital role in inquiry learning. *School Libraries in Canada, 22*, 3–5.

Kuhlthau, C. C. Maniotes, L. K., & Caspari, A. K. (2007). *Guided inquiry: Learning in the 21st century.* Portsmouth, NH: Libraries Unlimited.

Kyriakides, L., Creemers, B., Antounious, P., & Demetrious, D. (2010). A synthesis of studies searching for school factors: Implications for theory and research. *British Educational Research Journal, 26*(5), 807–830.

Lance, K. C., Rodney, M. J., & Hamilton-Pennell, C. (2000). *How school librarians help kids achieve standards: The second Colorado study.* Castle Rock, CO: Hi Willow Research and Publishing.

Lance, K. C., Rodney, M. J., & Hamilton-Pennell, C. (2002). *How school libraries improve outcomes for children: The New Mexico study.* Salt Lake City: Hi Willow Research and Publishing.

Langer, J. A. (2000). Excellence in English in middle and high school: How teachers' professional lives support student achievement. *American Educational Research Journal, 37*, 397–439.

Lee, E. A., & Klinger, D. A. (2009). Exemplary school libraries: The centre of all the action. *The Teaching Librarian, 17*(1), 20–22.

Lee, E. A., & Klinger, D. A. (2011, January). Against the flow: A continuum for evaluating and revitalizing school libraries. *School Libraries Worldwide, 17*(1). Retrieved from www.iasl-online.org/pubs/slw/jan2011.htm

Leithwood, K., Leonard, L. & Sharratt, L. (1998). Conditions fostering organizational learning in schools. *Educational Administration Quarterly, 34*(2), 243–276.

Literacy Coalition of New Brunswick. (2005, January 20). *School libraries fundamental to learning.* Retrieved from www.nb.literacy.ca/media/2005/jan20.htm

Louis, K. S., & Marks, H. N. (1998). Does professional community affect the classroom? Teachers' work and student experiences in restructuring schools. *American Journal of Education, 106*, 532–575.

McLaughlin, M. W., & Talbert, J. E. (2001). *Professional communities and the work of high school teaching.* Chicago: University of Chicago Press.

Montiel-Overall, P. (2008). Teacher and librarian collaboration: A qualitative study. *Library & Information Science Research, 30*, 145–155.

Oakes, J., & Lipton, M. (1999). *Teaching to change the world.* Boston: McGraw-Hill.

Oberg, D. (2009). Libraries in schools: Essential contexts for studying organizational change and culture. *Library Trends, 58*(1), 1–14.

Ontario Ministry of Education. (1982). *Partners in action: The Library Resource Centre in the school curriculum.* Toronto: Ontario Ministry of Education.

Ontario School Library Association. (2010). *Together for learning: School libraries and the emergence of the learning commons.* Toronto: Ontario School Library Association.

Preskill, H., & Catsambas, T. T. (Eds.). (2006). *Reframing evaluation through appreciative inquiry.* Thousand Oaks, CA: Sage Publications.

Todd, R. J. (2008). The dynamics of classroom teacher and school librarian instructional collaborations. *Scan, 27*(2), 19–28.

Wilson, P. J., & Blake, M. (1993, Spring). The missing piece: A school library media center component in principal-preparation programs. *Educational Administration and Supervision, 13*(2), 65–58.

7

PERSPECTIVES OF SCHOOL ADMINISTRATORS RELATED TO SCHOOL LIBRARIES

Deborah Levitov

INTRODUCTION: MIXED METHODS STUDY OF SCHOOL ADMINISTRATORS

This chapter presents findings of a mixed methods study that examined the experiences of two groups of administrators who participated in an online course, "School Library Advocacy for Administrators," respectively, in the summer of 2005 and the fall of 2006. The course was offered through Mansfield University in Mansfield, Pennsylvania, and was developed through an Institute of Museum and Library Services (IMLS) grant. The purpose of the course was to educate administrators about school library programs and the role of the librarian, and to subsequently create administrative advocates for school libraries. The purpose of the study was to explore how the administrators perceived the course made a difference in what they know about school library programs and how the information impacted their perspectives and actions in relationship to the library programs and the school librarians in their buildings.

LACK OF ADMINISTRATIVE AWARENESS

According to Brewer and Milam (2005), the results of a 2005 survey conducted by *School Library Journal* and International Society for Technology in Education showed that "library media specialists are key players in creating schools befitting the 21st century. It's up to the education leadership, as well as the community at large, to recognize, support, and fund their efforts."

Studies have shown a significant impact of school libraries on student learning (Lance & Loertscher, 2001; Todd & Kuhlthau, 2005a, 2005b; Todd, Kuhlthau, & Heinstrom, 2005) through assessment measures for inquiry learning. A Canadian study (Blackett & Klinger, 2006) showed correlations between the presence of professional staffing of the school library and higher student reading achievement scores (p. 57). Blackett and Klinger (2006) also reported that the presence of a school librarian was the "single strongest predictor of reading enjoyment for both grades 3 and 6" and that lack of professional library staffing is associated with less positive attitudes toward reading enjoyment (p. 57).

Another study by Todd, Kuhlthau, and Heinstrom (2005) suggests the additional impact of school libraries on student learning through assessment measures for inquiry learning. Part of the information literacy standards and the inquiry approach is the identification of learner needs and student learning through assessment (Harada & Yoshina, 2005; Kuhlthau, Maniotes, & Caspari, 2007).

Guided inquiry, the basis for American Association of School Librarians' (AASL) *Standards for the 21st-century learner* (2007), is at the heart of many school reform measures developed to address a critical need of learners. The AASL standards "mirror the same foundational elements of successful learners being promoted by other educational consortia, including the Partnership for the 21st Century Skills (2004) and the International Society of Technology in Education (2000–02)" (Zmuda & Harada, 2008, p. 86). These elements are also reflected in Common Core State Standards; "academic standards for K-12 education designed to prepare students for college and career readiness" with the goal of emphasizing and demonstrating student learning—especially higher order thinking skills (Kramer, 2011, p. 8).

Yet, school administrators remain unaware of available research findings that show the importance of school libraries to student learning, and are not knowledgeable of existing standards and guidelines and other readily available resources for guiding the development of school library programs. Consequently, many administrators are uninformed of the purpose of school libraries (O'Neal, 2004), which results in the ongoing threat to the continuation and existence of school libraries in K-12 education.

Based on this background knowledge, it was the intent of this research to determine if the offered course work for school administrators did impact their awareness regarding school library programs. The results of the study not only offered insights from the perspective of participating administrators, but also revealed implications of benefit to school librarians as they work with school administrators and develop and implement school library programs, advocate for those programs, and recruit others to do the same.

CONTEXT AND BACKGROUND OF THE STUDY

This study examined the experiences of two groups of administrators who participated in the online course, "School Library Advocacy for Administrators," respectively, in the summer of 2005 and the fall of 2006. The course was offered through Mansfield University in Mansfield, Pennsylvania, and was developed through an IMLS grant. The course content focused on educating administrators about school library programs and the role of the school librarian, and to subsequently create administrative advocates for school libraries (Kachel, 2003). The purpose of this study was to explore how the participating administrators perceived the course making a difference in what they knew about school library programs and how the information impacted their perspectives and actions in relationship to the library programs in their buildings.

The online course, "School Library Advocacy for Administrators," has been offered by Mansfield University since 2003 as a way of educating school administrators about school library programs. It is a unique means of helping educational administrators gain knowledge about school libraries through identified resources such as research studies, current literature, and program planning materials and standards. The course is 5 weeks long and requires a 15-hour time commitment from administrators with an option for professional development or graduate credit hours.

Administrators, through the use of course resources, examine research and literature related to school library programs, learn about the role of the school librarian, define information literacy, learn the importance of the student research process, and identify the key elements of exemplary library programs. They also learn how to apply course content to their individual schools, students, and teachers by developing program improvement plans for their libraries.

Thirteen administrators who enrolled in the online course and their school librarian agreed to participate in this study. Nine of the 13 administrators agreed to give telephone interviews after they had completed the course and implemented action plans developed within the context of the course.

RESEARCH QUESTIONS

The study examined the following questions related to the experience of 13 administrators enrolled in the course. When school administrators are provided with in-depth knowledge of school library programs established by research as well as frameworks of the profession, in what ways do they perceive that they

1. Gained information about school library programs
2. Changed their perceptions of library media programs
3. Changed their actions related to their building library media programs (e.g., through scheduling, staffing, program initiatives, professional assignments, evaluation, budgeting, in-services, communications, etc.)

The focus of the study seeks insights related to these questions through the perceptions of the administrator participants as well as through information provided by self-evaluation module surveys, course feedback forms, and action plans.

LITERATURE REVIEW

School librarians have held positions in schools since the early 1900s; yet, "to play a pivotal role in student achievement, they must be meaningfully built into the 'architecture' of the leadership in schools" (Zmuda & Harada, 2008, p. 26). There are extensive resources and literature available that can contribute to this goal and guide the development of excellent school library programs integral to the educational mission.

A fundamental document for quality school libraries is the AASL's *Standards for the 21st-century learner* (2007) and *Standards for the 21st-century learner in action* (2009a), which provide guidance for teaching, learning, and assessment in the school library program. These standards offer the following message for administrators:

The focus of these standards is on the learner, but implicit within every standard and indicator is the necessity of a strong school library media program (SLMP) that offers a highly-qualified school library media specialist (a term used interchangeably with librarian), equitable access to up-to-date resources, dynamic instruction, and a culture that nurtures reading and learn-ing throughout the school. (AASL, 2009a, p. 5)

This document also emphasizes the responsibility of all educators to realize the importance of "providing environments that support and foster successful learn-ing" (AASL, 2009a, p. 6). Necessary for students is equitable access to resources, opportunities to learn, a collaborative learning environment, and access to a quality library (AASL, 2009a, p. 6).

The AASL guidelines, published in *Empowering learners* (AASL, 2009b), pro-vide a framework for exemplary school library programs and professional practice. The guidelines characterize exemplary programs as an environment for learning. It is an environment where students and teachers can pursue learning goals and curriculum objectives as well as personal interests through resources that build and expand knowledge. In a study conducted by Ross Todd and Carol Kuhlthau, 99.4 percent of students, grades 3–12, "believe school libraries and their services help them become better learners" (Whelan, 2004, p. 46).

The role of the school librarian is included in the recommendations for exem-plary school library programs. According to *Empowering learners* (AASL, 2009b), the roles for the school librarian are those of leader, instructional partner, teacher, and program administrator (pp. 18, 19). Kuhlthau comments that "few educators have recognized the power of the school library as an integral element in designing the information age school . . . even though recent studies have shown a significant impact of school libraries on student learning (Lance & Loertscher, 2001; Todd & Kuhlthau, 2005a, 2005b)" (Kuhlthau et al., 2007, p. 10). Another study by Todd, Kuhlthau, and Heinstrom (2005) suggests the additional impact of school librar-ies on student learning through assessment measures for inquiry learning. Part of the information literacy standards and the inquiry approach is the identification of learner needs and student learning through assessment (Harada & Yoshina, 2005; Kuhlthau et al.; 2007). All is structured through existing curriculum and learning goals and involves "both short-term and long-term desires" (Marzano, Pickering, & Pollock, 2001) and supports the idea that, according to Pressley and McCormick (1995), effective learners and thinkers use background knowledge, apply learning strategies, are mindful of their own thinking, and are motivated.

ADMINISTRATORS' KNOWLEDGE OF SCHOOL LIBRARY PROGRAMS

It is important for school administrators to have an understanding of school library programs, including a grasp of the roles of the school librarian and their place in the academic plan of the school (Campbell, 1994; Hartzell, 2002; Oberg, Hay, & Henri, 2000; Rose, 2002). In a survey of 572 teacher librarians and 423 princi-pals (terms used in the survey), 90 percent of the librarians and 78 percent of the principals agreed that principals were inadequately trained in the management and function of school libraries (Wilson & Blake, 1993).

Traditionally, teachers and administrators have not been exposed to the kinds of school library programs proposed by the national standards for school libraries, nor are they well versed in the meaning of information literacy, the existence of informa-tion literacy standards, or the roles outlined for school librarians. According to sev-eral studies and surveys, conducted from 1989 to 2004, school principals at all levels,

Pre-K through 12, know very little about managing or sustaining effective school library programs and, therefore, are less likely to fund and support them (Campbell, 1991; Edwards, 1989; Lau, 2002; O'Neal, 2004; Wilson & Blake, 1993).

Support by the administrator is essential if the value of the school library program is to be recognized and capitalized upon, especially when the school librarian is not seen in a leadership capacity in the school setting (Wilson & Lyders, 2001). A 2003 Kentucky study (Alexander & Carey, 2003) reported fewer than 10 percent of the principals who responded had taken a college course that included content related to school librarian and principal collaboration. The Kentucky study went on to show that principals who had participated in such course work "rated the library media center significantly higher, 7.00 on a 10-point scale, than the principals who had not taken a course, who rated the value of the library media center at 4.97" (Alexander & Carey, 2003, p. 11). The finding of Alexander and Carey (2003) emphasizes the importance of providing formal training opportunities for administrators about school library programs. This is doubly important since administrators not only lack this kind of training in their administrative classes, but also lack this kind of information about school libraries in their teacher-training courses.

The principals' perceived "value of libraries" for students in the AASL KRC Research (AASL & ALA, 2003) seems illusive when not connected to student achievement or grounded in research; instead, it seems to reflect more of a "feel good" reason for valuing libraries on the part of administrators. This reiterates the need for administrators to have more knowledge about school library programs and related literature so they can provide informed, sustained support for such programs.

INFORMING SCHOOL ADMINISTRATORS ABOUT SCHOOL LIBRARY PROGRAMS

School administrators are key to impacting change for school libraries, yet finding ways to inform them about school libraries remains a challenge. When advocating for bottom-up change, Hall and Hord (2006) contend that those at the bottom can advocate for change but not without the ongoing support of administrators. They argue that such efforts will not be sustained since it is the administrators that must "secure the necessary infrastructure changes and long-term resource supports if use of an innovation is to continue indefinitely" (Hall & Hord, 2006, p. 13). The school administrator is pivotal as the building's instructional leader, instituting policies and establishing priorities such as policies that directly impact school library programs.

A study by Campbell (1991) revealed that much of what principals know about school libraries comes from their interaction with the school librarian on the job in the school setting. When 333 principals responded to a survey, 39 percent of those surveyed selected responses that indicated they learned what they knew about school libraries from either their current or former school librarian, while only 8 percent learned what they knew from college coursework (p. 56). In an effort to provide information for principals about school libraries whenever possible, Alexander and Carey (2003) point out that it is important for school librarians to "collaborate with principals and educate them about professional roles, responsibilities, and services" at every opportunity (p. 11).

Many studies have indicated that administrators lack knowledge about school libraries and the role of school librarians in education. Administrators do not see school librarians in a leadership capacity in the school. They are not aware of national standards for school library programs or information literacy standards. Recommendations from numerous studies have called for opportunities for administrators to be provided with better background knowledge about school library programs and the role of school librarian so they can make informed decisions for library program development and integration as well as serve as advocates for school libraries.

METHODOLOGY: MIXED METHODS APPROACH

Employing a mixed methods approach, this study made use of standardized responses from surveys, action plans, feedback sheets, and demographic information. In addition, it used descriptive/phenomenological methods to examine the lived experiences of the participants (Hatch, 2002) through interviews. Participants' perceptions, shared through semistructured interviews, were the result of their individual interpretations of the meanings assigned to events and to acquired knowledge. The interviews revealed how participants made meaning of their experiences related to a Mansfield University online course and how they put the resulting action plans to work (Seidman, 1998).

The interviews, surveys, self-evaluations, course feedback sheets, and action plans provide multiple perspectives of the participants' experiences. Standardized responses alone are not sufficient to accommodate individual, subjective differences; thus, the interviews help provide a deeper understanding of the participants' perceptions (Seidman, 1998). The chosen mixed methods research approach takes advantage of multiple sources of information that add depth to the interpretation (Greene & Caracelli, 1997, p. 10).

PARTICIPANTS

Originally, 40 administrators registered to participate in the Mansfield online course during 2005 and 2006. Twenty of the 40 enrollees actually completed the course during this time period and 3 finished at a later date. In the end, 23 enrollees (58% of the original 40) completed the online course and 17 (43%) did not complete the course. Completion of the course was somewhat higher (58%) in the summer of 2005 and the fall of 2006 than the completion rate (51%) for other courses offered from 2003 through 2007.

Thirteen of the 20 administrators who successfully completed the course agreed to participate in the study. In addition to the quantitative data gathered, a sampling of administrator participants were invited to participate in telephone interviews regarding their learning experiences. Nine administrators agreed to be interviewed for the study (four from summer 2005 and five from fall 2006).

Administrator participants were located in nine states representing various regions of the country (northeast region, four states; Midwest region, one state; southern region, one state; southwestern region, one state; and western region, two states). They represented the range of K-12 grade levels (eight elementary, one elementary–middle, one middle, one middle–high, and two high schools). Participants' years of experience as administrators ranged from one to nine years. Most administrators had worked with their current school librarian for 1–5 years, and 2 had worked with the same school librarian for 6–10 years. Nine of the 13 administrators had full-time school librarians, 3 had school librarians that were less than half-time, and 1 had a school librarian with a 4-day-a-week assignment. Nine of the 13 had fixed schedules, 2 had combination schedules, and 2 were flexible.

ASSUMPTIONS

The underlying assumption of this study is that school administrators have limited background knowledge about school libraries while, at the same time, they have power that influences the success of school library programs. For this study, interviews, examination of course feedback forms, self-assessments, surveys, and action plans were used to determine how the administrators perceived the background knowledge about school libraries influenced their perceptions and actions and how that knowledge served to motivate them to make changes in their programs.

LIMITATIONS

Limitations of the study included the virtual nature of the course and the study, with no face-to-face meetings. Also, the format of the course was predetermined, which included preestablished course surveys (e.g., general-demographic survey, module surveys, and course survey) and course content. The online survey developed for the study yielded uniformly high scores for all items. The short period of time between the administrators taking the course and putting their action plans into place (nine months for the 2005 participants and five months for the 2006 participants) also could be seen as a limitation.

In future studies, these limitations could be addressed in various ways. To capitalize on the course surveys, work could be done with the professor to devise alternative surveys that would be more conducive to data gathering and analysis with consistent language while still meeting the needs of Mansfield University. The online survey could be further analyzed to determine if different questions would provide more useable data. An effort could be made to select timing of courses for study that would allow more time for implementation of action plans.

Another limitation is the fact that participants received professional development funds for participating in the course. This could have compelled them to indicate more progress on their action plan out of obligation to meet the expectations linked to the staff development funds. Also, there was potential for the participating administrators to have a preconceived pro-library disposition by the sheer nature of signing up to take the course at the request of a teacher or an acting school librarian in their school. If they agreed to take the online course, the Mansfield student would get a scholarship. This could be addressed if the course were offered with no professional development funding and having the administrators take the course under circumstances where they were not recruited by Mansfield University students.

IMPROVEMENT PLAN (SUMMARY OF FINDINGS)

Administrators' Changed Perceptions

Administrators indicated that they acquired knowledge through the course modules about many topics on school library programs. The majority of administrator participants further indicated that these were areas they knew little about prior to the course. According to the administrators, this information provided new perspectives regarding their school library programs and librarian related to three themes: (a) changed perceptions for the school librarian and the program, (b) improved ability to communicate with the school librarian and others, and (c) increased awareness of what the administrator can do to support the school library program.

It appears, according to the comments of the administrators in the study, they came to better understand information literacy and how it relates to all academic standards. They acknowledged that the school librarian has a unique position and should be looked at differently when conducting appraisal and evaluation. As they indicated, this new level of understanding resulted in a change in their perceptions regarding the school librarian and the school library program.

The administrators indicated a new understanding of their responsibilities regarding the school library program. They suggested that the course heightened their expectations for the program and provided more awareness of what school librarian can contribute to instruction, teaching and learning, and collaboration. The descriptors used by the principals corresponded to the roles of the school librarian as outlined in *Information power* (AASL & AECT, 1998), the national guidelines developed by the American Association of School Librarians and the Association for Educational Communications and Technology in place at the time the course was developed.

Participants, in their comments, used words like *personality, communicator, energizer, cheerleader, voice, leader,* or *advocate* as important qualities needed by the school librarians. The administrators in this study suggested the pivotal role the school librarian must play, when they used these descriptive words and phrases, *move the program forward, win over the teachers, lead the cause, communicate and serve as the voice of the program.*

Another theme that emerged from the participants' responses was the change in their perceptions of the school librarian's role in teaching and learning. The administrators suggested the importance of appointing the school librarian to planning committees as a way of integrating the school library into the school academic plan of the school. They also suggested linking the library to school improvement plans and having the school librarian promote the use of technology.

The terms listed under Instructional Partner (e.g., collaborator, expert, involved, team member, integrator, communicator, facilitator, leader, credible, knowledgeable, and informed) are clearly focused on the school librarian as a team player. Administrators described the school librarian as someone working with teachers, planning instruction, and integrating the library program with classroom curriculum while contributing specialized skills.

Terms used frequently by the administrators corresponded to the role of information specialist. This role description reflected the unique expertise of the school librarian and appeared to be particularly important to the administrators, especially in the area of technology. They suggested the school librarian served as a central player in the use of technology and as a professional developer who helped teachers learn about and use technology in instruction.

Seeing the library as something essential to all teachers was also a change in perception indicated by administrators. They suggested that in order for all teachers to better use the school library and the librarian, in-service was required. Many also commented on the ability of the school librarian to bring a new perspective and focus to achieving standards—a new way of teaching. The administrators mentioned consistently that they had a new understanding of what the school librarian can do and how the library program can be integral to the academic program.

Several of the descriptors used by principals related to the roles of the school librarian can be placed under the general heading of "leadership" (e.g., facilitator, innovator, involved, cheerleader, voice, communicator, energizer, advocate, planner, expert, informed, and knowledgeable). These descriptors comprise over half of those used by administrators and stress the importance placed on the leadership role for school librarians. Many of the comments made by the administrators during the interviews emphasized the success of the action plan depended a great deal on the ability of the school librarian to implement the plan. They stressed the need for the school librarian to draw the teachers in, be an advocate for the library program, be available, and make sure teachers know they are there for them. Many administrators emphasized the importance of the school librarian serving a leadership role on building teams (e.g., curriculum, school improvement, etc.).

Administrators mentioned the role of "professional developer" as desirable for the school librarian, beyond the connection to technology. This again reflects expectations for the school librarian to serve in a leadership role. It aligns with the findings of McCracken (2001), wherein school librarian perceive the following factors as important in helping them expand their roles: supportive administrators and teachers; use of new technology, including the Internet; professional development opportunities; their own abilities and attitudes; adequate funding; and clerical support.

Administrators suggested they viewed the school library program in new ways. For two administrators, it was related to the environment of the center; they wanted it to be more inviting, larger, and more centrally located. For others, it opened their eyes to new opportunities such as grants and resources. The administrators also suggested there was a need for teamwork and an effort to build the library program through consensus.

They described the need to build stronger curriculum, using the library more and with a collaborative approach. As one administrator suggested, the school library should be a place where teachers go first instead of last. For many, it appeared the course had an impact on their perceptions of scheduling the library, the importance of time and access, and the concept that the library should not serve as just a drop-off point for students. Another administrator shared that she had concluded that staffing the library with volunteers was not a good option—something she had at one time considered.

According to one administrator, the course helped him better understand the language of the school librarian. It gave him a new way of looking at how she was involved in instruction. He described ways in which he was more informed and knowledgeable and more able to appreciate and support her efforts. The same administrator commented he would not have acted on a grant opportunity that came across his desk prior to taking the course, but his new awareness made him look at the grant as something viable for the library.

Communication is a key factor reflected in the comments by participants—communication with the school librarian, communication with teachers, and communication with others in the district and the community. As the administrators suggested, the course helped them understand the library program and made it easier to communicate that information to others. The administrators also specified that gaining a better understanding of the library program provided insight and focus when communicating with the school librarian. They suggested that this allowed for more shared expectations and facilitated better planning for the program.

Administrators indicated the course provided information that could be used to gain support for their plans and programs. As they commented, it helped them articulate the importance and value of the school library program and the librarian, justifying them to other administrators as well as teachers. Many of the administrators used the course as a vehicle for communicating with the school librarian not only about the program in general but also about the action plan for the library program.

The importance of regular communication with the school librarian was reflected in the comments of the administrators. In some cases, it was used to bring the school librarian along, helping them to update and improve their skills and perspectives. For others, it was used to better understand what the school librarian was already doing, resulting in more focus and better support by the administrator.

One administrator indicated that creating a job description for the school librarian was a vehicle for communicating the depth and breadth of the position, providing it with credibility. Administrators also expressed the importance of communication by the school librarian about their skills, their knowledge of resources available, and how they and the library program could help teachers meet academic goals for students. The administrators suggested it was essential for communications to go beyond the library—that the school librarian should be involved in many different aspects of the school and show support and involvement in the whole school program.

Another outcome of taking the course for the administrators was increased insight into what they, as administrators, could do to provide more support and guidance for the school librarian and the program. The administrators acknowledged their power to influence teacher attitudes and actions. They also recognized their influence over staffing and budgeting for the library program. They suggested their time and availability was important to show support and investment so teachers as well as the school librarian would know the library program was a priority for the administrator. They indicated that support by the administrator is key to making changes in how the library program is viewed and integrated in to the academic program. They acknowledged the important role played by them in supporting the school library and librarian.

The administrators' influence reached beyond the school to board members, district-level administrators, other principals, the superintendent, parents, and community. As one principal said, the course allowed her to be a catalyst for the program. Another administrator suggested it was possible to serve as a leader and an advocate. Administrators shared many examples of how they took action to make an impact on the library program by focusing on budgeting, staffing, and developing a relationship with the school librarian. They also expressed expectations for teachers to plan with the school librarian and integrate the use of the library into their teaching.

Administrators suggested that one outcome of taking the online course was more focused communication with the school librarian on a regular basis. They also expressed a better understanding of the role of the school librarian and the function of the library. They indicated that they sought out opportunities to communicate information about the library program with others such as teachers, other administrators, and school board members, sharing information through conversations, presentations, and meetings. Many suggested they were more watchful for opportunities for the library program (e.g., school and district initiatives, grant opportunities, working with the community, etc.).

Making more of an effort to understand how the school librarian could support the academic plan of the building was also emphasized by the administrators. Many indicated the importance of evaluating the library program. They also specified the need to fine tune the evaluation of the school librarian to better match the job. Through their comments, they indicated the importance of the administrator as an advocate for the library program. Many wanted to search out ideas for the library program and the school librarian from other districts as a means of helping to improve their programs.

A Shift in Language

The language used by the administrators in the interviews and the online course evaluation responses reveals a pattern of discourse that emphasizes what they used to know and think before taking the online course compared to what they know and think after taking the online course. Through their comments, they indicated moving from narrow views of school librarian's role to a broader understanding of varying roles. They also suggested a shift from seeing the library program as marginal and isolated to a central focus for the school. Staffing of the school library appears to become more of a priority with emphasis on wanting a full-time school librarian.

The administrators indicated that, before taking the online course, the school librarian served more as a babysitter, seen as an aide or helper. After taking the online course, they suggested a shift to seeing the school librarian as a collaborator and a teacher. They described viewing the school librarian in a broader role where he or she works with students and teachers, moves beyond the walls of the library, ties into all curriculum areas, and helps reach school academic goals. There was a shift from viewing the school librarian in traditional roles such as checking out books and finding resources to working collaboratively on research projects, being part of the teaching team, meeting standards, as well as providing professional development for teachers. From their perspective, the school librarian had moved from the traditional librarian to a leader with broader responsibilities and varying roles.

There was also a shift in language that indicates a different view of the library program. It is described as moving from being a marginal, isolated program to one that is central to the educational plan of the building. It is described as being the hub of the school and a system that should be developed and used collaboratively rather than as a stand-alone tool. The school library is presented as a place where teachers should go first rather than last. In the language of the administrators, the library program becomes high priority, indicating importance of funding and better staffing. Small and unattractive centers were described as liabilities and larger centers with inviting spaces were preferred.

The availability of the school librarian appears to become a higher priority after taking the online course. Efforts are discussed for moving away from "drop-off" or "pull-out" programs where students were left with the school librarians with little or no communication with teachers. The administrators suggested a need for more flexible schedules with time for the school librarian and teachers to collaborate. Use of volunteers to manage the center was no longer seen as feasible and full-time school librarian became a goal. Paraeducators were listed as necessary to help staff the library in addition to school librarians. Language moves from an emphasis on circulation statistics and the number of resources to how the program supports all content areas.

The shift in language from before the online course to after the online course serves as another indication that for these administrators, there was a change in their perspectives related to the library program. What cannot be determined is if this was a systemic change in their approach to their library programs that will endure over time or a change only in vocabulary that could be temporary.

CHANGED PERCEPTIONS

University-Level Coursework about Libraries/Librarians

Within the context of this study, the administrators who participated indicated that the course content was important not only to them but also would be valuable to other administrators and should be part of university-level administrative coursework. They assigned high ratings to content even though they did not give a high rating to the experience of taking an online course. They confirmed that they had not had content in their administrative courses that dealt with development and evaluation of library programs. The administrators, who rated themselves as not knowing the content of the course modules, consistently rated themselves as knowing the information after completing each module.

They suggested, through examples, how information was gained from the online course. They implied that they gained a better understanding of information literacy and awareness of information literacy standards. They indicated a better understanding of how the library program and the work of the school librarian can be linked to the classroom, the curriculum, and academic standards. Their comments supported the idea that the school library can play an important role in the educational plan for the school. The language used by the administrators revealed a contrast between what they knew, did, and thought before taking the online course compared with after taking the online course, indicating changed perspectives toward library programs.

Identifiable themes emerged from the data that suggests the administrators gained a better understanding of the role of the school librarian and their expectations changed for library program. They stressed the importance of communicating with others about the library program and communicating with the school librarian on a regular basis.

Administrators as Advocates for Librarians/Libraries

Advocacy for the program was a subtheme. The administrators indicated that it was important to help teachers realize the potential of the school librarian as a collaborator or co-teacher in meeting educational goals for students. They also identified themselves as playing an important role in supporting and advocating for the school library program. They acknowledged that their opinions and their expectations were significant in the eyes of the teachers in their building. They also emphasized the perceived need for planning for and evaluating the library program as well as the need for a more role-specific evaluation of the school librarian.

School Librarian and Administrator Hold Commonality

On a more personal note, administrators indicated appreciation for an opportunity to hear from other administrators and participate in professional development specifically for themselves. Their comments reflect the many demands that tug at school administrators as they work to meet the needs of students, parents, and teachers, and address demands from their districts as well as state and national requirements. They, like the school librarian, are often loners in their buildings. One administrator suggested the school librarian holds some commonality with the principal as another person who works with all teachers and all students and has to know the entire curriculum.

The administrators expressed concerns related to time, money, and staffing limitations that created challenges for accomplishing established goals. Often, as they indicated, their best intentions are stalled or pushed down on their priority list when another initiative or expectation takes precedence. These administrators revealed through their comments that they do care about the library program and they want to see the actualization of their action plans. At the same time, they suggest they cannot accomplish it alone—the school librarian has to play an important role and the teachers have to buy into the plan. Several gave examples of how they sought support for the library program from others (e.g., school board members, superintendents, parents, and other administrators).

In summary, the administrator participants in this study provided examples of how they changed their perceptions of library programs. They indicated how the Mansfield online course provided information that gave them new ideas and concepts about library programs that they did not previously know. They also suggested that they changed their actions toward their library programs and began to make changes related to their action plans. Within the confines of this study, for the 13 administrator participants, it appears the Mansfield course did make a difference for them and their school library programs.

IMPLICATIONS

Based on the findings of this study, the Mansfield online course does appear to offer a viable solution for informing educational administrators about school library programs. It also provides an avenue for filling a gap that exists in university-level educational administration coursework. It offers an alternative solution to in-depth information for school administrators about school libraries in a short time span, complete with strategies for applying the information.

As a 2003 Kentucky study revealed (Alexander & Carey, 2003), those who know more about school libraries have a more favorable view of programs. In this regard, finding ways to educate the large majority of the principals with no background information about school libraries is a worthy goal.

Solutions for Informing Administrators

A traditional solution for informing administrators about school library programs is through one-on-one contact with school librarian (Hartzell, 2002; McNeil & Wilson, 1999–2000). In this scenario, the school librarian raises the awareness of the administrator through his or her actions on behalf of the library program and through interactions with the administrator. This is a phenomenon that is corroborated in an article written by school librarian Carl Harvey II (2008). Harvey interviewed his principal who establishes he came to learn about school libraries from Harvey, and he has learned to value the program due to the work of his school librarian. This is a solution that has worked for many school librarians and principals.

Based on the premise that providing formal training opportunities for administrators related to school library programs is needed, Mansfield University in Pennsylvania provides a new and viable approach to informing administrators about school library programs through the online course, "School Library Advocacy for Administrators." It represents an attempt to raise the knowledge level of school administrators in relationship to school libraries through direct, sustained contact of a course, which has not been the norm.

Online tools that offer ease of access to information anywhere anytime provide potential for delivery options for content similar to that of the Mansfield online course. The Mansfield course was originally developed in 2003. Since then, many more options for course delivery have been made available. It is more conceivable now than ever that a virtual course can serve as a workable solution for informing administrators about school library programs. Capitalizing on the positive reaction to the content of the online course by administrators in this study, it is possible that similar offerings can supersede the more traditional solution of established administrative classes at the university level.

It is possible to make content similar to the Mansfield course available through state departments, districts, educational service agencies, special initiatives, and grants. The course could fulfill professional development requirements or graduate credit for building administrators anywhere in the country. Content similar to the Mansfield online course could be packaged with a set number of modules, to be delivered in a limited time frame, by trained instructors, and made available using delivery options best for the locale (e.g., Blackboard, Moodle, webinar, etc.). This would allow for flexibility of delivery and the potential for a wider audience.

The timing in the educational environment is conducive to restructuring the course to take advantage of initiatives like *Partnership for the 21st century skills* (2004), the AASL's *Empowering learners: Guidelines for school library media programs* (2009a) and *Standards for the 21st-century learner* (2007), *The national educational technology standards for students: The next generation* (2007), and the Common Core State Standards Initiative (2010). All are initiatives that can serve to bridge information of interest to administrators, teachers, and school librarians linked to the learning needs of the student that stress the process of inquiry and real-world learning.

Informing School Library Specialists

The words of administrators reflected in this study can serve to confirm the roles of the school librarian established by AASL national standards. Their words indicate certain qualities that school librarians can heed as important and relevant to the success of their library programs. The descriptors used by these administrators should be given serious consideration as school librarians examine their actions and evaluate the roles they are playing in their schools.

According to the administrators who participated in this study, in regard to school librarians, personality counts, leadership is key, advocacy is essential, and communication is imperative. It is also important for school librarians to realize they still must serve as a central source for educating school administrators about school library programs on a daily basis. It would be beneficial for library media specialists to participate in a course like the Mansfield online course, with or without their administrator. It could serve as either a good refresher course or as a source of new information.

Hall and Hord (2006) suggest that without the support of the administrator, bottom-up change cannot be maintained; while Senge (1999) and Smith (2002) maintain others need to help orchestrate change. Either way, school librarians need to contemplate the role of change theories when working with administrators to alter the way the library program is perceived and used in the school.

School librarians can use this study to see through the eyes of administrators and better align their library agendas to priorities of their administrators and learn to communicate in ways that resonate with what is important to these very busy, often overwhelmed, but key players.

CONCLUSIONS: RECOMMENDATIONS FOR FURTHER STUDY

The findings in this study show there is potential for further research related to the Mansfield online course and the administrators that have or will participate in the course. The Mansfield course is currently being used as a district initiative where several administrators are taking the course. A longitudinal study of the experiences of these administrators after taking the online course and the impact it has on their library programs over time would be useful. Determining if the course can continue without incentives would also be a topic to investigate.

Follow-up with the administrators who participated in this study would be beneficial. It would be helpful to determine if they are still using information learned from the course. Have they continued to apply the information in different settings with different circumstances? Have they continued to pursue action planning for their library programs? What kinds of changes have they continued to make in their programs over time? These are questions that could indicate whether or not the administrators who completed the online course continue to apply the information gained and continue to have similar perceptions of the library program as reflected in this study.

Examining the perspective of the school librarians in buildings where the administrator has taken the Mansfield online course would be another important basis for future research. Do these school librarians perceive that the course is successful in informing their administrators? Do they perceive the course made a difference in how the administrator relates to and supports the library program? It would also be valuable to have school librarians and administrators take the course together and conduct research that reflects their experience and the impact it has on their working relationship and the library program.

Another topic for research would be to investigate how administrators approach change in their buildings after completing the course. How does it align with various theories related to change? What strategies were most successful? Who was involved?

Examination of the discourse that emerged as the administrators discussed their experiences could be the basis of further research. Indications through comments of "before" and "after" perceptions and behaviors related to school library programs could be further studied for indications of whether or not a change in culture model was occurring for these administrators. Did the comments go beyond changes in vocabulary and become an established part of their approach to management and development of their library programs? Also, observation of the administrators for emerging types would be another aspect or potential research. How did they approach planning and evaluation of the library program? Were they enablers? Did they orchestrate? Were there differences and similarities?

Each of these research topics would extend this study. They could serve to give more insight into the value or potential value of the Mansfield online course, "School Library Advocacy for Administrators," as a viable solution to informing administrators about school library programs.

REFERENCES

AASL. (2007). *Standards for the 21st-century learner*. Chicago: ALA.

AASL. (2009a). *Standards for the 21st-century learner in action*. Chicago: AASL.

AASL. (2009b). *Empowering learners: Guidelines for school library media programs*. Chicago: ALA.

AASL & AECT. (1998). *Information power: Building partnerships for learning*. Chicago: ALA.

AASL & ALA. (2003). *Report of findings: KRC research*. Chicago: ALA.

Alexander, L., & Carey, J. (2003, November–December). Education reform and the school library media specialist: Perceptions of principals. *Knowledge Quest, 32*(2), 10–13.

Blackett, K., & Klinger, D. (2006). Canadian study strengthens the link between school library staffing and student achievement and reading enjoyment. *School Library Media Activities Monthly, 23*(3), 56–58.

Brewer, S., & Milam, P. (1995). SLJ's technology survey. *School Library Journal, 51*(6), 49–53.

Campbell, B. S. (1994). *High school principal roles and implementation themes for main-streaming information literacy instruction* (Doctoral dissertation). University of Connecticut, Storrs, CT.

Campbell, J. (1991). *Principal-school library media relations as perceived by selected North Carolina elementary principals and school library media specialists* (Doctoral dissertation). University of North Carolina, Chapel Hill, NC.

Common Core State Standards Initiative. (2010). *Preparing America's students for college and career*. Retrieved from www.corestandards.org.

Edwards, K. K. (1989). Principals' perceptions of librarians: A survey. *School Library Journal, 35*(5), 28–31.

Greene, J. C., & Caracelli, V. J. (1997). *Advances in mixed-method evaluation: The challenges and benefits of integrating diverse paradigms*. San Francisco: Josey-Bass.

Hall, G. E., & Hord, S. M. (2006). *Implementing change: Patterns, principles, and potholes*. Boston: Allyn and Bacon.

Harada, V. H., & Yoshina, J. M. (2005). *Assessing learning: Librarians and teachers as partners*. Westport, CT: Libraries Unlimited.

Hartzell, G. (2002). The principals' perceptions of school libraries and teacher-librarians. *School Libraries Worldwide, 8*(1), 92–110.

Harvey, Carl, II. (2008, December). Principal perspective, Part 2: The library media program. *School Library Media Activities Monthly, 25*(4), 53–55.

Hatch, J. A. (2002). *Doing qualitative research in educational settings.* Albany, NY: State University of New York Press.

ISTE. (2007). *The national educational technology standards for students: The next generation.* Washington, D.C.: Author. Retrieved from www.iste.org/Content/Naviga tionMenu/NETS/NETSRefresh Project/NETS_Refresh.htm

Kachel, D. E. (2003). Partners for success: A school library advocacy training program for principals. *Knowledge Quest, 32*(2), 17–19.

Kramer, P. (2011, September/October). Common core and school libarians: An interview with Joyce Karon. *School Library Monthly, 28*(1), 8–10.

Kuhlthau, C. C., Maniotes, L. K., & Caspari, A. K. (2007). *Guided inquiry: Learning in the 21st century.* Westport, CT: Libraries Unlimited.

Lance, K., & Loertscher, D. (2001). Proof of power: Recent research on the impact of school library media programs on the academic achievement of U.S. public school students. *ERIC Digests.* (ED 456861). Retrieved from http://www.ericdigests .org/2002-2/proof.htm

Lau, D. (2002, September). What does your boss think about you? *School Library Journal, 48*(9), 52–55.

Marzano, R. J., Pickering, D. J., & Pollock, J. E. (2001). *Classroom instruction that works: Research-based strategies for increasing student achievement.* Alexandria, VA: ASCD.

McCracken, A. (2001). *School library media specialists' perceptions of practice and importance of roles described in information power.* Chicago: ALA. Retrieved from http:// www.ala.org/ala/mgrps/divs/aasl/aaslpubsandjournals/slmrb/slmrcontents/volume 42001/mccracken.cfm

McNeil, A., & Wilson, P. P. (1999–2000). Preparing principals for the leadership role in library media centers. *Applied Educational Research Journal, 12*(2), 21–27.

Oberg, D., Hay, L., & Henri, J. (2000). The role of the principal in an information literate school community: Cross-country comparisons from an international research project. *School Library Media Research, 3.* Retrieved from http://www.ala.org/ala/ mgrps/divs/aasl/aaslpubsandjournals/slmrb/slmrcontents/volume32000/principal. cfm

O'Neal, A. J. (2004). Administrators' and media specialists' perceptions of the roles of media specialists in the schools' instructional programs: Implications for instructional administration. *Journal of Education for Library and Information Science, 45*(4), 286–306.

Partnership for 21st century skills. (2004). Tucson, AZ: Author. Retrieved from www.21stcenturyskills.org/

Pressley, M., & McCormick, C. (1995). *Cognition, teaching, and assessment.* New York: Harper Collins.

Rose, K. E. (2002). *Profiles in success: The leadership role of the principal as initiator, facilitator, and sustainer of change in Blue Ribbon elementary schools in Illinois* (Doctoral dissertation). Northern Illinois University, Dekalb, IL.

Seidman, I. (1998). *Interviewing as qualitative research* (2nd ed.). New York: Teacher's College Press.

Senge, P. M. (1999). *The dance of change: The challenges of sustaining momentum in learning organizations.* New York: Doubleday.

Smith, M. E. (2002, October). The myths of change management. *Performance Improvement, 41*(9), 30–32.

Todd, R., & Kuhlthau, C. (2005a). Student learning through Ohio school libraries, Part1: How effective school libraries help students. *School Libraries Worldwide, 11*(1), 63–88.

Todd, R., & Kuhlthau, C. (2005b). Student learning through Ohio school libraries, Part 2: Faculty perceptions of effective school libraries. *School Libraries Worldwide, 11*(1), 89–110.

Todd, R., Kuhlthau, C., & Heinstrom, J. (2005). *Impact of school libraries on student learning*. Institute of Museum and Library Services Leadership Grant Project Report. Retrieved from http://cissl.scils.rutgers.edu/research/imls

Whelan, D. L. (2003). Why isn't information literacy catching on? *School Library Journal, 49*(9), 50–53.

Wilson, P., & Blake, M. (1993, September/October). A study and a plan for partnership. *Emergency Librarian, 21*(1), 19–24.

Wilson, P., & Lyders, J. A. (2001). *Leadership for today's school library: A handbook for the school library media specialist and the school principal.* Westport, CT: Greenwood.

Zmuda, A., & Harada, V. H. (2008). *Librarians as learning specialists: Meeting the learning imperative for the 21st century.* Westport, CT: Libraries Unlimited.

8

A CONTENT ANALYSIS OF SCHOOL LIBRARIAN CONFERENCES: A SEARCH FOR EMPOWERING PROFESSIONAL DEVELOPMENT

Judi Moreillon

INTRODUCTION: CONTENT OF PROFESSIONAL DEVELOPMENT CONFERENCE OFFERINGS

This research study originated as an effort to solve a teaching problem and expanded into a larger concern for the school librarian profession, namely the content of professional development activities offered via state-level school librarian conferences. When a professional organization, in this case the American Association of School Librarians (AASL), releases new guidelines, it is important for state-level organizations to disseminate the goals and objectives of the national organization. In the summer of 2009, AASL released *Empowering learners: Guidelines for school library programs* (AASL, 2009), hereafter referred to as *EL*. This document spells out the five roles that school librarians must practice in order to facilitate effective 21st-century library programs.

Utilizing a stratified random sample, the researchers conducted a content analysis of conferences held in the 2010–2011 academic year. The researchers developed and tested a domain matrix based on *EL* descriptions of four of the five roles. (The leader role is embedded in the other four roles.) They then used the matrix to analyze the titles and descriptions of 12 conference program offerings. The results of the study showed that state-level conference-sponsored professional development is neither balanced nor aligned with the *EL*-defined roles and priorities for school librarians.

A LINE OF INQUIRY TO IMPROVE TEACHING IN HIGHER EDUCATION

How does teaching inform research and research inform teaching in higher education? Researchers are in a perpetual state of seeking, asking, and investigating researchable questions. Sometimes a question or problem will arise when a researcher makes connections between a new study published in the literature or an emerging trend and her own research interests. In addition to scholarship, most researchers are also responsible for teaching university students so questions related to teaching also arise. The content analysis study that is the subject of this chapter arose out of a teaching dilemma. The researchers were motivated to pursue a line of inquiry to improve education for school librarian graduate students. In the process, they shared the results of their study within the larger school librarian community in hopes of shedding light on a challenge, namely the content of professional development through conference participation.

In the United States, classroom teacher preparation and proficiency are timely topics. Researchers offer many strategies for linking student achievement to teacher quality (Tucker & Stronge, 2005). Some studies show that students who perform well on standardized achievement tests were taught by effective classroom teachers (Hanushek, 2011; Haycock & Crawford, 2008; Pascopella, 2006). A value-added approach is being applied to the study of educator proficiency (Isenberg & Hock, 2011). In fact, many school districts are tying teachers' pay to students' performance on standardized tests (Gonring, Teske, & Jupp, 2007; Stronge, Gareis, & Little, 2006). The shared belief in all of these studies is that students learn more in the company of excellent teachers.

In K-12 schools today, leadership is often described in terms of student achievement. School librarians, like classroom teachers, specialists, and administrators, must be part of the instructional team that makes a measurable impact on student learning. Researchers in our field call on school librarians to take instructional leadership roles and to adopt evidence-based practice in order to document student outcomes that result from learning through the library program (Pappas, 2008; Todd, 2003, 2008).

In this context, the AASL published *EL* (AASL, 2009) and delineated practices necessary to meet the needs of 21st-century learners. In *EL*, AASL spells out and prioritizes the five roles that school librarians must effectively enact in order to empower library users: leader, instructional partner, information specialist, teacher, and program administrator. It is essential, then, for AASL to disseminate information about new guidelines to practitioners in the field. In addition, the association must also ensure that practitioners fully understand how to implement and use the guidelines in order to improve practice (Sawchuk, 2010). State-level conferences are one strategy. In addition to offering professional development for practitioners, these conference sessions have the potential to expand learning opportunities for preservice school librarian attendees as well.

TOPIC AND PROBLEM OF CONFERENCE PROFESSIONAL DEVELOPMENT CONTENT

How do preservice and in-service school librarians learn how to enact the five roles described in *EL?* Learning and practicing these roles in the university classroom is important, but professional development must be available beyond coursework. Librarian educators and practitioners alike acknowledge the value of conference attendance as an accepted form of professional development for knowledge and skill development as well as networking purposes (Alaimo, 2004; Franklin & Stephens, 2008; Laughlin, 2010; Morse, 2008; Natarajan, 2008; Needham, 2008; Simmons & Fenton, 2010). After reviewing the literature on library and information science conferences, Harrison (2010) concluded that they serve as unique forms of professional development unavailable through other venues for continuing education.

One of the researchers involved in this study offered master's candidates course assignment credit for attending and reporting on a state-library conference experience.

When the researcher looked at conference offerings, she was unsure that candidates would avail themselves of the types of sessions that would significantly impact their professional development. Along with her colleague, the researchers wondered if state-level school library conference sessions indeed support the goals and objectives of the national organization, in this case, the five roles outlined in *EL*. They also wondered whether or not the number of sessions reflects the relative importance of each role as delineated in *EL*.

What kinds of professional development do preservice and practicing school librarians need in order to make a difference in student achievement? *EL* brings the association's previous guidelines *Information power: Building partnerships for learning* (AASL & AECT, 1998) into line with societal and educational change. *EL* focuses school librarians' contributions on partnering with stakeholders to make improvements in learning and teaching. In addition, AASL recognizes the increasing need for librarians to practice the "leader" role, which was added to the other four roles previously described in AASL guidelines documents. Serving as leaders, school librarians should be positioned to accept the "challenges and opportunities to empower learning through their roles as instructional partners, information specialists, teachers, and program administrators" (AASL, 2009, p. 46).

AASL has taken several steps to disseminate the guidelines. First, the association initiated Learning4Life (L4L), an implementation plan to disseminate both *EL* and the *Standards for the 21st century learner* (AASL, 2007). Before this study was conducted and the conferences under investigation had been held, AASL offered L4L and other sessions focused on the new guidelines at the 2009 AASL National Conference, the 2010 and 2011 ALA Midwinter meetings, the 2010 Annual Conferences, and the 2010 Fall Forum. However, many school librarian practitioners and preservice candidates are unable to travel to take advantage of the national association's professional development opportunities. A greater number are more likely to attend state-level conferences.

At the time of this writing, school librarian positions are threatened across the United States, Canada, and Australia. When state- and district-level budgets are cut, class size grows and educators who are not assigned to teach a specific number of students for each period of the day can be viewed as "nice-to-have" extras. In the United States, national initiatives such as White House petitions in support of school library programs and legislative efforts such as the Strengthen Kids' Interest in Learning and Libraries Act are attempts to stem the elimination of professional school librarian positions and stave off drastic cuts to school library program budgets.

RESEARCH QUESTIONS

The purpose of this content analysis study was to determine the degree to which state-level conference sessions for school librarians support professional development related to the five roles identified in *EL*. The researchers studied conference programs to learn about the options available to school library candidates and practitioners through the keynote speeches, workshops, and concurrent sessions in a sampling of conferences offered in the 2010–2011 academic year.

R.1. How do conference offerings align with and support the five roles of the school librarian as outlined in *EL* and how do these differ across conference types?

R.2. What are the major topics of state conference offerings available to school librarians and how do these offerings differ according to the conference type?

R.3. How do state-level library conference offerings support school librarians' development as leaders, the newest role defined by the national association, and does this support differ across conference types?

Through these questions, the researchers sought to learn the degree to which state-level conference professional development opportunities met the priorities for best practice set out by the national association.

In the school library field, research repeatedly points to the incongruence between guidelines for best practice and enactment of those guidelines by practitioners (McCracken, 2001). Studies have indicated misunderstandings in the roles of school librarians (Craver, 1986; McCracken, 2001; Pickard, 1993). Ervin (1989) found that although librarians believed in the roles as prescribed by *Information power: Guidelines for school library media centers* (AASL and AECT, 1988), they only practiced those roles occasionally. Both Craver (1986) and Pickard (1993) noted that practice seems to lag 10 years behind the roles as described in the literature. Neuman's (2001) study reported on the views of a panel of library stakeholders and found that the areas of teaching and learning and program administration seem to pose the greatest challenges for practicing librarians. McCracken (2001) studied school librarians' perceptions and practice of the roles described in *Information power* (AASL and AECT, 1988, 1998): instructional consultant/instructional partner, information specialist, teacher, and program administrator. She found that practitioners in the field believed that the roles were all important, but that they were unable to practice them for various reasons.

In the current financial and educational climate, can the profession afford a 10-year lag time between guidelines and implementation? Can school library advocates continue to circulate petitions and seek state and national legislation to preserve school libraries and professional librarian positions if practitioners are unable to enact best practices in their libraries? One possible use of results of this study is to encourage state- and district-level school library leaders and building-level practitioners to step up implementation of the *EL* guidelines in order to strengthen the impact of librarians' and library programs' on student achievement.

LITERATURE REVIEW

In a search of the literature, the researchers found relatively few studies in the library and information sciences field related to professional conferences. Several studies have analyzed national association conference offerings (Garner, Davidson, & Williams, 2008; Julien, 2007; Snelson & Talar, 1991). One study analyzed the offerings at Canadian provincial library conferences (Wilson, 2010). The researchers found just one outdated study that focused specifically on school library conferences (Eisenberg, Spitzer, Kingsley, & Darby, 1990).

There is, however, a current and growing body of research that suggests the positive impact of school librarians on K-12 student achievement. In a recent study conducted by Lance and Hofshire (2011), the researchers found that the presence of a school librarian in elementary schools correlates to higher standardized test reading scores or a quicker rise in scores among fourth-grade students. More specifically, research suggests that planning with teachers, co-teaching, teaching information and communication technologies, and providing in-services to teachers are among the library predictors of students' academic achievement on standardized tests, particularly in reading and language arts (Achterman, 2010; 2008, pp. 62–65).

Research has been conducted that relates to specific roles. Some researchers identify the information specialist role as having significant potential for school librarian improvement and leadership (Everhart, 2007; Everhart, Mardis, & Johnston, 2011; Johnston, 2011). Kachel et al. (2011) summarized the research findings of the school library impact studies (Library Research Service, 2011) and identified a positive correlation between classroom–library collaboration for instruction and increased student achievement in 15 out of the 21 studies they reviewed. Mardis and Hoffman (2008) found a positive relationship between middle school science collections, collaboration between librarians and science teachers, and students' achievement in science.

Developing instructional partnerships is one way school librarians enact a leadership role in their schools (Haycock, 2010; Moreillon, 2007, 2012; Todd, 2011; Zmuda & Harada, 2008). Learning about leadership in their coursework can develop graduate students' self-perceptions as leaders (Smith, 2011). When they enact the leader role, school librarians have the opportunity to serve as change agents in their schools (Dow, 2010).

METHODOLOGY: CONTENT ANALYSIS

Duke and Martin (2011) identified five quality indicators for a content analysis study. First, researchers must offer a clear purpose and rationale for their study. Second, they must thoroughly describe the sample and its context. Third, it is incumbent upon researchers to define the variables through referencing the rationale for the study or the theoretical framework. Fourth, there should be at least two coders who reach a high rate of inter-rater reliability. Finally, the researchers must develop a set of procedures to make valid inferences from the content under examination. This study meets these criteria.

Preparation of the Analysis

For this problem-based content analysis study, the researchers used an official document of school librarianship, *EL*. They developed a domain matrix (Figure 8.1) based on four of the five roles as topic domains. (The leader role is embedded in the other four roles.). They also developed subcategories in each domain using the descriptions of the roles outlined in *EL*.

Using conference keynotes, workshops, and concurrent session titles and descriptions as sampling units, the researchers field tested the matrix on three state conference programs held in the previous year until they reached an 85-percent interrater reliability. Each researcher analyzed conference programs independently from the others. Then they met to compare their coding. For any discrepancies, they first negotiated the role to which the session applied and then the subcategory into which it fit. In all cases, two of the three researchers agreed and the session was coded with the majority decision. When the researchers did not reach consensus, they noted that session as a "disagreement." It took three trials and revisions to the matrix before the researchers consistently reached the 85-percent interrater goal.

Category	Code	Topic	Details/Notes
Instructional partner	1.0		
	1.1	Policy, practice, or curricula development	Including in-service and/or professional development for teachers
	1.2	Collaborative assignments matched to academic standards	If technology not involved
	1.3	Collaborative assignments promoting critical thinking	
	1.4	Collaborative assignments promoting technology/ information literacy	
	1.5	Collaborative assignments promoting social skills/cultural competencies	
	1.6	Instructional design: Objectives, goals, and assessments	
	1.7	Learning commons: 24/7 learning environment	
Information specialist	2.0		
	2.1	Technology tools to supplement school resources	Including databases, not hardware
	2.2	Creation of engaging technological learning tasks	Activities in which the students engage, Skype, and student-created book trailers
	2.3	Communication tools: Students, teachers, and global learning community	Cloud computing, user choices, Web 2.0, and teacher-created book trailers
	2.4	Emerging technologies	Trends, Second Life, applications, and QR codes
	2.5	Information literacy	Citation generators
	2.6	Software and hardware evaluation	Free, if software stored on library computers/devices
	2.7	Technology data analysis	
	2.8	Information ethics/copyright	Cyberbullying, netiquette, and Internet safety
Teacher	3.0		
	3.1	Promotion of critical thinking	
	3.2	Literacy skills	Including storytime, storytelling, readers' theater, oral history, and writing

(*Continued*)

Category	Code	Topic	Details/Notes
	3.3	Research skills	Including content-area lessons, content-area instructional design (objectives, goals, and assessment), and IL w/o technology
	3.4	Pleasure reading motivation	Including booktalks, reading incentive programs, new literature, live author visits, and book clubs
	3.5	Multiple reading formats: Graphic novels, periodicals, audiobooks, and eBooks	
	3.6	Peer learning	
	3.7	Trends in literature	
	3.8	Social/cultural competencies for students	
	3.9	Author/illustrator/poet talking about their own work	
Program administrator	4.0		
	4.1	Collection development/ collection management	Cataloging, vendors, and any tool that must be purchased
	4.2	Program mission, plan, and policies	Intellectual freedom, disaster preparedness, social/cultural competencies that affect policies and standards, and broad educational issues
	4.3	Staff management	
	4.4	Budget	Grant writing and grants
	4.5	Physical and virtual space	Decisions made "behind the scenes" that impact users' virtual access
	4.6	Partnerships with stakeholders and sister organizations	PTA, NEA, etc.
	4.7	Partnerships with other librarians/professional associations	Library-only associations
	4.8	Continuing education	
	4.9	Personal skills: Communication, interviewing	
	4.10	Marketing/advocacy	

Figure 8.1 Domain Matrix

Through the testing process, the subtopics under each role were further refined. The researchers returned to *EL* and clarified for themselves and each other that they had fully described each subtopic and could use it consistently to categorize conference sessions. It was particularly important that three researchers conducted this study. When they did not reach consensus, the uneven number helped the investigators determine a category based on two out of the three researchers' codes.

Sample

The researchers utilized a stratified random sample to analyze 12 conferences sponsored or cosponsored by school library state associations. To identify the sample, they created a matrix of all state-library conferences in the United States and organized it by three conference types: state-level school library association-only conferences (SLOCs), state-level association conferences in which school librarians were a unit within a larger library organization (FLACs), and conferences in which state-level school librarian organizations partnered with a nonlibrary association (NLOCs). In all cases, the NLOCs were joint school library–technology association conferences.

Using a random number, the investigators identified conferences for inclusion in the sample by counting off to that number. They secured the 2010–2011 conference programs from each of the state organizations in the sample via the association's website or by emailing a contact given on the site. If they were unable to access a program after two attempts, they repeated the sampling and secured a replacement program. They repeated this process until they reached approximately 24 percent of the state conferences in each category. The final sample in each of the three conferences categories included SLOCs ($n = 7$), FLACs ($n = 4$), and NLOCs ($n = 1$).

For the state-level association conferences in which school librarians sessions were mixed in with sessions targeted to other types of libraries and for the conference cosponsored with a technology association, the researchers identified all sessions with content that might inform a school librarian about school library–related issues. Sessions that were not clearly relevant to a school librarian audience were not analyzed. Also, the researchers counted and analyzed only the first instance of a session offered multiple times during a single conference.

All totaled, the researchers analyzed the titles and descriptions of 615 conference sessions. The researchers followed the procedures they established in the preparation phase of the study when they developed and field tested the domain matrix. Additionally, the researchers randomly selected one of the conference programs to reanalyze approximately 8 weeks after the initial analyses, which they independently recoded with 90 percent or greater agreement to the first analysis.

Findings

The researchers posited that the domain matrix they developed for this study could be used by other researchers and practitioners for similar analyses. In the article on which this chapter is based, the bulk of the investigators' analysis was "devoted to explanations and interpretations within the text" (Beck & Manuel, 2008, p. 61). To frame their discussion, they displayed their findings visually in tables that showed the number and percentages of program sessions across conference types, conference offerings alignment with four of the roles for school librarians, major subtopics presented in all state-library conference programs, and major topics showcased in each conference category.

The investigators found that the teacher role followed by the program administrator role were the roles most frequently showcased in conference offerings. Subtopics in the teacher role dominated SLOCs, program administrator topics were most predominant at FLACs, and information specialist role sessions were the most prevalent at NLOCs. The instructional partner role was underrepresented in all three conference categories and garnered only 6.69 percent of all of the offerings in the study sample. The researchers provided a rationale for not attempting to assess the leader role. They felt that a conference title and description was insufficient information to determine the session's potential to address the leader role. They also posited that the leader role is embedded in the other four roles.

IMPROVEMENT PLAN

In 2006, when representatives from each state affiliate participated in the AASL Vision Summit, these school librarian leaders ranked four of the five roles in this order: instructional partner, information specialist, teacher, and program administrator (AASL, 2009, p. 16). The findings from this content analysis suggest that state-level conferences are not in alignment with that vision. Conference programs in this sample were unbalanced in their offerings, and the instructional partner role was the least featured of all. If the national association's priorities for the future of the profession lie with the instructional partner role, then none of these conferences effectively promoted AASL's guidelines.

The researchers had several suggestions for improvement. First, in the future and in relationship to the original problem identified for this study, the researchers will ask graduate students who are attending conferences for course assignment "credit" to develop a professional development plan based on the five roles described in *EL* and their self-perceived needs before attending a conference. Students will be required to use the domain matrix to analyze the conference program and target specific sessions based on their professional development goals. The researchers will guide students to consider sessions that focus on the instructional partner and information specialist roles rather than focusing only on the more traditional roles of teacher and program administrator. They may also suggest sessions with the words "leader" or "leadership" in the title or description. In their reports and reflections on conference attendance, graduate students be asked to connect their professional development plans with their discussion of the content of the sessions they attended.

The domain matrix developed, tested, and utilized to analyze this random sample proved to be an effective tool for the researchers. Individual conference attendees can use the matrix to analyze conference programs and focus their conference-based professional development activities. State conference planning committees can use this instrument to analyze the content of their previous conferences. They can select or solicit specific types of conference programs for future conferences in order to balance offerings related to all of the roles. Planning committees can develop a strategy for considering how the "leader" role is addressed through their conference programs as well. Practitioners and researchers can also use this matrix to categorize their own conference proposals. They can consider including relevant keywords in their session descriptions in order to clarify the alignment of their proposals with national guidelines.

CONCLUSIONS: STATE-LEVEL CONFERENCES ARE IMPORTANT FOR EMPOWERING PROFESSIONAL DEVELOPMENT

On the basis of this study, the school librarian profession can consider which of the roles has the most potential to strengthen the work of practitioners in the field. If conferences privilege one or more roles over the others, how does that affect the dissemination of best practices? If conference presenters neglect one or more of the roles, what are the consequences? Are one or more roles most critical to enlisting advocates for school librarians or for preserving the profession? Do conference offerings signal the value placed on various aspects of school librarians' work? Even though library conference sessions are only a piece of the formal professional development picture for school librarians, they may indicate professional priorities and expand or limit the opportunities provided to improve our profession.

Professional development via library conferences is limited by program session offerings. If conference planners do not perceive that certain types of keynote, workshop, or session topics will attract participants, they may reject proposals that fail to align with their perceptions about what is needed to draw an audience. The researchers only had access to the program sessions that were selected by the conference program committees and published in the conference programs. Some program committees could have been composed of few or no school librarians and, therefore, may not have considered AASL's roles in the proposal selection.

Further research in the area of professional development provided at state-level conferences could include interviews with conference program committees and organizers to access their insider perspectives on the quality of sessions offered as well as issues related to selecting conference sessions from the proposals submitted. To further validate the domain matrix, it could be field tested with program committees, conference presenters, and participants in order to determine its usefulness to various stakeholder groups. A comparison between state-level and national conference offerings would also be fruitful.

State-level conferences are an important piece of the professional development puzzle for school librarians. National- and state-level associations, their governing bodies, and members of the school library community at large may be wise to consider the meaning and ramifications of unbalanced representation of the roles in conference offerings. When state-level conferences bring conference programs into alignment with national guidelines and priorities, more empowering professional development could be more accessible to a greater number of preservice and practicing school librarians alike.

REFERENCES

AASL. (2007). *Standards for the 21st century learner*. Chicago: American Library Association. Retrieved from http://ala.org/aasl/standards

AASL. (2009). *Empowering learners: Guidelines for school library media programs*. Chicago: American Library Association.

AASL and AECT. (1988). *Information power: Guidelines for school library media centers.* Chicago: American Library Association.

AASL and AECT. (1998). *Information power: Building partnerships for learning.* Chicago: American Library Association.

Achterman, D. L. (2008). *Haves, halves, and have-nots: School libraries and student achievement in California.* Denton, TX. UNT Digital Library. Retrieved from http://digital.library.unt.edu/ark:/67531/metadc9800/m1/

Achterman, D. L. (2010). Literacy leadership and the school librarian. In S. Coatney (Ed.), *The many faces of school library leadership* (pp. 67–84). Santa Barbara, CA: ABC-CLIO.

Alaimo, R. (2004). Top six reasons to attend a conference. *Knowledge Quest, 33*(1), 34–35.

Beck, S. E., & Manuel, K. (2008). *Practical research methods for librarians and information professions.* New York: Neal-Shuman.

Craver, K. W. (1986). The changing instructional role of the high school library media specialist: 1950–1984. *School Library Media Quarterly, 14*(4), 183–191.

Dow, M. (2010). Making schools better: School librarians' roles in aggressive reforms—What is our official position? *Knowledge Quest, 38*(5), 78–82.

Duke, N. K., & Martin, N. M. (2011). 10 things every literacy educator should know about research. *The Reading Teacher, 65*(1), 9–22.

Eisenberg, M. B., Spitzer, K. L., Kingsley, I., & Darby, C. (1990). *Trends & issues in library & information science 1990.* Syracuse, NY: ERIC Clearinghouse on Information Resources.

Ervin, D. (1989). The effect of experience, educational level, and subject area on the philosophical acceptance, the perceived assumption, and the perceived barriers to implementation of the instructional and curricular role of the school library media specialist. Doctoral dissertation, Univ. of South Carolina. *Dissertation Abstracts International, 50*(09A), 2767.

Everhart, N. (2007). Leadership: School library media specialists as effective school leaders. *Knowledge Quest, 35*(4), 54–57.

Everhart, N., Mardis, M., & Johnston, M. (2011). National Board Certified school librarians' leadership in technology integration: Results of a national survey. *School Library Media Research, 14.* Retrieved from http://www.ala.org/aasl/aaslpubsandjournals/slmrb/slmrcontents/volume14/everhart_mardis

Franklin, P., & Stephens, C. G. (2008). Membership matters! *School Library Media Activities Monthly, 24*(5), 42–44.

Garner, J., Davidson, K., & Williams, V. K. (2008). Identifying serials trends through twenty years of NASIG conference proceedings: A content analysis. *Serials Review, 34*(2), 88–103.

Gonring, P., Teske, P., & Jupp, B. (2007). *Pay-for-performance teacher compensation: An inside view of Denver's ProComp Plan.* Cambridge, MA: Harvard Education Press.

Hanushek, E. A. (2011). The economic value of higher teacher quality. *Economics of Education Review, 30*(3), 466–479.

Harrison, R. (2010). Unique benefits of conference attendance as a method of professional development for LIS professionals. *The Serials Librarian, 59*(3/4), 263–270.

Haycock, K. (2010). Leadership from the middle: Building influence for change. In S. Coatney (Ed.), *The many faces of school library leadership* (pp. 1–12). Santa Barbara, CA: Libraries Unlimited.

Haycock, K., & Crawford, C. (2008). Closing the teacher quality gap. *Educational Leadership, 65*(7), 14–19.

Isenberg, E., & Hock, H. (2011). *Measuring of value-added models for IMPACT and TEAM in DC public schools, 2010–2011 school year.* Washington, D.C.: Mathematica Policy Research.

Johnston, M. P. (2011). School librarians as technology integration leaders: Enablers and barriers to leadership enactment (Unpublished doctoral dissertation). The Florida State University, Tallahassee, FL.

Julien, H. (2007). The Association for Library and Information Science Education (ALISE): Past, present, future. *Education for Information, 25,* 131–140.

Kachel, D. E. et al. (2011). *School library research summarized: A graduate class project.* Mansfield, PA: School of Library & Information Technologies Department, Mansfield University.

Lance, K. C., & Hofschire, L. (2011, September 1). Something to shout about: New research shows that more librarians means higher reading scores. *School Library Journal.* Retrieved from http://www.schoollibraryjournal.com/slj/home/891612-312/something_to_shout_about_new.html.csp

Laughlin, K. (2010). Feasting on professional development. *Alki, 26*(2), 25–27.

Library Research Service. (2011). *School library impact studies.* Retrieved from http://www.lrs.org/impact.php

Mardis, M., & Hoffman, E. (2008). Collection and collaboration: Science in Michigan middle school media centers. *School Library Media Research, 10.* Retrieved from http://www.ala.org/aasl/aaslpubsandjournals/slmrb/slmrcontents/volume10/mardis_collectionandcollaboration

McCracken, A. (2001). School library media specialists' perceptions of practice and importance of roles described in *Information Power. School Library Media Research, 4.* Retrieved from http://www.ala.org/ala/mgrps/divs/aasl/aaslpubsandjournals/slmrb/slmrcontents/volume42001/mccracken.cfm

Moreillon, J. (2007). *Collaborative strategies for teaching reading comprehension: Maximizing your impact.* Chicago: American Library Association.

Moreillon, J. (2012). *Coteaching reading comprehension strategies in secondary schools: Maximizing your impact.* Chicago: American Library Association.

Morse, J. M. (2008). The side effects of conferences. *Qualitative Health Research, 18*(9), 159–160.

Natarajan, R. (2008). On attending conferences. *IEEE Computer, 41*(2), 107, 108.

Needham, M. (2008). From the president. *Florida Media Quarterly, 33*(3), 4.

Neuman, D. (2001). Re-visioning school library media programs for the future. *Journal of Education for Library and Information Science, 42*(2), 96–115.

Pappas, M. L. (2008). Designing learning for evidence-based practice. *School Library Media Activities Monthly, 24*(5), 20–23.

Pascopella, A. (2006). Teachers are still the most important tool. *District Administration, 42*(8), 20–23.

Pickard, P. W. (1993). The instructional consultant role of the school library media specialist. *School Library Media Quarterly, 21*(2), 115–121.

Sawchuk, S. (2010). Teaching, curricular challenges looming. *Education Week, 29*(17), 16–19.

Simmons, R., & Fenton, J. (2010). Why we attend WLA conferences. *Alki, 26*(3), 5.

Smith, D. (2011). Educating preservice school librarians to lead: A study of self-perceived transformational leadership behaviors. *School Library Media Research, 14.* Retrieved from http://www.ala.org/aasl/aaslpubsandjournals/slmrb/slmrcontents/volume14/smith

Snelson, P., & Talar, S. A. (1991). Content analysis of ACRL conference papers. *College & Research Libraries, 52*(5), 466–472.

Stronge, J. H., Gareis, C. R., & Little, C. A. (2006). Teacher pay, teacher quality: Attracting, developing, and retaining the best teachers. Thousand Oaks, CA: Corwin Press.

Todd, R. J. (2003). Irrefutable evidence. *School Library Journal, 49*(4), 52–55.

Todd, R. J. (2008). A question of evidence. *Knowledge Quest, 37*(2), 16–21.

Todd, R. J. (2011). "Look for me in the whirlwind": Actions, outcomes and evidence. In D. V. Loertscher & B. Wools (Eds.), *Knowledge building in the learning commons: Moving from research to practice to close the achievement gap* (pp. 34–50). Conference Proceedings of the Treasure Mountain Research Retreat #17,Osseo, MN. Spring, TX: LMC Source.

Tucker, P. D., & Stronge, J. H. (2005). *Linking teacher evaluation and student learning.* Alexandria, VA: Association for Curriculum and Supervision.

Wilson, V. (2010). Something for everyone? A content analysis of provincial library association conference sessions. *Partnership: The Canadian Journal of Library and Information Practice and Research, 5*(1), 1–13.

Zmuda, A., & Harada, V. H. (2008). *Librarians as learning specialists: Meeting the imperative for the 21st century.* Santa Barbara, CA: Libraries Unlimited.

9

SCHOOL-BASED TECHNOLOGY INTEGRATION AND SCHOOL LIBRARIAN LEADERSHIP

Marcia A. Mardis and Nancy Everhart

INTRODUCTION: SOLUTIONS TO TECHNOLOGY-RELATED SCHOOL CHALLENGES

Cooperative inquiry (CI), a form of participatory qualitative research used in community building and social work has been, to date, unused with school librarians and in very few schools. Through the lens of formative leadership theory, the researchers studied the ability of six new school librarians trained in CI and leadership, to assemble collaborative problem-solving school teams to identify and institute solutions to technology-related school challenges. Participants experienced various degrees of success in the CI process based on internal and external factors, but most gained positive recognition among their colleagues by exhibiting traits of formative leaders.

TECHNOLOGY INTEGRATION

Technology integration is an increasingly crucial element of teaching and learning that requires school-based leadership in order to be consistent, relevant, and a connector between various aspects of students' learning experiences. Many theorists and researchers have argued that school librarians are well positioned to assume a leadership role in technology integration (e.g., Everhart & Dresang, 2007; Hughes-Hassell & Hanson-Baldauf, 2008; McCracken, 2001; Vansickle, 2000). School librarians have been continually directed to assume leadership roles in their schools via the professional guidelines of state, national, and international organizations. However, research-based strategies to successfully exercise technology integration leadership are yet to be developed.

Library education has traditionally been at the forefront of embracing new technologies, but only in the last decade or so have library and information studies (LIS) programs been developed that focus on leadership—particularly in a school library context. The Institute of Museum and Library and Services (IMLS) has served as a catalyst for leadership education vis-à-vis National Leadership Grants and the Laura Bush 21st Century Librarian Program. Project LEAD is one such

IMLS program, developed and implemented over three phases, at the Florida State University's School of Library and Information Studies.

Phase one of Project LEAD involved constructing a 12-credit leadership curriculum for school librarians with emphases on technology integration, instructional leadership, literature appreciation, and general leadership. Once the curriculum was developed, in phase two, 30 outstanding teacher leaders throughout Florida were selected for a cohort that completed the curriculum as part of a 45-credit master's degree. The cohort structure, along with the grant funding, allowed for additional leadership opportunities for participants such as attending a state and a national conference and summer leadership workshops with recognized experts on campus. Given all the advantages of the Project LEAD program, the question remained: Would graduates enact a leadership role when they took a position as a school librarian? In a study of the Project LEAD cohort (Smith, 2011), it was revealed that the one area in which school librarians felt most confident to lead was technology integration; so it was determined to focus on this leadership as an area for further research.

To answer the question of school librarians' abilities to translate coursework and observations of technology integration leadership into their own practice, IMLS funded a follow-up project, Project Leadership in Action (LIA). Project LIA was a two-phased project. The first phase included surveying National Board Certified and other school librarians to determine the extent to which they were able to engage in technology leadership activities. Initial analyses of survey results (Everhart, Mardis, & Johnson, 2010) indicated that, overall, most school librarians not only were successful in exercising some technology leadership, but were also often challenged in realizing their full leadership potential due to situational and external factors.

The second phase of Project LIA, reported here, was a series of in-depth case studies in which six graduates of Project LEAD were followed into their first school librarian positions to determine their abilities to act as leaders. Armed with a small stipend to acquire necessary materials with their work, these new school librarians were tasked with assembling a school-based team to investigate an agreed upon technology problem. Because of their new status as school librarians, it was acknowledged that their leadership would be developing and the research would likely reflect formative stages.

To organize and guide their investigations, the school librarians used CI, a leadership-in-action research methodology that includes leadership development as part of the process, as it was determined to be uniquely suited to answer the research question. CI research aims to engage and empower practitioners as they partner with academics in documenting, interpreting, and disseminating insights from their own experience (RCLA, n.d.) and is not known to be applied in any library setting. Project LIA provided an excellent arena in which to test this powerful research methodology, which supports leadership in action. Their experiences form the foundation to answer the driving research question and related subquestions of this study.

RESEARCH QUESTIONS

How can CI methodology be used to evaluate the outcomes of education for school librarianship leadership in technology integration?

1. To what extent are new school librarians able to exercise formative leadership to organize and convene CI groups in their schools?
2. What are the factors common to successful CI process led by school librarians?
3. How do new school librarians feel about the CI process integrated with their own leadership styles and abilities?

The lack of application of this extremely relevant methodology and research findings to the LIS field provides the opportunity to increase the research capacity of LIS. Many LIS schools desire and need to conduct studies on the impact of their educational programs that extend beyond alumni surveys. Because it is prohibitive to conduct intensive case studies at graduates' place of employment, CI may provide a compromise solution.

THEORETICAL FRAMEWORK: FORMATIVE LEADERSHIP THEORY

Formative leadership theory, developed by Ash and Persall (2000), is based on the belief that there are numerous leadership possibilities and many leaders within a school. Leadership is not role-specific, reserved only for administrators; rather the job of the school leader is to fashion learning opportunities for the faculty and staff in order that they might develop into productive leaders. This theory of leadership supports the view of the school librarian as leader. It is grounded in the belief that educators should enhance not only student learning but also the learning of the adults within the school.

The formative leader must possess a high level of facilitation skills because team inquiry and learning and collaborative problem solving are essential ingredients of this leadership approach. Imagining future possibilities; examining shared beliefs; asking questions; collecting, analyzing, and interpreting data; and engaging the faculty in meaningful conversation about teaching and learning are all formative leadership behaviors. In order to determine how library education can prepare school librarians for a leadership role in technology integration, this theory guided this research.

In light of the possibilities and challenges inherent in technology integration leadership, this study seeks to explore ways in which school librarians can effectively assert, enact, and document participatory practices designed to respond to consensually identified school needs within the context of existing school culture. By integrating the lens of formative leadership to view the CI process in school librarian–led technology integration, this study lends insight into the education, skills, and dispositions needed to be successful in this role.

LITERATURE REVIEW

With increased demands for school librarians to accept technology leadership roles crucial to interactive technologies and a participatory culture in schools (Asselin, 2005), there is a need for research-based strategies to enable them to lead a new generation of learners. It is necessary to explore the concept of leadership in schools, focusing particularly on formative leadership and the leadership roles of school librarians as well as technology integration and its intersection with leadership.

Leadership in Schools

Today's information and technology–rich environments require schools to be true learning organizations where all students have the opportunity to engage in challenging and interesting academic work as a result of instructional strategies and cutting-edge technologies. Leaders of these organizations have to create learning opportunities that enable the faculty and staff to participate in anticipating and leading productive change.

To be effective instructional leaders, all members of the school community must lead, expect leadership, and facilitate leadership skills in others. The resulting climate is called formative leadership. According to Ash and Persall (2000), the principles underlying formative leadership theory are

1. Team learning, productive thinking, and collaborative problem solving should replace control mechanisms, top-down decision-making, and enforcement of conformity.
2. Teachers should be viewed as leaders and school principals as leaders of leaders. Leaders must be viewed as asking the right kinds of questions rather than knowing all the answers.
3. Trust should drive our working relationships. Leaders must not assume that the faculty, staff, and students will try their best to do their worst. The leader's job is to drive out fear.
4. Leaders should move from demanding conformity and compliance to encouraging and supporting innovation and creativity.
5. Leaders should focus on people and processes, rather than on paperwork and administrative minutiae. Time should be spent on value-added activities.
6. Leaders should be customer-focused and servant-based. Faculty and staff are the direct customers of the principal, and the most important function of the principal is to serve his or her customers.
7. Leaders should create networks that foster two-way communication rather than channels that direct the flow of information in only one direction.
8. Formative leadership requires proximity, visibility, and being close to the customer. Leaders should wander about the school and the surrounding community, listening and learning, asking questions, building relationships, and identifying possibilities.
9. Formative leadership is empowering the people within the school to do the work and then protecting them from unwarranted outside interference.
10. Formative leadership requires the ability to operate in an environment of uncertainty, constantly learning how to exploit systemic change, rather than maintaining the status quo (para. 11).

School Librarians and Leadership

A school library leader can be defined as someone who proactively inspires or engages others to achieve shared goals within a school. The American Association of School Librarian's (AASL, 2009b) strategic plan seeks to have school librarians universally recognized as indispensable leaders and the leadership role is prescribed for the first time in the *Empowering learners: Guidelines for school library programs* developed by AASL (2009a). These guidelines delineated multiple opportunities for school librarians to act as leaders and collaborators and notes that school librarians display leadership through modeling and promoting the use of technology for learning. School librarians are charged "to play a leading role in weaving such skills throughout the curriculum so that all members of the school community are effective users of ideas and information" (AASL, 2009a, p. 49). It is this "weaving" or the integration of technology into the curricular areas where the school librarian based on their knowledge of pedagogical principles, their interdisciplinary perspective on the school curriculum, their training as information experts, and their experience in forging cooperative partnerships with classroom teachers can serve as a leader and valuable asset to their schools (Asselin, 2005; Vansickle, 2000).

Despite the abundance of research that has suggested the need for and the importance of school librarians to be a proactive leaders in schools, the leadership role of the school librarian in technology integration has been left undefined for school administrators, teachers, and, often, for the school librarians themselves (Asselin, 2005; Everhart & Dresang, 2007).

The formative leadership role expressed by AASL is supported by research. For example, the compendium of statewide studies of school libraries and student achievement, *School Libraries Work* (Scholastic Research Results, 2008), indicated that there have been at least 16 statewide studies that examined leadership as a school librarian role. According to these studies, and many others completed over a substantial period of time (Achterman, 2008; Mardis, 2007; McCracken, 2001; Slygh, 2000), school librarians who acted as leaders had programs that impacted student success in reading and science, thereby making school libraries important components of schools.

For many school librarians, leadership education prepares them to take on leadership. The Project LEAD curriculum was developed specifically to teach leadership skills to school librarians using the guidelines established by the National Board for Professional Teaching Standards (Everhart & Dresang, 2007). The final evaluation of the program established that school librarians could be taught leadership skills and how to apply those skills to their practice. The preservice school librarians who participated in the program also noted that using technology training was a key element in the leadership development (Smith, 2011).

METHODOLOGY: PARTICIPATORY RESEARCH

Participatory research is a form of qualitative research that best allows researchers to develop interpersonal relationships during studies. It takes place when the researcher collecting the data actively participates in the intervention. Generally speaking, participatory research concentrates on creating meaningful experiences during the research process (Ospina, Dodge, Godsoe, Minieri, Reza, & Schall, 2004). CI, the method upon which this project is based, is a form of participatory research designed for institutions responsible with social transformation, like schools. CI is an emergent process that contributes to the acquisition and creation of knowledge grounded in participatory research practice, deepens the leadership potential of all participants, and strengthens trusting and collaborative partnerships and relationships among group members (Oates, 2002). It is designed to bridge the perspectives and approaches of diverse stakeholders in a situation (Ospina, El Hadidy, & Hofmann-Pinilla, 2008); in this case, the CI process is being used to merge the participation of school librarians, teachers, technology personnel, administrators, and other key school stakeholders in solving a mutually agreed-upon problem: What is an issue facing our school community that can be addressed with technology? CI participants go through the phases of inquiry together multiple times, cycling between action and reflection in an effort to "heal" their divergent points-of-view into a common solution.

CI fosters mutual respect among its coinvestigators because all participants are involved in making research decisions; there is no particular individual leading the study. The opinions and reactions of all participants are equally important; in CI, everyone is a coinvestigator into the research problem and they rely on one another to complete the research process. The use of cycles of action and reflection aids study participants in understanding their biases and how they influence the products of their research. CI adds a humanistic quality to scientific inquiry by seeking the opinions of those who are truly experiencing the research questions. Participants often find their research creates empathetic connections (Kovari et al., n.d.).

The experience of CI requires coinvestigators to share how they react to particular situations and sensitive topics. As such, coinvestigators must build a trustworthy rapport. While some researchers may regard these experiences as insignificant and not objective, according to Reason and Heron (2004, para. 48), researchers can "develop their attention so they can look at themselves—their way of being, their intuitions and imaginings, their beliefs and actions—critically and in this way improve the quality of their claims to four-fold knowing." Reason and Heron (2004) define this process as "critical subjectivity." Critical subjectivity is an additional strength of CI. With critical subjectivity, coinvestigators can be objective without having to disregard their personal experiences. Instead, coinvestigators use their personal knowledge and the experiences they have shared with others to gain an authentic perspective of a particular issue along with others who are involved in the same task.

Because CI is a methodology and a method, the philosophy behind CI guides the way data are collected; group members share the values of the endeavor and then, in concert, compile information and develop strategies for implementing solutions, gathering data, and making adjustments to enactment.

PROCEDURE

This study reports the experiences of six school librarians who are leading CI projects in their schools. The participants were recent graduates of the Florida State University's School of Library and Information Studies and in their first year as school librarians. All of the participants had been teachers for at least three years.

The first phase of the project, training in the CI process, was coordinated over a two-day period by a team of two facilitators from the Research Center for Leadership in Action (RCLA), Wagner School of Public Service, New York University (NYU)—nationally recognized experts in CI. The training mirrored some of the dynamics of CI as well as offered experience with the tools and methods that the school librarian facilitators would employ during the CI process in their schools. The NYU facilitators introduced fundamental principles of CI as an action research and adult learning methodology along with concepts of how to start a CI group, how to choose an inquiry question, the role of action and reflection, and the importance of holding the validation principles through the inquiry. An exercise of a mini-inquiry resulted in an overarching question: "What is an issue in our school that might be addressed with technology?" Examples were provided on how each school librarian facilitator could tailor the research question to their own site and methods for moving the inquiry ahead.

Several hours into the training, the facilitators noted discomfort among the group that led to a discussion of some of the anxieties members of the research team were holding regarding CI facilitation. The group expressed the need to have more clarity on the task ahead, the time frame, and the outcomes of the project. With the help of RCLA facilitators, they identified possible challenges they might face in their schools—lack of time, managing authority and power, and lack of clarity from school members on what they could learn and/or obtain from participating in the process. The training concluded on a positive note with the group expressing an appreciation for the experience provided and what they had learned. By the end, the school librarians offered rich and creative ideas on how to initiate their own CIs and demonstrated readiness to go ahead and develop their projects.

Once back at their schools, participants were responsible for selecting and cultivating their own school-based teams. Teams were comprised of teachers, administrators, and technology personnel; the composition of each team was unique. After the team was established, the school librarian held a series of meetings, organized using the CI model, during which team members identified and agreed upon a need in their school that could be met with technology. Each school was given $6,000 to finance their technology projects. Participants recorded activities and reflections relating to CI in journals, submitted to the researchers on Blackboard, which were analyzed. Five journal entries were prompted by questions provided by the researchers that were both descriptive and reflective, asking participants to not only record their activities but also to reflect on the leadership styles and development as new professionals.

For reasons of privacy, each of the participants will be referred to by pseudonym in this research report.

Validity and Reliability

Validity is established in several ways in CI studies. Face validity is established because the natural process of people communicating and expressing their opinions is recorded. Content validity is established because the people who participate are the experts in their own situations. Only they can express exactly how they feel about a situation or activity in which they have participated. Furthermore, the use of cycles (Figure 9.1) is a benefit in CI because the cycles increase validity. During the cycles, the coresearchers participate in action and reflection. This increases validity because each time a topic is examined, the results are either confirmed or revisited until all coresearchers are satisfied with the results.

Representing all of the cycles of action and reflection and the information gathered during the meetings in the same context that it was presented ensures reliability. All participants take notes when CI studies are done properly. These notes are compared and compiled into a final report for the approval of all participants. Following this process ensures information is not inadvertently excluded or misinterpreted.

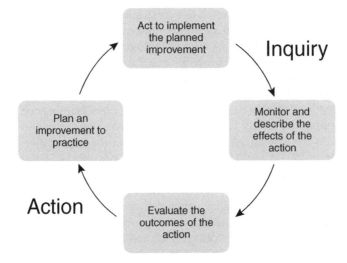

Figure 9.1   Cycle of Cooperative Inquiry

IMPROVEMENT PLAN

The six participants in this CI study (Table 9.1) experienced varying degrees of success in implementing both the research process and the technology projects in their schools. Three representative cases, representing high, intermediate, and low levels of implementation success, are presented here with recommendations for improving practice.

CONCLUSIONS: QUESTIONS ANSWERED THROUGH COOPERATIVE INQUIRY

For school librarians, CI can be a powerful means to develop the cultural competencies and awareness necessary to lead effectively in a variety of educational and political contexts (Kasl & Yorks, 2010; Seidl, 2007). The CI process allows school librarians to merge the perspectives of diverse stakeholders at every stage of using information and communications technology in addressing a mutually agreed-upon problem. This study, a pioneering effort in the use of CI in a school library setting, provides definitive research findings that are a starting point for future researchers and practitioners. Through this process we were able to answer our research questions:

How can CI methodology be used to evaluate the outcomes of education for school librarianship leadership in technology integration?

CI is a viable methodology to evaluate the outcomes of library education for school librarianship in technology. The process of action and reflection, coupled with the concept of participant researchers, allows for data to be collected in an unobtrusive manner. The cycle of action and reflection can be spread out or condensed, depending on the needs of the participants. It is helpful to provide prompts

Table 9.1 Summary of Participants' Cooperative Inquiry Experiences

Group Factor	Case 1: Penny	Case 2: Christine	Case 3: Jennifer
School Type	Elementary	Middle	Elementary
Level of Implementation Success	High	Intermediate	Low
Team Members	Third-grade teacher, first-grade teacher, principal, assistant principal, former parent who is a technology expert, and community volunteer	Principal, network manager, instructional TV teacher, social studies teacher, math teacher, music teacher, and language arts teacher	Fifth-grade teacher, second-grade teacher, parent liaison, volunteer coordinator, and technology coordinator
Question	How can teachers quickly and easily integrate technology into their instruction?	How can we increase student motivation?	How can parents be taught the importance of technology to their child's education?
Project Description	Developed a technology-rich media center, met with classes every two weeks, and taught students along with their teachers how to integrate new hardware or software by modeling	Used handheld devices to motivate students in after-school tutoring to approach learning in a different way	Designed workshops for parents to learn basic computer skills such as e-mail, social networking, and filling out job applications
Main Group Issues	Worked well together since a similar process has been being used in district and faculty were more committed than administration.	Team members remained professional even when two members left to go to other schools and network manager who was originally supportive, blocked the download of apps once tablets were purchased.	Interpersonal conflict, erratic attendance, group reformulation, members' discomfort with technology, negativity, group had to be disbanded and another formed.

(Continued)

Table 9.1 (Continued)

Cooperative Inquiry Implications	Efficient meetings as a result of following agenda and planning next steps.	Made it clear it was a group process and school librarian became very confident as process evolved.	Principal not a member of the team, team members also parents, and team members solicited at a faculty meeting and not strategically invited.
Best Practice	Pre- and postdata collected to determine impact, faculty buy-in of the process, and CI group is representative of school.	Tracked four students with pre- and posttest scores, maintain confidence, and realize school librarian's role as a facilitator.	Continue to ask engaging questions to reinforce that this is a group process.
What Participants Would Do Differently	Examine implementation by specific grade levels	Move more quickly through the process, facilitate faster decision-making, and conduct anecdotal student interviews throughout the project	Select team members according to commitment and ability to get along with others and make sure principal is on the team
Recommendations for School Librarians from Participants	Form a committee that covers all areas of expertise in your school	Determine how you are going to collect data to determine impact from the beginning	Record the meetings so you have accurate information and have a plan B
Leadership Implications	Process has helped participant gain confidence, become an integral part of the school community, and a leader in the profession; named to several school leadership teams.	Process was empowering; asked to join school leadership team.	Process caused school librarian to further reflect on his/her leadership style; appointed to lead discussions on how to spend significant technology funding school has received.

at various points for focused reflection as this leads to a richer discussion and also allows for data comparison among cases.

1. **To what extent are new school librarians able to exercise formative leadership to organize and convene CI groups in their schools?**

The new school librarians (including the other three cases not reported here) exhibited most of the formative leadership traits, mainly through strategic selection of their CI teams, skillful discussion facilitation, and consistent administration of the CI process. Jennifer's difficulty could be traced to allowing the group to self-select, rather than to deliberately invite influential and diligent members of the school community who would move the project forward. Even with persistent reminders that Jennifer was a facilitator and not the leader of the team, her team continued to look to her to set the meeting agendas and order of events. She also described group dynamics as very poor. Given that the CI participants were first year school librarians in these schools, it is understandable how team selection could be challenging. However, those who were successful built teams that were a cross-section of the faculty and also included the technology coordinators and principal.

2. **What are the factors common to successful CI process led by school librarians?**

Participants who led a successful CI process noted careful team selection, sensitive and diplomatic discussion facilitation, and professional follow-through as determining factors. Meetings were held on specified dates, begun on time, recorded, and resulted in action items that were completed. The participants emphasized group ownership of the problem and the process, particularly the elements of formative leadership. This well-conducted process helped the CI teams focus on the work at hand, i.e., to address problems in their schools with technology and quickly and collaboratively propose possible solutions.

Another factor that contributed to those who were less successful was that they did not have a well-defined question to pursue. Two participants decided almost immediately to seize the opportunity of the $6,000 funding to purchase iPads that did not evolve directly from the CI process but a perceived need. Although this was contrary to the spirit, if not the goals, of the research, we did not interfere with the participant researchers but let the process unfold naturally.

Training in the CI process was essential. The skills on how to be an effective listener, facilitation, focusing the group, diversifying their CI group, discussing scenarios, and modeling of the process were all reported as being helpful in achieving their goals for their project.

3. **How do new school librarians feel about the CI process integrated with their own leadership styles and abilities?**

It became clear throughout this project that, for new school librarians, leadership involves both forming their insights into the culture of their schools as well as influencing their colleagues' ideas of what school librarians can and should do. The education they received in the Project LEAD program gave them the confidence to tackle their new positions as school librarians from the perspective of a leader—particularly in the area of technology integration. The CI process gave them a technique to share this leadership and inspire others.

Although the results of the CI process in this project can be deemed successful, it should be noted that facilitators might face some challenges in schools that could make a process like CI seem counterintuitive. School structures are hierarchical, driven by action, and framed by concrete objectives and learning standards. Many teachers today are hindered by a shortage of time and resources and are not often given the opportunity to experience participatory decision-making and inquiry. One of the highly successful participants remarked, "I found that I had to re-think and revise many of the activities to relate to the school setting. It felt very 'corporate' to me." Based on comments like these, the researchers are currently investigating an adaptation to the CI process model that might be more compatible for school librarian leaders.

Despite some minor snags with CI, impressing their new coworkers with their abilities to organize and follow through was a source of pride and a sense of success for participants. In this way, as new librarians, the participants may well be experiencing the model of development by first building strength as an entry-level program manager and organizer (i.e., aspects of the *Empowering learners'* program administrator role) to demonstrating their knowledge of tools and resources (i.e., aspects of the *Empowering learners'* information specialist role). As their projects progressed, participants, even those deemed less successful in overall implementation, evolved to take on the integrated instructional partner role (AASL, 2009a), and ultimately the leader role (AASL, 2009a). Regardless of the labels assigned to their experiences, the participants each experienced a traceable progression through the CI process that reflected the traits of formative leadership.

REFERENCES

AASL. (2009a). *Empowering learners: Guidelines for school library media programs.* Chicago: American Library Association.

AASL. (2009b, January). *Strategic plan.* Retrieved from http://www.ala.org/aasl/abouta asl/aaslgovernance/aaslstrategicplanning/spgoals

Achterman, D.L. (2008). *Haves, halves, and have-nots: School libraries and student achievement in California* (PhD dissertation). University of North Texas, Denton, TX.

Ash, R.C., & Persall, J.M. (2000). The principal as chief learning officer: Developing teacher leaders. *NASSP Bulletin, 84*(616), 15–22.

Asselin, M. (2005). Teaching information skills in the Information Age: An examination of trends in the middle grades. *School Libraries Worldwide, 11*(1), 17–36.

Everhart, N., & Dresang, E.T. (2007). Integrating research results and National Board Certification standards into a leadership curriculum for school library media specialists. *Journal of Education for Library & Information Science, 48*, 271–283.

Everhart, N., M. Mardis, and M.P. Johnston. 2010. The leadership role of the teacher librarian in technology integration: Early results of a survey of highly certified teacher-librarians in the United States. In *Diversity Challenge Resilience: School Libraries in Action, Proceedings of the 12th Biennial School Library Association of Queensland Conference, the 39th International Association of School Librarianship Annual Conference Incorporating the 14th International Forum on Research in School Librarianship, September 27 – October 1.* Brisbane, Australia: International Association of School Librarians. IASL. [CD-ROM].

Hughes-Hassell, S., & Hanson-Baldauf, D. (2008). Information and communication technology use by North Carolina school library media specialists: Perceived competencies and barriers. *School Library Media Research, 11.* Retrieved from http://www.ala.org/ala/mgrps/divs/aasl/aaslpubsandjournals/slmrb/slmrcontents/volume11/hughes_hassell.cfm

Kasl, E., & Yorks, L. (2010). "Whose inquiry is this anyway?" Money, power, reports, and collaborative inquiry. *Adult Education Quarterly, 60*(4), 315–338.

Kovari, V., Hicks, T., Ferlazzo, L., McGarvey, C., Ochs, M., Alcantara, L., et al. (n.d.). *Leaders as lead learners—A CI into the question: How can we be more effective in helping others become more strategic, conceptual, and creative in their thinking.* New York: New York University. Retrieved from http://wagner.nyu.edu/leadership/reports/files/LeadersLearners.pdf

Mardis, M.A. (2007). School libraries and science achievement: A view from Michigan's middle schools. *School Library Media Research, 10.* Retrieved from http://www.ala.org/ala/aasl/aaslpubsandjournals/slmrb/slmrcontents/volume10/mardis_school librariesandscience.cfm

McCracken, A. (2001). School library media specialists' perceptions of practice and importance of roles described in information power. *School Library Media Research, 4.* Retrieved from http://www.ala.org/ala/aasl/aaslpubsandjournals/slmrb/slmrcontents/volume42001/mccracken.htm

Oates, B.J. (2002). Co-operative inquiry: Reflections on practice. *Electronic Journal of Business Research Methods, 1*(1), 27–37. Retrieved from http://www.ejbrm.com/volume1/issue1/p27

Ospina, S., Dodge, J., Godsoe, B., Minieri, J., Reza, S., & Schall, E. (2004). From consent to mutual inquiry. *Action Research, 2*(1), 47–69.

Ospina, S., El Hadidy, W., & Hofmann-Pinilla, A. (2008). Cooperative Inquiry for learning and connectedness. *Action Learning, 5*(2), 131–147.

Reason, P., & Heron, J. (2004). *A layperson's guide to co-operative inquiry.* Retrieved from http://www.bath.ac.uk/carpp/publications/coop_inquiry.html

RCLA. (n.d.). *Cooperative inquiry.* Retrieved from http://wagner.nyu.edu/leadership/reports/cooperative.php

Scholastic Research Results. (2008). *School libraries work!,* 3rd edition. Retrieved from http://www.scholastic.com/content/collateral_resources/pdf/s/slw3_2008.pdf

Seidl, B. (2007). Working with communities to explore and personalize culturally relevant pedagogies: Push, double images, and raced talk. *Journal of Teacher Education, 58*(2), 168–183.

Slygh, G.L. (2000). *Shake, rattle, and role! The effects of professional community on the collaborative role of the school librarian* (Doctoral dissertation). University of Wisconsin, Madison, WI.

Smith, D. (2011). Educating preservice school librarians to lead: A study of self-perceived transformational leadership behaviors. *School Library Media Research, 14.* Retrieved from http://www.ala.org/aasl/aaslpubsandjournals/slmrb/slmrcontents/volume14/smith

Vansickle, S. (2000). Educating preservice media specialists: Developing school leaders. *School Libraries Worldwide, 6*(2), 1–20.

10

CROSSING THE LANGUAGE BARRIER:
THE POTENTIAL FOR SCHOOL
LIBRARIANS IN FACILITATING
CROSS-CULTURAL TEACHING AND
LEARNING IN THE SCHOOL LIBRARY

Andrew J.M. Smith and Nancy J. Brown

> How does one stop reading the exterior signs of a foreign tribe and step into
> the inwardness, the viscera of their meanings? Every anthropologist under-
> stands the difficulty of such a feat; and so does every immigrant.
>
> —*Hoffman, 1989, p. 209*

INTRODUCTION: ENGLISH LANGUAGE LEARNERS

This chapter describes the shifting population demographics and highlights the
increasing number of English language learners (ELLs) within schools, as well
as the changing face of the school library and the challenges these factors create
within the school. The authors' research is a review of the literature describing
the role of the school librarian as a pivotal resource for learners and teachers, and
provides examples of successful strategies from the research in the area of materials,
instructional strategies, programming, and technology. They answer two leading
questions for more than a decade: "Why does our school need a library when we
have access to so much information from our classrooms via the Internet?" And,
"What does a new learning commons look like?"

THE MULTICULTURAL SCHOOL

Reports from the latest census indicate there are an increasing number of foreign-
born residents in the United States. Mexico provides the largest percentage of
foreign-born residents (29%), but 28 percent come from Asia, 23 percent from
other Latin American and Caribbean countries, 12 percent from Europe, and 4

Portions of this chapter were previously published in Nancy Brown, Build with what they
 have: Including limited English proficient Chinese children in the elementary school
 media center, *New Review of Children's Literature and Librarianship*, 12(1), 19–31.
 Reprinted with permission.

percent from Africa, with the remainder from Northern America and Oceania (Grieco et al., 2012).

Data for school-age children show that in 2009, more than 21 percent spoke a language other than English at home (U.S. Census Bureau, 2012). Although the numbers vary by region from almost 12 percent in the Midwest through 18 percent in the South and 21 percent in the Northeast to over 33 percent in the West, even the smaller numbers suggest the necessity of a reconsideration of teaching and learning.

Nor is this trend confined to the United States, with a recent report on schools in the United Kingdom revealing that, on average, one in six students at the elementary level and one in eight students at the secondary level speak a language other than English at home (Department for Education, 2012). Although the underlying problem is the same, the variety of languages spoken by school-age children in the United Kingdom varies, with the most commonly spoken languages including Punjabi, Urdu, Bengali, Gujarati, Somali, Polish, Arabic, Portuguese, Turkish, and Tamil, but with sizable numbers of students speaking Shqip (Albania and Kosovo), Igbo (Nigeria), Luganda (Uganda), Sinhala (Sri Lanka), and Amharic (Ethiopia).

Providing a quality education for the rapidly increasing numbers of ethnically and linguistically diverse children is a significant issue that must be addressed by educators at all levels (Brock, McVee, Shojgreen-Downer & Dueñas, 1998). The increasing enrollment of students who do not speak English as their first language challenges schools to provide programs and materials to address the unique needs of this multifaceted special population.

PROBLEMS FOR FOREIGN-BORN STUDENTS

A growing number of children entering U.S. schools are experiencing difficulties learning to read and becoming literate because they are not native speakers of English. When addressing the specific educational needs of ELLs, educators have debated whether instruction should be primarily in the student's native language or in English and when to make a transition from bilingual to English-language-only classrooms. A more crucial issue, however, is how to merge English language instruction with subject matter instruction (Greenwood, 2001). The question is how to successfully design instruction that develops literacy skills in English while at the same time promoting second-language acquisition. Arreaga-Mayer (1998) describes features of effective instruction. These include implementation with heterogeneous groups; promotion of high levels of student engagement; activation of higher-order cognitive processes; opportunities for students to engage in extended English discourse; applicability to small and class-wide groups; social acceptance by teachers, students, and parents; and respect for cultural and linguistic diversity. Consequently, combining effective instructional interventions with features of language-sensitive teaching appears to maximize opportunities for ELLs to become literate.

Rance-Roney (2010) notes that it is critical that we seek innovative and effective skill improvement approaches that increase the rapidity of content literacy development for ELLs while simultaneously developing the four language skills of writing, reading, listening, and speaking. School librarians are in positions within their schools that allow them to work collaboratively with teachers to address these language skills, playing pivotal roles in working to effectively meet the educational needs of the many linguistically and culturally diverse children in American classrooms. York (2008) observes, "Chances are good that the majority of school librarians and media specialists have worked with or will work with students who have limited or no English language background" (p. 26).

THE ROLE OF THE SCHOOL LIBRARIAN IN STANDARDS-BASED EDUCATION

School librarians are in positions within their schools that allow them to play pivotal roles in working to effectively meet the educational needs of the many linguistically and culturally diverse children in American classrooms. School librarians are equipped with the knowledge to establish collaborative relationships, enabling them to support the work of English for speakers of other languages (ESOL) teachers and to provide media center resources and programming for limited English proficient (LEP) students.

The American Library Association (ALA) and American Association of School Librarians (AASL) have made clear statements about the importance of instructing students, identifying student's information needs, and fostering a community of lifelong learners. AASL's *Standards for the 21st-century learner* (2007) notes that today's learners must use skills, resources, and tools that equip students to do the following: (1) inquire, think critically, and gain knowledge; (2) draw conclusions, make informed decisions, apply knowledge to new situations, and create new knowledge; (3) share knowledge and participate ethically and productively as members of our democratic society; and (4) pursue personal and aesthetic growth.

By addressing these important standards, the school librarian can be instrumental in gathering the resources needed to not only provide direct support for immigrant students learning English, but to also work closely with ELL educators to help the students bridge the educational gap (Armour & Corona, 2007). American Association of School Libraries' President Cassandra Barnett (2010) says, "With such high concentrations of ELLs in our schools, school library media specialists (teacher-librarians) are in the unique position to make significant contributions to this unique student population. Clearly resources, both in materials as well as certified and trained school library media specialists, can greatly impact the success of English language learners" (p. 2).

McCarthey, Dressman, Smolkin, McGill-Franzen, and Harris (2000) conclude that a diverse student population will resemble a multicultural quilt, created from the diverse experiences and backgrounds of children and teachers, stitched together by their contacts with one another within the seams of schools. Such a creation can be firmly bound by literature, technology, dialogue, creative thinking, and collaborative efforts. The elementary school librarian is well equipped to create such a quilt by applying these resources and approaches to working with LEP students.

School librarians are guided by clearly stated, basic standards established for serving non-English speaking children. The authors of *Information power: Guidelines for school library media programs* (1998) note, "The mission of the library media program is to ensure that students and staff are effective users of ideas and information." This mission is accomplished by

1. Providing intellectual and physical access to materials in all formats
2. Providing instruction to foster competence and stimulate interest in reading, viewing, and using information and ideas

3. Working with other educators to design learning strategies to meet the needs of individual students (AASL & AECT, 1998, p. 6)

The ALA and AASL have made clear statements about the importance of instructing students, identifying student information needs, and fostering a community of lifelong learners (AASL and AECT, 1998). These respected professional organizations have established four distinct roles of the school media specialist:

1. *Teacher* collaborates with faculty, instructs students, is knowledgeable about current research on teaching and learning, serves as curricular leader and participant on the school's instructional team, updates professional skills, and demonstrates skills to help students access, evaluate and use information from multiple sources.
2. *Instructional partner* identifies links across student information needs, curricular content, and learning outcomes; takes a leading role in developing policies that guide students to develop a full range of information abilities; and designs authentic learning tasks.
3. *Information specialist* provides leadership and expertise in acquiring and evaluating information resources in all formats, brings an awareness of information issues into collaborative relationships with teachers and administrators, models learning strategies for students, and masters sophisticated electronic resources.
4. *Program administrator* exhibits proficiency in management of staff, budgets, equipment, and facilities; defines the policies of the library media program; is an advocate for the library media program; and plans, executes, and evaluates the program.

A fifth role, that of *leader*, was added by AASL in 2009, with the acknowledgement that the creation of a truly effective school library program requires a more overt and all-encompassing form of leadership than simply taking a leading role in instructional decisions. The leadership definition also expands the role of the school librarian beyond the individual library into the local and global learning community. A new ordering of the now five roles of the school librarian results in leader, instructional partner, information specialist, teacher, and program administrator (AASL, 2009).

The mission statement of the library media program as stated in *Information power* encourages all school librarians to be inclusive in purchasing materials for the media center and in offering programs within the center to address the needs and interests of LEP students. *Information power* moved from providing resources for students to creating a community of lifelong learners. School librarians are to provide materials in numerous formats for individual students and create a community of lifelong learners.

However, school librarians face a number of challenges in addressing the needs and interests of special populations. First, managing the numbers of students in an economic and political climate in which funding does not keep up with growth is an enormous task (McCarthey et al., 2000). Second, with continuing mobility patterns of both teachers and children, it is unlikely that teachers will teach in the same community in which they live. This geographic consideration may cause the teacher to feel disconnected from the students' life experiences. Third, school librarians must cultivate a point of view dedicated to building firm foundations of reading and writing for children whose first language is not English.

School librarians, by the nature of their profession, have always been advocates of literacy, and for many years, they have recognized the potential importance of literature in enabling children to become lifelong readers (Bishop & Blazek, 1994). According to *Information power*, the mission of the library media specialist (school librarian) is to ensure "that students and staff are effective users of ideas and information." Moyer and Small (2001) observe that if information literacy programs are to be effective, they must stimulate intellectual curiosity, develop self-confidence for research activities, and encourage a desire for continued information exploration throughout life. Making this valuable connection between reading, literature, literacy, and information retrieval is an important professional responsibility of the school librarian. Making the connection with students who speak English as a second language heightens that responsibility.

THE CHANGING ENVIRONMENT: FROM SCHOOL LIBRARY TO LEARNING COMMONS

Rapidly evolving technologies have given rise to a debate among professionals about the very nature of a traditional school library. For generations, the school library has housed shelves and shelves of books to serve the reading and research interests of students. However, today's digital natives have grown up with laptops, tablets, smartphones, and a world of information only a click away. Students are increasingly expected to express their understanding using images, video, and animation in addition to plain text (Regan, 2008, p. 10).

The concept of a school library is evolving from a repository for books to a center for learning or "learning commons," an area within a school that serves the needs of the 21st-century learner. Why does our school need a library when we have access to so much information from our classrooms via the Internet? What does this new learning commons look like? Waskow (2011) notes, "These have been leading questions for almost a decade, and nationally recognized professionals have explained that it has yet to be defined, much less described" (p. 8). Architect Doug Westmoreland provided further insight with a description of the design process for the new library for Glen Allen High School in Henrico, Virginia. There was a general consensus that students wanted an atmosphere more closely resembling that of a commercial bookstore. The design committee suggested a more open environment for supervision and flexibility, but with smaller delineated instructional spaces. Informal furniture groupings were created in designated areas of the room where various types of instructional technology were provided for group or individual learning opportunities, including laptops, whiteboards, and projection equipment (Martin, Westmoreland, & Branyon, 2011).

Cushing Academy in Ashburnham, Massachusetts, sparked heated discussion within the profession when it dramatically redesigned its library into a radically different learning commons beginning in 2007 (Corbett, 2011). More and more schools and school librarians have begun the discussion to transform the traditional library into a facility that better meets the needs of 21st-century learners. It is in this environment that the school librarian must collaborate with classroom teachers and create the learning space that ensures equal access and opportunity for all students.

LEARNER CHARACTERISTICS

When working with immigrant children, it is important to remember that each student's response and behavior in school are "a result of the complex interaction of his or her cultural background, individual nature, and length of time that student has been in the host country" (Ioga, 1995, p. 17). The following observations regarding the nature of Chinese-speaking children in elementary schools in the United States are not meant to stereotype, but to present what has been observed by other researchers and to give an indication of the ways in which these students may differ from their native-born counterparts.

New ELLs are diverse and need lots of individual attention. The stereotype of the "overachieving Asian student" can be as damaging as any other stereotype (Barbieri, 2002). School is central to Chinese students' lives. We must make it relevant, valuable, and joyful, welcoming families to participate whenever they are available (Barbieri, 2002). The school and community can assist parents of LEP children to understand the path to school achievement (Constantino, 1994). By working from the knowledge and understandings of the parents, schools can create programs to serve parents in helping their children assimilate into the classroom and perform at an equal level with their classmates while maintaining their native culture.

However, Fu (2003) cautions American teachers to be aware that many Chinese believe that the best way to help their children's education is to manage to send them to a good school. In the author's experiences in a school in New York's Chinatown, she observes, "Once they put their children in a good school, then it is the task of teachers to educate them, not the parents. Volunteering in the school, assisting on a field trip, or corresponding with the teachers regularly about their children's education may sound strange or even be seen as intrusive in the eyes of many Chinese parents" (Fu, 2003, pp. 158, 159). Chinese-speaking students may prefer more structure-oriented lessons, are less likely to voice their opinions or ask questions, tend to hide their abilities, and tend to seek conformity and group dependence (Cortazzi & Jin, 1996).

STRATEGIES FOR SUPPORTING ELLs FROM THE RESEARCH

An examination of the research reveals an array of examples of instructional methods and outcomes that specifically serve ELLs, in both the elementary and high school environment.

Books and Instructional Materials

- *Provide good materials:* Coonrod & Hughes (1994) observe that children who are culturally and linguistically different present a special challenge to early childhood educators. Kiefer (2001) notes that children's experiences with good books can play an enormous role in smoothing the transition from beginning reading to fluent reading. Such transitions often begin with books available in the school media center and with a collaborative effort between the ESL (English as a second language) classroom teacher and the school library media specialist, encouraging second language acquisition through reading and understanding the printed word.

- *Bilingual picture books:* Barbieri (2002) notes that saturating students with bilingual literature, picture books, age-appropriate technology, and nonfiction texts will make English acquisition more desirable, more joyful, and easier. Such books should affirm the student's culture and be reflected positively in both words and pictures. "Offer books that encourage cumulative language development as well as those with a phonetic approach—a both/and rather than an either/or approach" (Ioga, 1995, p. 35). Dickinson and Hinton (2008) remind teacher librarians to use valid and responsible vendors when buying international materials to ensure the materials are authoritative and accurate. Dietrich and Ralph (1995) observe educators should help students explore their own cultures and contribute to intercultural understanding. A continuing dialogue should result in the classroom through the use of culturally diverse literature to enhance student involvement in the curriculum and in multicultural controversies.

- *Simple English language picture books:* Muchisky (2007) observes that perhaps the most important acquisitions for the library collection are good-quality multicultural books, especially picture books. Moorefield-Lang, Anaya, and Shirk (2010) concur noting, "With everything from low-level picture books to age- and grade-appropriate books, ELL students can choose books that fit their own levels of reading and move up as they are ready" (p. 23). Hi-lo books for older readers; upper elementary students should have these books available as they are much more age-appropriate.

- *Informational books:* Naidoo (2005) emphasizes the importance of nonfiction books for language acquisition and as a means of collaboration with ESOL teachers, particularly in sheltered instruction.

- *Big books (www.teacherbigbooks.com):* Oversized books are important tools for emergent readers, shared readers, and those learning a language.

- *Wordless picture books:* These help students who are just learning to read practice storytelling in their home language and in English.

Instructional Strategies

- *Storybooks:* Children's literature selections allow students to enjoy and replicate actual and vicarious life experiences of others right in the classroom. Storybooks act as "mirrors and windows on a global community" (Cox and Galdo, 1990, p. 582). Faltis (1989) summarizes the advantages of using storybooks for language minority students. First, storybooks are excellent sources for both vocabulary and concept development, because the words tend to be presented in contexts supported with pictures and other kinds of extralinguistic clues. Second, they provide a context for verbal interaction, particularly the important sequence of elicitation–response–evaluation. Third, they teach children about attitudes and behaviors that are valued in society. Elementary school librarians are able to share wonderful stories with children and should include stories that actively involve LEP children.

- *Multicultural literature:* Researchers have observed the value gained from collaboration between students in the ESL environment. Dietrich and Ralph (1995) emphasize students need to connect what is in the text to what they already understand. Multicultural literature should become a primary vehicle for generating discussion and for literacy acquisition. The literary work becomes the shared body of experience, allowing students to respond from the perspectives of their individual cultural backgrounds.

- *Poetry:* Involve the ESL children by encouraging simple poetry using their available English-language vocabulary. The school librarian may consider posting these poems on a special bulletin board in the media center showcasing student work.

- *Literature-inspired creative expression:* Hosli (2000) discusses the use of intermodal learning activities with LEP children. The author encourages the natural use of the different art disciplines of visual art, music, dance, literature, and theater. "Working with art means to find and offer the art disciplines which help people to better express their own themes; or to approach, meet, and become acquainted with unknown theme" (Hosli, 2000, p. 17).

- *Storytelling:* Von Franz (1970) speaks of storytelling as the international language of all ages, or all races and cultures. The universal themes found in good literature give children a sense of solidarity with all people. They transcend cultural attitudes. Craft and Bardell (1984) note that hearing, telling, writing, and drawing stories helps the language development of second-language learners. In retelling stories they have heard told and read to them, their unconscious knowledge directs their language production. Dietrich and Ralph (1995) concur noting that literature and the ensuing discussion permit students to read, think, and become actively engaged with the texts. The school librarian can work with the LEP teachers to include LEP students in reader's theater and radio productions. Kulleseid (1986) places a strong emphasis on multisensory ways of knowing and noted this leads to the importance of providing access to information in many media. School library media specialists must also create opportunities for individualized or small-group instruction so that students' unique and individual pathways to learning may be discovered, made explicit, and stimulated (Kulleseid, 1986, p. 46).

Programming to Support ELLs

- *Parent/grandparent nights in the school library:* Invite extended families to visit the school to see the progress their children have made. Showcase books, art, music, and technology the students have been using to learn their new language.

- *Book clubs and literature circles:* ELLs develop confidence through participating in a verbal exchange where they can discuss books in a relaxed setting. Encourage students to bring prewritten notes to meetings. This will give students practice writing in English and may make them more comfortable when speaking (Blair, Brasfield, Crenshaw, & Mosedale, 2011). When children and youth engage in conversations with peers and adults about texts they have read, they become more aware of their own beliefs, their learning, and the learning process (Moreillon & Cahill, 2010).

- *Morning announcements via closed-circuit TV:* Include ELLs by having them tape book reviews, poetry readings, songs, or minilessons about their countries. Taping in advance will lessen the anxiety to have perfect English and give them the opportunity to edit their final presentation.

- *Student-produced materials:* The school librarian should consider working with the children to produce graphic novels or comic strips illustrating the story. Books can be cataloged and checked out to other students through the library's Online Public Access Catalog (OPAC).

- *"Family treasure" booklets:* Using objects of cultural and personal relevance that the children brought from home, stories can be generated from the original telling in the student's native language into English in small-group contexts, transcribed, illustrated, and uploaded to a website for permanent sharing, rereading, and exchange. These booklets provide an opportunity for identity formation, pride of family and culture, and the acquisition of rudimentary technology skills, which all work to motivate and engage young learners in the development of early literacy (Roessingh, 2011).

Technology Applications and Projects

- *DVDs in both the home language with English subtitles and in English with home-language subtitles:* These encourage students to develop their literacy skills in one language while making connections to the other spoken language (Blair et al., 2011).

- *Mp3 players or other audio devices: Playaways* (prerecorded mp3 players) are also valuable so that students can listen to all required texts while they read, since students can understand spoken English before written English (Adams, 2010).

- *iPods* and *iPads:* Using either of these devices as a delivery method is a natural fit for a school librarian, as they are tools for a collaborative venture with classroom teachers and provide an enticement to engage teachers with the library skills curriculum. Podcasts, pronunciation recordings, and language exercise can then be used at any time by any user (Patten & Craig, 2007). Valuable free or inexpensive downloadable applications for the iPad include *TranslateIt*, providing one-click translations of text from one language to another, and *Notes 'n More,* which allows students and teachers to generate to-do lists, notes, voice memos, pictures, and videos and then collect the disparate file types into folders. Such a program can provide a valuable aid to serve as a digital graphic organizer.

- *iMovie or movie maker:* Students can write, produce, and edit presentations by collaboratively using their English skills.

- *Pathfinders or Webquest (www.webquest.org):* Lists of valuable websites can be prepared by the school librarian and made available to the ELL for easy reference.

- *Flip video (www.theflip.com):* This relatively inexpensive, easy-to-use video camera will have ELLs and other students clamoring to have their voices heard.

- *Kindles, Nooks, and other eReaders:* Allow for the easy download of eBooks and, not only are searchable, but can provide read-along audio.

- *Doodle Buddy and other computer-aided drawing programs:* Bermudez and Palumbo (1994) discuss the importance of using emerging technologies and updated information to enhance literacy education for ELL students. The authors conclude that levels of fluency, knowledge, motivation, and interest can be addressed individually through the use of age-appropriate technology applications.

- *TeacherWeb (www.teachersweb.com) or Weebly (www.weebly.com):* Add an ELL section with links to online translators, dictionaries, and foreign newspapers to the library's Web page. Create a link to the International Children's Digital Library (http://en.childrenslibrary.org/) where students can read books in more than 50 languages (Adams, 2010). The Web page can also allow students to showcase book reviews.

- *Animoto (www.animoto.com):* It can be used instead of traditional booktalking to hook ELL students by integrating media into language learning (Collins, 2010).

- *Prezi (www.prezi.com):* Software that creatively goes beyond PowerPoint's presentation capabilities.

- *Moodle (www.moodle.org):* It enables students to meld great literature and the power of Web 2.0. Using this site, ELLs can collaborate about content, research information, create online projects, and converse with those from unfamiliar cultures.

- *Glogs (www.glogster.com) and online posters:* Integrate text, photos, audio, and video encourage creativity while helping ELLs organize and present concepts in English.

- *Skype (www.skype.com):* It allows students to connect various school communities using live communication through computer-to-computer phone calls. It encourages language exchange through a global community.

Practical Matters

- *Illustrations and signage:* Communication in the school library media center can be facilitated through the use of prominently posted signs and pertinent information. The media specialist should direct, involve, and encourage LEP children by posting relevant signs and directions throughout the media center in the child's native language.

- *Foreign language cataloging:* Adamich (2009a, 2009b) highlights the importance of equality of access and the ways in which metadata can be displayed within the OPAC in another language. This allows better access to ELLs and can also provide more relevant and helpful examples when students are learning about metadata and searching for information.

CONCLUSIONS: CULTURALLY RESPONSIVE LEADERS

Students need culturally responsive school librarians who focus on 21st-century skills for all students, including immigrant students learning English. Basic principles for culturally responsive leadership in school libraries are articulated by multicultural educators who know that social equity is more important than ever, as the number of diverse and underserved students increase each year. Ethnicity, race, disability, gender, language, and socioeconomic status define diverse students who enter school libraries every day. Since school librarians interact with *all* students within a school, it is a natural fit to look toward our school library personnel to model culturally responsive leadership for educators within their school and communities (Summers, 2010). School librarians must focus on enhancing their professional competencies and promote positive intercultural interactions between students in order to create the best learning environment in the 21st century.

Years ago, at a National Council of Teachers of English conference in St. Louis, Maya Angelou spoke about teachers. "Unless we recognize that all children are our children," she said, "we are missing the point." The lives of teachers in the United States are enriched by working with students and families from diverse cultures. Immigrant children bring a rich cultural and linguistic heritage to American schools. The school librarian is in a unique position to provide resources, programming, and appropriate technology to support English language acquisition by these special children. At a time when there is pressure to remove professionally qualified staff from school media centers, it is essential that school librarians lead the way in helping these new Americans succeed in education and in life.

REFERENCES

AASL. (2007). *Standards for the 21st-century learner*. Chicago: American Library Association. Retrieved from http://www.ala.org/ala/mgrps/divs/aasl/guidelinesandstandards/learningstandards/standards.cfm

AASL. (2009). *Empowering learners: Guidelines for school library media programs*. Chicago: American Library Association.

AASL and AECT. (1998). *Information power: Guidelines for school library media programs*. Chicago: American Library Association.

Adamich, T. (2009a). Making and managing metadata in K-12: Foreign language cataloging, non-native English speakers, and equitable access. *Technicalities, 29*(2), 7–11.

Adamich, T. (2009b). The purpose of cataloging for matters of equitable access: Spanish-language cataloging and "everyday" approaches for non-native English speakers. *Knowledge Quest, 37*(5), 42–47.

Adams, H. (2010). Welcoming America's newest immigrants: Providing access to resources and services for English language learners. *School Library Monthly, 27*(1), 50, 51.

Armour, L., & Corona, E. (2007). Providing support for English language learner services. *Library Media Connection, 25*(6), 34–37.

Arreaga-Mayer, C. (1998). Language sensitive peer-mediated instruction for culturally and linguistically diverse learners in the intermediate elementary grades. In R. M. Gersten & R. T. Jimenez (Eds.), *Promoting learning for culturally and linguistically diverse students* (pp. 73–90). Belmont, CA: Wadsworth.

Barbieri, M. (2002). *Change my life forever: Giving voice to English-language learners*. Portsmouth, NH: Heinemann.

Barnett, C. (2010). *AASL survey reveals U.S. school libraries lack materials to support needs of ELLs*. Chicago: American Library Association. Retrieved from http://www.ala.org/ala/newspresscenter/news/pressreleases2010/january2010/survey_ells_aasl.cfm

Bermudez, A., & Palumbo, D. (1994). Bridging the gap between literacy and technology: Hypermedia as a learning tool for limited English proficient students. *Journal of Educational Issues of Language Minority Students, 14*(1), 165–184.

Bishop, K., & Blazek, R. (1994). The role of the elementary school library media specialist in a literature-based reading program. *School Library Media Quarterly, 22*(3), 146–150.

Blair, C., Brasfield, A., Crenshaw, K., & Mosedale, A. (2011). School librarians bridging the language gap for English language learners. *School Library Monthly, 27*(6), 34–37.

Brock, C. H., McVee, M. B., Shojgreen-Downer, A. M., & Dueñas, L. F. (1998). No habla inglés: Exploring a bilingual child's literacy learning opportunities in a predominantly English-speaking classroom. *Bilingual Research Journal, 22*(2–4), 175–200.

Collins, J. (2010). Transform global literature circles with Web 2.0. *Library Media Connection, 29*(2), 24–25.

Constantino, R. (1994). It's like a lot of things in America: Linguistic minority parents use of libraries. *School Library Media Quarterly, 22*(2), 87–89.

Coonrod, D., & Hughes, S. (1994). Using children's literature to promote the language development of minority students. *Journal of Educational Issues of Language Minority Students, 14,* 319–332.

Corbett, T. (2011).The changing role of the school library's physical space. *School Library Monthly, 27*(7), 5–7.

Cortazzi, M., & Jin, L. (1996). Culture of learning: Language classrooms in China. In H. Coleman (Ed.), *Society and the language classroom* (pp. 86–104). Cambridge, England: Cambridge University Press.

Cox, S., & Galda, L. (1990). Multicultural literature: Mirrors and windows on a global community. *Reading Teacher, 43*(8), 582–589.

Craft, A., & Bardell, G. (1984). *Curriculum opportunities in a multicultural society.* London: Harper and Row.

Department for Education. (2012, January). *Schools, pupils and their characteristics.* London:Author.Retrievedfromhttp://www.education.gov.uk/researchandstatistics/datasets/a00209478/dfe-schools-pupils-and-their-characteristics-january-2012

Dickinson, G., & Hinton, K. (2008).Celebrating language diversity to improve achievement. *Library Media Connection, 26*(7), 5.

Dietrich, D., & Ralph, K. (1995). Crossing borders: Multicultural literature in the classroom. *Journal of Educational Issues of Language Minority Students, 15*(Winter), 1–8.

Faltis, C. J. (1989). Code-switching and bilingual schooling: An examination of Jacobson's new concurrent approach. *Journal of Multilingual and Multicultural Development, 10*(2), 117–127.

Fu, D. (2003). *An island of English: Teaching ESL in Chinatown.* Portsmouth, NH: Heinemann.

Greenwood, C. (2001). Class wide peer tutoring learning management system. *Remedial and Special Education, 22*(1), 34–53.

Grieco, E. M., Acosta, Y. D., de la Cruz, G. P., Gambino, C., Gryn, T., Larsen, L. J., Trevelyan, E. N., & Walters, N. P. (2012). *The foreign-born population in the United States: 2010.* Washington, D.C.: U.S. Census Bureau. Retrieved from http://www.census.gov/population/foreign/

Hoffman, E. (1989). *Lost in translation: A life in a new language.* New York: Penguin.

Hosli, E. K. (2000). *"I have got something to say, but I don't know your language yet!": Intermodal learning in multicultural urban education.* New York: Peter Lang.

Ioga, C. (1995). *The inner world of the immigrant child.* New York: St. Martin's Press.

Kiefer, B. (2001). Understanding reading. *School Library Journal, 47*(2), 49–52.

Kulleseid, E. (1986). Extending the research base: Schema theory, cognitive styles, and types of intelligence. *School Library Media Quarterly, 15*(1), 41–48.

Martin, A., Westmoreland, D., & Branyon, A. (2011), New design considerations that transform the library into an indispensible learning environment. *Teacher- Librarian, 38*(5), 15–20.

McCarthey, S., Dressman, M., Smolkin, L., McGill-Franzen, & Harris, V. J. (2000). How will diversity affect literacy in the next millennium? *Reading Research Quarterly, 35*(4), 548–552.

Moorefield-Lang, H., Anaya, G., & Shirk, D. (2010). ELL students and the library or ELL estudiantes en la biblioteca. *Library Media Connection, 29*(3), 22, 23.

Moreillon, J., & Cahill, M. (2010). Literature for life: When cultures meet. *School Library Monthly, 27*(2), 27–29.

Moyer, S. L., & Small, R. V. (2001). Building a motivation toolkit for teaching information literacy. *Knowledge Quest, 29*(3), 28–32.

Muchisky, B. (2007). English language learner-friendly library media centers. *School Library Media Activities Monthly, 24*(4), 29–31.

Naidoo, J. C. (2005). Informational empowerment: Using informational books to connect the library media center program with sheltered instruction. *School Libraries Worldwide, 11*(2), 132–152.

Patten, K., & Craig, D. (2007). iPods and English-language learners: A great combination. *Teacher Librarian, 34*(5), 40–44.

Rance-Roney, J. (2010). Jump-starting language and schema for English-language learners: Teacher-composed digital jumpstarts for academic reading. *Journal of Adolescent and Adult Literacy, 53*(5), 386–395.

Regan, B. (2008). Why we need to teach 21-st century skills: And how to do it. *MultiMedia&Internet@Schools, 15*(4), 10–13.

Roessingh, H. (2011). Family treasures: A dual-language book project for negotiating language, literacy, culture, and identity. *Canadian Modern Language Review, 67*(1), 123–148.

Summers, L. (2010).Culturally responsive leadership in school libraries. *Library Media Connection, 28*(5), 10–13.

U.S. Census Bureau. (2012). Table 236. Children who speak a language other than English at home by region: 2009. *The 2012 statistical abstract: The national data book.* Retrieved from http://www.census.gov/compendia/statab/cats/education.html

Von Franz, M.L. (1970). *An introduction to the interpretation of fairy tales.* New York: Spring Publications.

Waskow, L. (2011). The journey from library media center to learning commons. *Teacher-Librarian, 38*(5), 8–14.

York, S. (2008). Culturally speaking: English language learners. *Library Media Connection, 26*(7), 26–27.

11

VIEWS FROM RESEARCH: FROM IDEOLOGY TO ACTION

Mirah J. Dow

INTRODUCTION: WHAT MUST WE SAY ABOUT SCHOOL LIBRARIES?

School libraries matter if schools are to successfully engage in a new "Common Core" (2010) of national learning standards that include inquiry-based learning, instruction in multiple literacies, and require effective modeling of differential teaching that meets the needs of diverse learning communities. Ten chapters in this book, which came together as a result of a year-long project to identify researchers and their recently completed studies that address issues relevant to why school libraries matter, are quintessential to describing guided inquiry, project-based learning involving collaboration between school librarians and classroom teachers in general studies, language development and reading comprehension, and information technology.

THE PURPOSE

The purpose of this collection of research is to "shine a bright light" on the importance of school librarianship and the American Association of School Librarians' (AASL) standards and guidelines that are models of excellence for student learning. The "bright light" generated by quantitative and qualitative research methodology exposes the importance of school librarians necessary to help today's children and youth to become prepared to graduate from high school job-ready, college-ready, and/or career-ready, regardless of their income, race, ethnic, language background, or disability status. It points out that as the Internet continues to transform society into a dynamic, global environment, school libraries and state-licensed school librarians are needed more than ever before to provide specialized knowledge about information retrieval, communication, and design. The contents of this book, along with published documentation of other significant school library research, make clear that there is abundant evidence that school librarians are highly specialized educators ready to lead in the United States' educational reform efforts. School librarians are ready because colleges and universities have long been involved in delivery of programs to prepare professional librarians. To express this view from research, what can and will advocates and informed stakeholders say to convince others that school libraries matter? Chapter 11 summaries key findings from all the chapters.

THE PREMISE

There must be advocacy for education that enables students to cut through taken-for-granted assumptions and to look through lenses of various ways of knowing, seeing, feeling, and interpreting their experiences. This century's students must be taught by educators who know and understand that it is imperative to be interested in education, not in schooling in its traditional forms of memorization and recitation. We must convince all educators, as well as educational policy makers at local, regional, and national levels, that school librarians are educated and prepared to provide leadership and "know-how" when it comes to teaching students to reach out for meanings and to learn how to learn. We must make clear that school librarians are essential to enabling students in today's schools to learn and achieve. School librarians have an irreplaceable role in helping all students to graduate from high school job-ready, college-ready, and/or career-ready. We must be clear that school librarians will be critically effective in the upcoming development of new school accountability practices that communicate educational achievement of *all* students.

The chapters in this book have several features in common—all are designed to improve advocacy and to stimulate curiosity and innovation in future researchers. All chapters are outlined in a similar structure beginning with an introduction to an educational topic or social problem that is then followed by a relevant literature review, research questions, and description of quantitative and/or qualitative methods used in the investigation, limitations, findings, conclusions, and suggestions for future study. This structure provides readers, future advocates, and researchers with evidence-based details that can be used in stating a request or making a case for fully funded school library programs and employment of professional school libraries, or proposing a new study. Each chapter's literature review cites and describes numerous empirical studies that serve to articulate much about the philosophy and pedagogy of librarianship and the value of professionally prepared school librarians. All the chapters in the book provide highly qualified "voices" of professional judgment about the national threat to quality education that comes with elimination or replacement of professional librarians with nonprofessionals. The conclusions in each chapter can become significant talking points and/or specific points for reference when communicating with school administrators and others who are, or hopefully soon will be, involved in making important, positive decisions relevant to future economic recovery and the restoration of school library programs.

THE PRACTICES

How are we to understand and communicate about the instructional method school librarians call "guided inquiry"? Further, how does "guided inquiry" differ from what is sometimes called "traditional education"? It is important to understand that "guided inquiry" is the term used to single out a particular kind of pedagogy, one concerned about perception, emotions, imagination, and how they relate to knowing, understanding, and feeling about the world. How are we to understand and to communicate about human "information behavior"? "Information behavior" is the term to describe the human capacity that people have to need, seek, give and use information in different contexts. Answers and action are at the heart of this book in the form of responses, both direct and indirect, to these and other relevant questions. Further, at the heart of the book is a new initiation into articulating why school libraries matter. What follows is a summary of main points from the chapters about the professionalism of school librarians.

SCHOOL LIBRARIES MATTER

While thorough understandings about the knowledge, skills, and professional dispositions of school librarians comes from reading each chapter in this book, advocates need clear, concise, and research-based statements that capture the evidence that explains why school libraries matter. The following are nine research-based, useful statements drawn from the content of this book:

1. **School librarians matter because professional school librarians have professional dispositions that support student learning and development. School librarians use their professional dispositions as a pathway to model student learning dispositions.**

Individuals including state-licensed teachers, principals, school psychologists, school librarians, and other school specialists in U.S. public schools must have and demonstrate content knowledge, skills, and dispositions necessary for facilitating student learning based on various professional and/or accrediting agency standards. The National Council for Accreditation of Teachers Education defines "professional dispositions" in the following statements:

> Professional attitudes, values, and beliefs demonstrated through both verbal and non-verbal behaviors as educators interact with students, families, colleagues, and communities. These positive behaviors support student learning and development. NCATE expects institutions to assess professional dispositions based on observable behaviors in educational settings. The two professional dispositions that NCATE expects institutions to assess are fairness and the belief that all students can learn. Based on their mission and conceptual framework, professional education units can identify, define, and operationalize additional professional dispositions. (NCATE, 2010–2012)

The impetus for Chapter 1 research by Bush and Jones (2010) is based on a study titled "Exploration to identifying professional dispositions of school librarians: A Delphi study" and the 2007 publication of the AASL's *Standards for the 21st-century learner* complete with dispositions in action for the student learner. Findings in the Bush and Jones study include a vision for professional dispositions of school librarians recognized predominantly for their quality teaching except from a distinctly school library perspective (in contrast to professional dispositions of classroom teachers). The chapter provides a self-assessment tool recommended for use in school library education and/or as an evaluation tool designed for use in school librarian evaluations by school administrators. The self-assessment tool can serve as a checklist for all school librarians and their classroom teacher colleagues. The tool is an adaptation for the school library field based on findings in the Bush and Jones study and an internal document by McMahon and Quiroa (2009) in the reading and language department at National-Louis University.

Bush and Jones's research on professional dispositions reveals that in the teacher education literature, interest in professional dispositions began and ended with teacher preparation programs and entry-level teachers. Their chapter boldly points out that only in school librarianship are professional dispositions viewed as a pathway to modeling student learning dispositions. Bush and Jones assert that school librarian professional dispositions distinctively include (1) caring, collegiality, and collaboration in interactions and community; (2) commitment to intellectual freedom, leadership, and professional ethics; and (3) willingness to model *dispositions in action for 21st-century standards for learners* (AASL, 2007).

2. **School librarians matter because professional school librarians have a knowledge base and practices (skills) that locate them along with students and other educators in an environment for learning, Vygotsky's zone of proximal development.**

School librarianship is much more than simply knowing how to check books in and out. Chapter 2 presents a philosophy of school librarian pedagogy and clarifies the knowledge base of school librarians. School librarians' professional knowledge base is philosophically located, with humanities and social sciences roots, in the area of educational research (e.g., student learning, teacher training, teaching methods, and classroom dynamics), and library and information science research. Library and information science research has as it goal learning how humans become informed or construct meanings through intermediation between inquirers and recorded records. School librarians' understandings of human information behavior represents an educational constructivist approach to teaching and learning shared by many educators, wherein individual students are viewed as actively constructing an understanding of their worlds, heavily influenced by the social world(s) in which they live. School librarians' understandings of human information behavior makes them unique in comparison to other educators because school librarians bring specialized, research-based understandings of sense-making and an information search process to the learning environment. School librarians' professional practices based on knowledge of information behavior are necessary for "Common Core" (2010) standards-based expectations for information retrieval skills as well as for digital, visual, textual, and technological skills.

Educational constructivism builds on the work of educational constructivist theorists including the theory of Lev Vygotsky (1978) who asserted that new cognitive skills should first be practiced by children in social interaction with a more experienced adult until the skill is mastered and internalized and the child is able to exercise the skill independently. Vygotksy's (1986) "zone of proximal development" (p. 86) enables school librarians to identify the place or gap in learning, the distance between dependent and independent problem solving, where school librarians should locate their specialized efforts with children and youth and their classroom teachers. As the second chapter in this book by Dow and Lakin describes, school librarians frequently train and collaborate with teachers in joint efforts to teach students to recognize an information need; search for, access, and evaluate information; and use information to develop and communicate new ideas for resolution of human problems.

Through the lens of annual yearly progress (AYP) data, the Dow and Lakin chapter (Chapter 5) creates a new "picture" of the presence (employment) or absence (elimination) of school librarians in schools. They describe their study titled "School librarian staffing levels and student achievement as represented in 2006–09 Kansas annual yearly progress data" (Dow, Lakin, & Court, 2012). In this study, this hypothesis was tested: Higher and more stable levels of school librarian allocation will yield greater levels of proficiency and greater positive change in proficiency when controlling for differences in prior performance, school characteristics, and student demographics. It articulates study findings that provide support for the researchers' hypothesis through a quantitative analysis of four years (2006–2009) of Kansas AYP data and state-licensed personnel records. The study revealed higher student proficiency rates in five content areas (reading, mathematics, science, history/government, and writing) with at least a part-time school librarian (preferably, a full-time school librarian) in the school building. Dow and Lakin suggest that it is possible that all assignments in today's schools may not encourage sense-making or support a process approach to research. They conclude that a challenge for educational leaders is to make certain teachers and school librarians are clear about how to collaboratively teach resource-based assignments that enable students to experience guided use of information from elementary through high schools and on to college.

3. School librarians matter because professional school librarians partner with other educators to provide information literacy instruction.

Successful integration of information literacy instruction requires collaboration and partnerships between school librarians and classroom teachers. In a classroom teacher–school librarian partnership, the classroom teacher brings expert knowledge of specific content areas and assumes responsibility for determining what, when, and how to teach specific aspects of the content and the school librarian brings expert knowledge of resources and assumes responsibility for facilitating information literacy instruction in the context of the content area. Through trusting, working relationships, and shared vision and shared objectives, student learning opportunities can be created that integrate subject content and information literacy. Through co-planning, co-implementing, and co-evaluating students' progress throughout the instructional process, student learning can be improved in all areas of the curriculum. However, this collaborative relationship between classroom teachers and school librarians is not often well known or well understood by classroom teachers, school administrators, and other educational decision-makers.

Chapter 3, including standards-based concepts of instructional partnering and a literature review of collaboration theory, is based on a study titled "Classroom-library collaboration: Factors influencing understanding and practice." This is a case study of preservice elementary education college students enrolled in a course designed to teach them about the roles and responsibilities of state-licensed school librarians. The purpose of the course thoroughly described in the chapter is an introduction to collaboration strategies for teaching reading comprehension and enriching children's appreciation of literature, identifying resources for literature-based instruction across the curriculum, and collaboration between the classroom teacher and school library media specialist in planning and teaching resource-based research. To determine whether the new course achieved its purpose, the researcher asked: Are elementary education majors' perceptions of school librarians as partners in teaching changed through a 1-credit hour course taught by library school faculty?

On the basis of findings in this study, it is evident that a university-based, elementary education course taught by library school faculty that focuses on co-teaching strategies for classroom teachers and school librarians can improve preservice elementary education teachers' perceptions about the school library program and school librarians' involvement in teaching reading and research skills. This study revealed that some preservice elementary education teachers are no strangers to the professional knowledge and skills of school librarians. Some participants in the study seemed to recognize upon beginning the class that school librarians assist classroom teachers to learn new computer technology; school library programs are a critical part of the literacy program; school principals should set expectations for classroom–library collaboration; and that when school librarians and classroom teachers collaborate for instruction, student's achievement should increase. This study provides evidence that a course about school libraries and the instructional role of school librarians included in teacher education requirements is worth the investment.

4. School librarians matter because professional school librarians allow school libraries to be used by students for information work and information play.

Global reach and advances in all areas of life are possible as new computer technologies are developed. School librarians are uniquely positioned to teach young people who eagerly adopt and modify technological innovations to suit their own social and learning needs. School librarians must model and teach guided inquiry and technology skills that enable *all* students to adapt to their environment while increasing cognitive and social growth. Research has been needed that investigates the information behavior of young people who use information and communication technologies to seek personal information, particularly in school libraries. It is professional school librarians who are well positioned to know about the everyday life information seeking practices of students. Without their research, it is likely difficult for educators and others to fully anticipate what types of information youth need. With school librarian research, it is possible for schools to shift to dynamic educational informatics (e.g., human–computer interactions, information science, computer science, etc.) in schools that can lead to improved instruction across the curriculum. This may be necessary to prepare students for life beyond high school. If so, what does it mean for school libraries?

Chapter 4 describes a case study conducted by Franklin, a National Board Certified school librarian, at a unique high school site, a newly constructed, highly technological high school with a school library designed with today's digital learners in mind. The chapter includes a detailed map of this unique, new library. Some may view this school as having the best of everything as we know it now. Franklin's research is conducted in recognition of how this school and students exist at a high socioeconomic level of society that is above that of the majority of citizens in today's society. Her research is nevertheless important because it captures a "slice" of society that needs to be better understood in order for education, school libraries in particular, to better serve *all* school-aged members of today's society. After all, don't we want the best information and technology educational experiences for *all* students while enabling them to be smart and safe?

Students attending this high school come from affluent families. At the time of the study, because the school was new, school policies at this site were still in development. For example, students at this site were not required to physically attend class. (Class attendance is a requirement in many schools and continues to be a school rule that no student should break unless with an approved request to be excused.) These students have the opportunity to stay at home and to take advantage of teacher-approved, alternative ways to take exams or make up learning activities.

The emerging picture of the everyday life information practices of students in this location is one of students enjoying access to computer technologies including students' own mobile devices that allow them to freely search for items of a personal information nature such as their scores/grades on class assignments and tests, information about college admission requirements, information about favorite athletic teams, music groups, online shopping, online news, Facebook, YouTube, and to use court records to investigate local driving tickets or arrests.

Student participants in this study revealed that they prefer to use cell phones and smartphones instead of library computers; they use their own mobile devices as another screen to bypass the district-required Internet filtering system. Students reported that until attending school at this site, their primary reason for visiting the school library was to print assignments and projects. Because the school librarians embrace usage of cell phones, smartphones, and other electronic devices, students in the study visited the library to do both assignment-related information work and information play but not waste time or lose intellectual "ground" when it came to completion of assignments and projects.

According to students and school librarian participants in the study, students at this school prefer "instructional models" to help them accurately and successfully complete written assignments, and they seek models from their school librarian to satisfy this need. Consequently, a new instructional model that allows freedom to complete work in alternative formats (in contrast to traditional formats such as memory and recite, read and write reports, etc.) calls for a new instructional methodology referred to in this study by school librarians as "inferencing," a method that enables students to analyze and compare potential final product choices for assignments. School librarians at the study site were uniquely positioned to infuse a sense of information work and information play into learning as they acknowledged and assisted students with personal information seeking practices in the school library settings. This study grounded in information behavior theory and a specialized understanding of information and technology provides invaluable data that can be used to better understand everyday life information practices and to create new, technologically modern approaches to teaching and using information inquiry methods.

5. **School librarians matter because professional school librarians continually conduct research, communicate empirical evidence, and take action based on the positive impact of school libraries and librarians on student achievement and school improvement.**

At a time when school budgets are cut and licensed personnel are being slashed, it is urgent that educational law and policy makers recognize and use what can be learned from empirical evidence about the importance and the positive impact of state-licensed school librarians and school library programs on student learning and achievement. Available evidence reveals that school librarians are, in this century, essential to teaching and learning. Without a doubt, the view that school libraries matter is articulated in a significant body of professional literature and can be used to advocate for employment of state-licensed school librarians and fully funded school library programs. While all chapters in the book and many more provide solid views from school library research, there are three chapters in this book that operationalize these terms: conduct, communicate, and take action.

Chapter 2 by Dow and Lakin describes a research model for using state AYP data to investigate student proficiency rates in all content areas in relationship to the presence (employment) or absence (elimination) of state-licensed school librarians. Their method can be replicated in any states not only to investigate impact of school librarians but also to investigate impact of presence (employment) or absence (elimination) of other licensed personnel such as school specialists in the areas of music, art, physical education, journalism, psychology, or school counselors.

Chapter 5 by Lance and Hofschire is an overview of school library impact studies. It begins with an outline of seven sets of circumstances that define the existing context of American public education that are likely to define the circumstances of future school library programs. The researchers discuss research questions typically asked and answered in recent school library impact studies and highlight many key findings. After pointing out challenges inherent in available data sources, Lance and Hofschire recommend on the basis of research-based evidence a five-step plan of action to improve local school library programs including (1) creation of partnerships with school administrators and other teachers; (2) confident sharing of research about the impact of school libraries and librarians; (3) establishing, redefining, and reinforcement of the positive roles that school librarians and library programs play in the school; (4) creating and reporting new local measures of school library output and outcomes; and (5) documenting through action-research local impact of teaching 21st-century skills on student learning and expanding options for large-scale measurement of teaching 21st-century skills on what students need to learn.

Chapter 6 by Lee and Klinger brings an international research perspective to the discussion of school improvement. In 2004, the Literacy and Numeracy Secretariat, a branch of the Ministry of Education Ontario, Canada, was formed and has been engaged in supporting school and district-based efforts to improve teaching and learning, with the majority of the efforts being directed toward literacy. Lee and Klinger share their mixed methods approach to investigation of school library programs that were identified as exemplary by the Ontario Library Association. These researchers discovered that it was not specific components of a library program as one would look for in a standards-based approach that made school library programs exemplary. Instead, it was the interaction between the program and the school context that made school library programs exemplary. They created a continuum of three consistently found features that appeared central to the functioning of exemplary libraries: (1) the role of the school library and the school librarian within the school context, (2) school librarians who focused on teaching, and (3) school librarians who were agents of change through the collaborations they initiated and the programs they developed or offered. This continuum recognized two supportive mechanisms: the school administration and financial support for the school library and the teacher librarian.

6. **School librarians matter because professional school librarians interact with all students and teachers and have knowledge of the school's curriculum.**

As all chapters in this book point out, school librarians are key players in creating schools befitting the 21st century. Without a federal mandate that each school employ state-licensed school librarians, the decision to fund state-licensed school librarians and school library programs depends on state and local educational leadership, as well as on the community at large. School administrators have key roles in shaping local educational practices and proprieties. Yet, research shows that school administrators, including school-building principals and district superintendents, are often unaware of research-based evidence indicating the positive impact of school libraries on student learning nor are they knowledgeable of professional standards and guidelines for developing school library programs. This lack of awareness poses an ongoing threat to the continuation and existence of school libraries in K-12 education.

Chapter 7 by Levitov describes school library research that investigated outcomes of an online, university-based, graduate-level course for school administrators designed to educate school administrators about school library programs and the role of the librarian, and subsequently to create administrative advocates for school libraries. The results of the study not only offered insights from the perspective of participating administrators, but also revealed implications in terms of benefits to school librarians as they work with school administrators to develop and implement school library programs, advocate for those programs, and recruit others to do the same. As a result of the course investigated by Levitov, benefits to school librarians and to students in schools included administrators' suggestions of the importance of the school librarian's role in teachings, serving on site-based curriculum committees to integrate the school library into the school's improvement plan, and in promoting use of computer technology.

Through the online, graduate-level course investigated by Levitov, school administrators began to view the library as something essential to all teachers and students. Participants in the study suggested that school librarians provide professional development (in-service sessions) devoted to increasing awareness of best professional practices by school librarians and to the improvement of communication and collaboration between and among school librarians and other educators and administrators. It became obvious to some administrators enrolled in the course that school librarians share some commonality with the school principal, as another person who works with all the teachers and students and who must be knowledgeable about the entire curriculum.

7. **School librarians matter because professional school librarian's knowledge and practices undergo continual improvement and change processes.**

In the United States, teacher preparation and proficiency are important, current topics. This book includes four chapters that provide examples of school library research conducted at the level of higher education to inform and improve teaching in higher education and/or to encourage heightened responsibility for professional development by national and state professional organizations. Chapter 3 by Dow, Davis, and Vietti-Okane describes a qualitative study to determine the effectiveness of a college course designed to prepare future elementary education teachers to work collaboratively with school librarians to teach reading and other content areas. Chapter 7 by Levitov describes a qualitative study to determine the effectiveness of a graduate, college course designed to inform school administrators about the standards and guidelines for school librarianship and research-based evidence of the positive impact that school librarians have on student learning and achievement. Chapter 9 by Mardis and Everhart describes a participatory, qualitative research study using cooperative inquiry (CI), both a methodology and a method, to study the abilities of school librarians to assemble collaborative problem-solving school teams to identify and institute solutions to technology-related school challenges.

Chapter 8 by Moreillon describes a forth study in this book devoted to conducting research to inform and improve teaching in higher education for and about school librarianship. This study using content analysis methods was designed to analyze and evaluate state-level school librarian conference sessions on the basis of criteria for the five roles (leader, instructional partner, information specialist, teacher, and program administrator) of school librarians identified in *Empowering learners: Guidelines for school library programs* (AASL, 2009), and to answer the question "What kinds of professional development do preservice and practicing school librarians need to make a difference in student achievement?" The researchers studied conference programs to learn about the options available to school library candidates and practitioners through conference keynote speeches, workshops, and concurrent sessions in a sampling of conferences offered in the 2010–2011 academic year. The results of the study showed that state-level, conference-sponsored, professional development was neither balanced on the basis criteria for the five roles and priorities of school librarians, nor was it aligned with the *Empowering learners* (AASL, 2009) roles and priorities for school librarians. This finding, while negative on the one hand, provides positive implications for future improvement of school librarian professional development. It highlights the importance of professional development for school librarians and articulates a clear call to action by national- and state-level associations, their governing bodies, and members of the school library community to offer empowering professional development to a greater number of pre- and in-service school librarians.

8. **School libraries matter because professional school librarians provide leadership for computer technology integration in schools.**

In this day and age, computer technology integration is a vital aspect of teaching and learning. Computer technology integration requires school-based leadership to be consistent, relevant, and to make connections between various aspects of students' learning experiences. The Institute of Museum and Library Services (IMLS) has served as a catalyst for leadership education through National Leadership Grants and the Laura Bush 21st-Century Librarians Program. Chapter 9 by Mardis and Everhart describes Project LEAD, an IMLS-funded program, developed and implemented over three phases at the Florida State University's School of Library and Information Studies. One phase of Project LEAD included development of a 12-credit leadership curriculum for school librarians with emphases on technology integration, instructional leadership, literature appreciation, and general leadership, and completion of the leadership curriculum as part of a master's degree by 30 Florida teachers. Another IMLS project, Project Leadership in Action, was funded to investigate the outcomes of the leadership curriculum by answering the question "Would graduates enact a leadership role when they took a position as a school librarian?"

Through the lens of formative leadership theory, the researchers studied the ability of six school librarians trained in CI, a form of participatory qualitative research frequently used in community building and social work, to assemble collaborative problem-solving school teams to identify and institute solutions to technology-related school challenges. It was discovered that one area where school librarians were most confident to lead was technology integration. This study, a pioneering effort in the use of CI in a school library setting, provides definitive research findings that are a starting point for future researchers and practitioners. First, CI is a viable methodology to evaluate the outcomes of library education for school librarian leadership in technology. Second, new school librarians are for the most part able to exercise formative leadership to organize and convene CI groups in their schools. Those who were most successful built teams comprised of a cross-section of the faculty and included the technology coordinators and principal. Third, new school librarians felt that the CI process integrated with their own leadership styles and ability. Researchers noted, however, that CI facilitators might face some challenges in schools that could make a process like CI seem counterintuitive. This conclusion was based on the recognition that school structures are hierarchical, driven by action, and framed by concrete objectives and learning standards. Many teachers today are hindered by a shortage of time and resources and are not often given the opportunity to experience participatory decision-making and inquiry.

9. **School librarians matter because professional school librarians model cross-cultural teaching and learning and social equity as they interact with all students in schools.**

Providing a quality education that leads to student learning and achievement for the rapidly increasing numbers of ethically and linguistically diverse children is a significant educational issue. In the United States, there are increasing numbers of foreign-born residents. Data about school-age children shows that in 2009, more than 21 percent spoke a language other than English at home (U.S. Census Bureau, 2012). Chapter 10 by Smith and Brown describes a review of literature that highlights the role of the school librarian as a pivotal resource for learners and teachers and provides examples of successful strategies from the research in the area of materials, instructional strategies, programming, and technology. They answer two leading questions for more than a decade: "Why does our school need a library when we have access to so much information from our classrooms via the Internet?" And, "What does a new learning commons look like?"

As Smith and Brown point out, schools need school librarians because it is the school librarian's professional responsibility to make connections for *all* students between reading, literature, literacy, and information retrieval. Making these connections with students who speak English as a second language heightens school librarians' responsibilities. Further, many of today's students have grown up with laptops, tablets, smartphones, and a world of information only a click away. All students are expected to express their understanding using images, video, and animation in addition to plain text. Students need culturally responsive school librarians who focus on 21st-century skills for *all* students, including immigrant student learning English. Basic principles for culturally responsive leadership in school libraries are articulated by multicultural educators who know that social equity is more important than ever. As Smith and Brown put it, it is a natural approach to look toward school librarians who interact with *all* students within a school to model culturally responsive teaching and leadership.

CONCLUSIONS: CHARACTERISTICS OF A PROFESSIONAL SCHOOL LIBRARIAN

An important aspect to consider when making a case that school libraries matter is the difference between a professional and a technician or paraprofessional. Paraprofessionals do not have the status of professionals. Paraprofessionals have some defined duties, but they do not have the overall responsibility for instruction or decision-making that is required by professional school librarians. While paraprofessional are important and needed to assist students, classroom teachers, and school librarians in today's schools, it is necessary to point out that this book has highlighted the professional work of school librarians who are educated and credentialed to provide instruction as well as selection and management of library resources and services. Throughout the book, the terms "state-licensed" and "endorsed" are used to indicate a professional school librarian who has completed a licensure process. Licensed personnel requirements and credentials vary from state-to-state, but the characteristics of a professional can be held constant across the United States and beyond. According to Flexner (1915), a profession is characterized by a body of knowledge, a body of literature, professional associations, an accreditation or licensure process, a system of education, and a system of ethics. In other words, a member of a profession has a unique culture and education.

A review of the nine statements in this chapter will make clear that school librarians matter. While reading the book, one can conclude that school librarians have all the characteristics central to a profession as described by Flexner (1915). School librarians as members of the library and information profession (Greer, Grover, & Fowler, 2007; Rubin, 2010) are experts in an area of knowledge that is applied to professional practice. The knowledge that school librarians master is recorded and available through a body of literature, which is organized, stored, indexed, and retrievable using the terms specific to their area of specialization. School librarians have professional organizations and associations that provide forums for the exchange of knowledge in their area and for dissemination of new knowledge related to practice. Librarians have professional schools where the body of knowledge, the literature, the ethics and values, the system of literature, and the culture of school librarianship is systematically conveyed to prospective members of the profession. School librarians have a form of authentication, a way to identify individuals who have gained professional knowledge of their specialization, through the accreditation of library and information programs of higher education granted by the American Library Association and the AASL. As library and information professionals, school librarians have a code of ethics, *Code of ethics of the American Library Association* (last amended July 22, 2008), that articulates a common thread of high standards for the profession.

The time has come for state-licensed school librarians in America to assume positions of authority and responsibility along with other educators in teaching today's students. This book provides authoritative library and information science research addressing the school librarian's position as an essential school leader, school-wide resource person, and collaborator who partners with classroom teachers in the design and delivery of instruction. The research in this book serves to make the case that recent, erratic trends of reducing school librarians' hours, or eliminating school librarians all together, will harm students and their abilities to do the kind of research and writing expected in jobs, college, and other postsecondary experiences. For the good of educational reform and improvement of education of *all* this century's students, school librarians should be named along with other teachers in future reauthorization of the Elementary and Secondary Education Act (P. L. 89–10, 1965). With official recognition and inclusion in the law, school librarians will be employed in every school building where they can use their specialized knowledge and skills to improve every student's learning. Without official recognition and inclusion in the law, school librarians are likely to continue to be reduced or eliminated in many schools across the United States.

School librarians' expertise is very important in a democratic society. With information and the skills to evaluate and use it, citizens can seek effective help, correct abuses, enjoy basic human functioning, and benefit from resources around them. With information, professional and scholarly bodies of knowledge can grow and expand through creation of new scientific knowledge and professional practices. School libraries *do* matter!

REFERENCES

AASL. (2007). *Standards for the 21st-century learner.* Chicago: American Library Association. Retrieved from http://www.ala.org/aasl/sites/ala.org.aasl/files/content/guidelinesandstandards/learningstandards/AASL_LearningStandards.pdf

AASL. (2009). *Empowering learners: Guidelines for school library media programs.* Chicago: American Library Association.

ALA. (2008). *Code of ethics of the American Library Association.* Chicago: American Library Association. Retrieved from http://www.ala.org/advocacy/proethics/codeofethics/codeethics

Bush, G., & Jones, J. L. (2010). Exploration to identify professional dispositions of school librarians. *School Library Research, 13.* American Library Association. Retrieved from http://www.ala.org/aasl/sites/ala.org.aasl/files/content/aaslpubsandjournals/slr/vol13/SLR_ExplorationtoIdentify.pdf

Common Core State Standards Initiative. (2010). *Common core state standards (CCSS).* Retrieved from http://www.corestandards.org/the-standards

Dow, M. J., Lakin, J. M., & Court, S.C. (2012). School librarian staffing levels and student achievement as represented in 2006–2009 Kansas Annual Yearly Progress Data. *School Library Research, 15* American Library Association. .Retrieved from http://www.ala.org/aasl/sites/ala.org.aasl/files/content/aaslpubsandjournals/slr/vol15/SLR_StaffingLevelsandStudentAchievement_V15.pdf

Elementary and Secondary Education Act (P. L. 89–10, 1965). *U.S. Statutes at Large, 79*, 27–58. Retrieved from http://www.nctic1p.org/files/40646763.pdf

Flexner, A. (1915). *Is social work a profession?* Paper presented at the National Conference on Charities and Correction.

Greer, R. C., Grover, R. J., & Fowler, S. G. (2007). *Introduction to the library and information professions.* Westport, CT: Libraries Unlimited.

McMahon, S. E., & Quiroa, R. (2009). *Scholarly and professional dispositions self-assessment: Reading and language students.* Wheeling, IL: Reading and Language Department Internal Document, National College of Education, National-Louis University.

NCATE. (2010–2012). Professional dispositions. In *NCATE Glossary.* Washington, D.C.: NCATE. Retrieved from http://www.ncate.org/Standards/NCATEUnitStandards/ NCATEGlossary/tabid/477/Default.aspx

Rubin, R. E. (2010). *Foundations of library and information science* (3rd ed.). New York: Neal-Schuman.

U.S. Census Bureau. (2012). Table 236. Children who speak a language other than English at home by region: 2009. *The 2012 statistical abstract: The national data book.* Retrieved from http://www.census.gov/compendia/statab/cats/education.html

Vygotsky, L. (1978). *Mind in society: The development of higher psychological processes.* Edited and translated by M. Cole, V. John-Steiner, S. Scribner, & E. Souberman. Cambridge, MA: Harvard University Press. (Original work published 1934).

INDEX

Academic achievement, impact of school libraries: American public education, 65–68; five-step improvement plan, 73–75; importance of collaboration, 72; moving beyond student achievement studies, 71–72; review of the literature, 69–72; school libraries and student achievement, inputs/outputs, 69–71; staffing data, methodological challenges, 73; typical school library research questions, 68–69

"Action research" strategies, 75

Adolescent developmental tasks (Havighurst), 51, 61

American Association of School Librarians (AASL), 2–5, 39, 68, 74–75, 86, 92–95, 98, 104, 109–12, 117–18, 126–27, 134, 139–40, 151, 153–54, 160, 163

American Library Association (ALA), 139

American public education, 65–68; absence of reliable, dedicated federal funding, 66; advent of computers and the internet, 67; advent of eBooks, eReaders, and tablet computers, 67–68; partnership for 21st-century skills, 68; school staffing trends, 66; site-based management, 65–66; standards-based state tests, 66–67; typical school library research questions, 68–69

ANCOVA method, 28, 34

Animoto, 146

Behavioral psychology, 21, 27

Books and instructional materials, ELL, 142–43; big books, 143; bilingual picture books, 143; informational books, 143; provide good materials, 143; simple English language picture books, 143; wordless picture books, 143

Bruner, J., 22–23

Child-as-apprentice theory, 23

"Children's Literature" (course), 41–42

Classroom–library collaboration, 41, 43, 48–49, 113, 156

Code of ethics of the American Library Association, 163

Cognitive psychology, 21

Collaborations to support school improvement: administration and financial support, 83; best practices, 85; concept of continuous school improvement, 80; developmental program evaluation approach, 81; education, reform and accountability, 79–80; educative or advocacy role of teacher librarian, 87–88; exemplary library programs, 83–86; integration through collaboration, 86; multistaged case study approach, 82; reductions in school library resources and staffing, 80; school libraries, 81–86; sections, survey, 82; teacher agency/efficacy, 79

Collaboration theory: "classroom-library collaboration: factors influencing understanding and practice," 40, 155

Collaborative problem solving, 123, 125–26, 160–61

Collaborative strategies for teaching reading comprehension: Maximizing your impact, 41

Colorado Student Assessment Program (CSAP), 69–71

Common Core State Standards, 20, 28–29, 92; initiative, 20, 104

Computer literacy, 67

Constructivism, 21–23; in education and sociology, 21–22; in library and information science research, 22; theories of information behavior, 22; ZPD (Vygotsky's), 22–23

Cooperative inquiry (CI), 123, 130–34, 160–61; *See also* Technology integration and school librarian leadership

Delphi study methodology: communication, 8; e-mail communication, 8; informed consent form, 8; open-ended qualitative research design, 9; panelists, 8; research design, 7–8; research findings and plans of action, 8–14; results, 9; self-assessment tool, 11–14; specific strengths, 7

Dewey, J., 6, 21–22

"Dialogic interface," 27

Digital literacy, 67

Dispositions in action for 21st-century standards for learners (AASL), 154

Doodle Buddy, 145

Educational constructivism, 21–23, 154

Elementary and Secondary Education Act, 66, 163

Elementary Teacher and the Library Media Specialist: Partners in Teaching Literature Appreciation and Information Literacy, 39, 43

E-mail communication, 8

Emporia State University (ESU), 39

Empowering learners: Guidelines for school library programs (AASL), 51, 62, 94, 104, 109, 126, 134, 160

English for speakers of other languages (ESOL), 33, 139, 143

English language learners (ELL), 25, 70, 72, 137–39, 142–46; books and instructional materials, 142–43;

instructional strategies, 143–46; practical matters, 146; programming, 144–45; technology applications and projects, 145–46

eReaders, 145

ETS-PRAXIS exam, 41

Everyday life information seeking (ELIS) practices: concept of, 53; data collection, 54; findings, 59–60; generalizability, substantive validation, and reliability, 57; methodology, 53–58; newly constructed school: rivals and rule testing, 54; notion of "transferability," 57; physical and virtual technologies, use of, 60–61; preference of own cell phones, 58; print and virtual documentation, 57; Savolainen and the Theoretical Framework, 52–53; school librarian interviews, 55–56; in school libraries, 52–53; school library map, 55; specific type of instructional model, 58; student focus group sessions, 56–57; students in school library, 51; study limitations, 58; technologies, 51–52; teenage students, 52; teens in technological school library, 53; theory (Savolainen), 51–53; unique study site and population, choice for, 53–54; of upper-income high school students, 61–63; virtual documentation, 57

Exemplary library programs, 83–86, 93, 158–59

Exploration to identifying professional dispositions of school librarians: A Delphi study, 8, 153

Five-step improvement plan, 73–75; new measures of outputs and outcomes, 75; partnerships with administrators and teachers, 73; research about impact of school libraries and librarians, 73–74; roles of school library and librarian, 75; teaching 21st-century skills on student learning, 75

FLACs, 116–17

Flip video, 145

Formative leadership, 126

Glogs, 146

"Guided inquiry," 23, 92, 151–52, 156

Habitus and *way and mastery of life,* 51–52

The Handy 5, 26

High School Graduation, 24
Human nature and conduct (Dewey), 6

IMovie or movie maker, 145
Information and communication
  technologies (ICTs), 51, 67–68, 72,
  113, 156
Information behavior, 19–22, 27–28,
  33–34, 51–53, 153–54, 156–57;
  definition, 21; research, 19
Information literacy, 67
*Information power: Building partnerships
  for learning* (AASL & AECT), 111
*Information power: Guidelines for school
  library media programs,* 139
Information search process (Kuhlthau), 19,
  27–28; "uncertainty principle," 28
In-service, 46, 71, 93, 98, 110, 113, 159
Institute of Museum and Library Services
  (IMLS), 91–92, 123–24, 160–61
Instructional best practice guidelines
  (AASL), 39
"Instructional models," 61–62, 157
Instructional partner, 39–49, 94, 98, 110,
  112–14, 117, 134, 140, 155, 160
Instructional partnerships in preservice
  elementary education teachers:
  case study methodology, 43–44;
  "Children's Literature" (course), 41–42;
  collaboration theory, 40–41; course
  learning activities, 42; elementary
  teacher and school library partner course,
  41–42; ETS-PRAXIS exam, 41; findings,
  46; limitations, 44–45; partnering in
  instruction, 39–40; pre- and post-survey
  and procedure, 43–44; preparing future
  teachers, 39; research questions, 42
Instructional strategies, ELL: literature-
  inspired creative expression, 144;
  multicultural literature, 143–44; poetry,
  144; storybooks, 143; storytelling, 144
International Society of Technology in
  Education, 92
iPads, 62, 67, 133, 145
iPods, 145

Kansas criterion-referenced assessments,
  26
Kansas statewide assessments (KSDE), 25
K-12 education, 92, 159
Kelly, G. A., 21–22
Kindles, 67, 145
"Know thyself," 5

Language barrier, crossing: center for
  learning or "learning commons," 141;
  challenges, 140–41; culturally responsive
  leaders, 146–47; English language learners
  (ELLs), 137; foreign-born students,
  problems for, 138–39; information power,
  140–41; innovative and effective skill
  improvement approaches, 138; leader,
  role of, 140; learner characteristics, 142;
  library media program, mission statement,
  140; multicultural school, 137–38; school
  media specialist, roles of, 140; standards-
  based education, role of librarian, 139–41;
  strategies for supporting ELLs from the
  research, 142–46
Laura Bush 21st Century Librarian
  Program, 123
Learning4Life (L4L), 111
Library and information science (LIS), 7,
  19–22, 25, 33–34, 41, 49, 52–53, 110,
  112, 123, 125, 154, 163
Literacy and Numeracy Secretariat (LNS),
  79, 158

Mansfield University, 91–92, 96–97, 104
Metatheories, 21
Moodle, 104, 146
Mp3 players/audio devices, 145

National Assessment of Educational
  Progress (NAEP), 70, 72
National Board for Professional Teaching
  Standards, 10, 127
National Council for the Accreditation
  of Teacher Education (NCATE), 1, 6,
  14, 153
*The national educational technology
  standards for students: The next
  generation,* 104
National Louis University, 14, 154
NLOCs, 116–17
"No Child Left Behind," 24, 66, 75, 79
Nooks, 67, 145

Obama, Barack (President), 20
1-credit hour course, 41, 156
Open-ended qualitative research design, 9
"Overachieving Asian student" stereotype,
  142

"Panelists," 3, 8
Partnering in instruction, 39–40; classroom
  teacher–school librarian partnership,

40; integration of information literacy instruction, 39–40

Partnership for the 21st century skills, 92, 104

Piaget, J., 22, 62

Practical matters, ELL, 146; foreign language cataloging, 146; illustrations and signage, 146

Preservice, 4, 14–15, 39–49, 110–11, 118, 127, 155–56, 160; *See also* Instructional partnerships in preservice elementary education teachers

Prezi, 146

Productive thinking, 126

Professional development conference offerings: classroom teacher preparation and proficiency, 110; domain matrix, 114–15; findings, 116–17; improvement plan, 117–18; instructional partnerships, developing, 113; leadership in K-12 schools, 110; literature review, 112–13; methodology: content analysis, 112–13; preparation of the analysis, 113–16; preservice and in-service, 110–11; problems, 110–11; research questions, 111–12; sample, 116; state-level conferences, importance in, 118; teaching in higher education, 109–10

Professional dispositions of school librarians: concept of professional dispositions, 3–5; definition, 153; Delphi study methodology, 7–14; dispositions, definition (Katz), 6; dispositions in action, 1–3; grasp of identity within a communal culture (Freud's), 3; identification of, 15; NCATE definition of dispositions, 6; "panelists" in the Delphi study methodology, 3; question of professional dispositions, 5; research goal, 1; review of the literature, 6; school library media program (SLMP), 4; self-identify professional dispositions, 2

Professional learning communities, 80

Professional school librarian, 162–63

Program administrator, 94, 100, 110–12, 115, 117, 134, 140, 160

Programming, ELL, 144–45; book clubs and literature circles, 144; "family treasure" booklets, 145; morning announcements via closed-circuit TV, 144; parent/grandparent nights, 144; student-produced materials, 145

Project LEAD, 123–24, 127, 133, 160–61, 166

Project Leadership in Action (LIA), 124

Psychoanalytic psychology, 21

Research Center for Leadership in Action (RCLA), 124, 128–29

Scaffolding (Bruner), 23

School administrators: as advocates for librarians/libraries, 102–3; assumptions, 97; changed perceptions, 97–98; commonality, school librarian and administrator, 103; communication, 99; content, school librarian and principal collaboration, 95; implications, 103–5; importance of communication with librarian, 100; improvement plan/findings, 97–102; informing school library programs, 95–96; informing school library specialists, 104–5; instructional partner, 98; knowledge of school library programs, 94–95; lack of administrative awareness, 91–92; limitations, 97; Mansfield course, 104; mixed methods approach, 91, 96; participants, 96–97; "professional developer," role of, 99; professional development funds, 97; recommendations, 105–6; research questions, 93; "School Library Advocacy for Administrators," online course, 92–93; shift in language, 101–2; solutions for informing administrators, 104; university-level coursework about libraries/librarians, 102; "value of libraries" for students, 95

School libraries/librarians, importance of, 153–62; cross-cultural teaching and learning and social equity, 161–62; information work and information play, 156–57; knowledge and practice, 159–60; knowledge base and practices (skills), 154–55; leadership for computer technology integration, 160–61; partnership for information literacy instruction, 155–56; professional dispositions, 153–54; research for student achievement and school improvement, 158–59; wide knowledge of the school's curriculum, 159

"School library impact studies," 34

School Library Journal, 91

School library media program (SLMP), 4, 11, 13, 46, 93
School library media specialist (SLMS), 62
"Selves" (Agosto and Hughes-Hassell's (2006a) theoretical model), 61
Sense-making (Dervin's), 27
Skype, 114, 146
SLOCs, 116–17
Social learning theory (Bandura), 23
Standards for the 21st-century learner (AASL), 2–4, 8, 42, 92–93, 104, 139, 153
Standards for the 21st-century learner in action (AASL), 4, 93
Structure-oriented lessons, 142
Student achievement, ZPD theory: Annual Yearly Progress: Federal Mandate, 24; *The Handy 5,* 26; High School Graduation, 24; Kansas criterion-referenced assessments, 26; students' growth: state-level example, 24–27; 2010 Kansas statewide assessments (KSDE), 25
Students with disabilities (SPED), 25
The system of professions: An essay on the division of expert labor, 2

TeacherWeb, 146
Team learning, 126
Technology applications and projects, ELL, 145–46; Animoto, 146; Doodle Buddy and other computer-aided drawing programs, 145; DVDs in both subtitles, 145; flip video, 145; Glogs, 146; iMovie or movie maker, 145; iPods and iPads, 145; Kindles, Nooks, and eReaders, 145; Moodle, 146; Mp3 players/audio devices, 145; Prezi, 146; Skype, 146; TeacherWeb, 146

Technology integration and school librarian leadership: cooperative inquiry (CI), 123, 128, 130–34; "critical subjectivity," 128; formative leadership theory, 125–26; improvement plan, 130; leadership in schools, 126; participants' CI experiences, 131–32; participatory research, 127–28; procedure, 128–30; Project LEAD, 123–24; Project Leadership in Action (LIA), 123–24; research questions, 124–25; school librarians and leadership, 126–27; solutions to technology related school challenges, 123; technology integration, 123–24; validity and reliability, 129–30
Traditional education, 126
Transferability, notion of, 57
True stories (Atwood), 7

Vygotsky, L., 19–35, 154

Zone of proximal development (ZPD) theory (Vygotsky's), 19, 22–23, 154; ANCOVA method, 34; AYP data, 20; Common Core State Standards, 28–29; constructivism, 21–23; cutting school librarians, 19–21; information behavior, 19, 21; information search process (Kuhlthau), 27–28; interactionist approach, 23; Kansas grade span by trend cross tabulation, 32; methodology, 27–29; presence or absence of school librarians, 34–35; research findings, 29–33; sense-making (Dervin), 27; student achievement, 24–27; 2006–2009 Kansas overall distribution trends across three, 30–31; 2010 Kansas statewide assessments (KSDE), 25

ABOUT THE EDITOR
AND CONTRIBUTORS

NANCY J. BROWN, PhD, served as coordinator of the School of the School Library Media Technology Unit in the College of Education at Georgia State University in Atlanta, Georgia. She is an experienced K-12 school librarian, particularly in multilingual schools. Her research addresses the needs of immigrant students, educating and training preservice school librarians, and information literacy for children and young adults.

GAIL BUSH, PhD, is a professor emerita in education, from National Louis University, Chicago, where she served as professor in the reading and language department, director of the school library program, and director of the Center for Teaching through Children's Books. Her academic background includes a bachelor's degree in anthropology, master's degree in library science, and doctorate in educational psychology. Her doctoral research, focusing on educator collaboration, is discussed in *The school buddy system: The practice of collaboration* (ALA, 2003).

TONYA DAVIS, MAEd, MLS, has been a national faculty in the School of Library and Information Management at Emporia State University in Emporia, Kansas. She served as a classroom teacher at Rex Elementary and Ruth Clark Elementary in Haysville, Kansas, and a school librarian at Swaney Elementary School in Derby, Kansas, where she currently teaches.

MIRAH J. DOW, PhD, is an associate professor in the School of Library and Information Management at Emporia State University in Emporia, Kansas, where she currently is director of the PhD program and previously served as coordinator of the School Library Media Program. She served five years, two years as chair, on the American Association of School Librarians' Legislation Committee.

NANCY EVERHART, PhD, is an associate professor at the Florida State University College of Information, where she is director of the School Library Media

Program, Project LEAD, and the PALM (Partnership Advancing Library Media) Center. She served as president of American Association of School Librarians, 2010–2011.

LORI L. FRANKLIN, MLS, a school librarian for the past 16 years, National Board Certified teacher, national faculty, and PhD candidate at the School of Library and Information Management, Emporia State University in Emporia, Kansas, is the school librarian at Olathe East High School, Olathe, Kansas, a school recently chosen as one of 20 model high schools by the International Center for Leadership in Education. She is coauthor of *Information literacy and information skills instruction: Applying research to practice in the 21st century school library* (Libraries Unlimited, 2011).

LINDA HOFSCHIRE, PhD, is a research analyst at the Library Research Service (LRS) at Colorado State Library. Prior to joining LRS, she conducted research and evaluation in the field of education and mass communication.

JAMI L. JONES, PhD, is an associate professor in the Department of Library Science at East Carolina University in Greenville, North Carolina. She is coauthor (with Gail Bush) of *Tales out of the school library: Developing professional disposition* (Libraries Unlimited, 2010), and books and articles on the role of the school librarian in preventing dropout, nurturing resilient students, and fostering creative school library programs.

DON A. KLINGER, PhD, is an associate professor in the Faculty of Education at Queen's University in Kingston, Ontario, Canada. He is a founding member of the Assessment and Evaluation Group at Queen's University, and a member of the Psychometric Expert Panel for the Education Quality and Accountability Office in Ontario (responsible for provincial testing of students). He served as a member of the Ontario Educational Research Panel, was a member of the writing team for the second edition of the *Personnel evaluation standards*, and cochair of the writing team revising the *Student evaluation standards* for the Joint Committee on Standards for Educational Evaluation.

JACQUELINE MCMAHON LAKIN, PhD, is an education program consultant in information management at the Kansas State Department of Education in Topeka, Kansas, and an instructor in the School of Professional and Graduate Studies at Baker University in Overland Park, Kansas.

KEITH CURRY LANCE, PhD, is a consultant who works with libraries and related organizations as a researcher, statistician, public speaker, proposal writer, and facilitator. He was the founding director of the Library Research Service at the Colorado State Library in 1987, where he served until he retired in 2007. He is focused on consulting both independently and with the RSL Research Group based in Louisville, Colorado.

ELIZABETH A. LEE, PhD, is an associate professor in the Faculty of Education at Queen's University in Kingston, Ontario, Canada. Her research interests are in the areas of reading comprehension, visual literacy, information literacy, and school librarians. She published five representative publications in the past five years including a journal article with Dr. Don A. Klinger in *School libraries worldwide* titled "Against the flow: A continuum for evaluating and revitalizing school libraries" (2011).

DEBORAH LEVITOV, PhD, worked in school libraries in Lincoln Public Schools for 25 years. For the past seven years, she has been managing editor of ABC-CLIO/Libraries Unlimited, *School Library Monthly*. She is the editor of *Activism and the School Librarian: Tools for Advocacy and Survival* (2012) published by Libraries Unlimited.

MARCIA A. MARDIS, PhD, is an assistant professor at the Florida State University College of Information, where she is the assistant director of the PALM (Partnership Advancing Library Media) Center. She is one of the authors of the 2007 AASL *Standards for the 21st-century student learner*.

JUDI MOREILLON, PhD, is an assistant professor in the School of Library and Information Studies at Texas Woman's University in Denton, Texas. She is author of two American Library Association publications: *Collaborative strategies for teaching reading comprehension: Maximizing your impact* (2007) and *Coteaching reading comprehension strategies in the secondary schools: Maximizing your impact* (2012).

ANDREW J.M. SMITH, PhD, a native of Scotland, is an assistant professor in the School of Library and Information Management at Emporia State University in Emporia, Kansas, where he is the coordinator of the School Library Licensure Program and teaches in the areas of children and young adult's librarianship, and cross-cultural teaching and learning.

ANGELA VIETTI-OKANE, MLS, is a national faculty in the School of Library and Information management at Emporia State University in Emporia, Kansas. She served as a classroom teacher and then a school librarian at Monticello Trails Middle School in Shawnee, Kansas, and school librarian at Pioneer Ridge Middle School, Shawnee, Kansas. She currently teaches at Horizon Elementary School, Shawnee, Kansas.

Made in the USA
Monee, IL
01 September 2021

77146533R00111